*Untended Gates: The Mismanaged Press*

# UNTENDED GATES
*The Mismanaged Press*

NORMAN E. ISAACS

*New York*   COLUMBIA UNIVERSITY PRESS   1986

Library of Congress Cataloging-in-Publication Data

Isaacs, Norman E., 1908–
Untended gates.

Bibliography: p.
Includes index.
1. Press—United States. I. Title.
PN4867.I8 1986 071'.3 85–13296
ISBN 0–231–05876–4

Columbia University Press
*New York Guildford, Surrey*
Copyright © 1986 Columbia University Press
All rights reserved

Printed in the United States of America

c 10 9 8 7 6 5 4 3 2

*This book is Smyth-sewn and printed on permanent and durable acid-free paper.*

To Millie, Roberta, and Steve
—and all the others
who believe devoutly in
a free and responsible press

# CONTENTS

*Untended Gates: The Mismanaged Press*

## CHAPTER 1

# "I've Got a Crazy on the Line"

"CAN I ASK you a personal question?" said one of Jim Detjen's classmates. "Shoot," said Jim. It was late afternoon in early May, 1978, during the weekly ethics seminar at Columbia University's Graduate School of Journalism. "Well," said the student, "what are you doing back in school?" The question had been bound to arise. Early that week the Pulitzer Prizes had been announced and word had raced through the student body that, while it hadn't won a prize, an environmental series Jim Detjen had written for a mid-state New York newspaper had remained in prize consideration right up to the final jury vote. Jim was 29, thoughtful, poised, and clearly a sound professional in little need of any journalism school. He mulled over the question for half a minute. What then came was typical of him, a well-organized and concise explanation.

"The paper I was on isn't big," he said. "It has about 40,000 circulation. Many on the staff are young and inexperienced. They make a lot of mistakes and there are a lot of protest calls. Every time there was a protest call whoever was on the city desk would take it. The call might have something to do with a fouled-up obit, or a wrong date for a meeting, or a totally warped quote. The city editor or his assistant would cup a hand over the mouthpiece of the telephone, turn and shout so everybody could hear, 'I've got a crazy on the line.' No matter what the goof-up, the caller was always a 'crazy.' It got under my hide and that was the kind of thing that drove me out of there—and to here."

What followed was excited, passionate discussion, a lot of it missing the real import, but that was to be expected. Even Jim was not fully aware that his act had been a protest against journalism's biggest continuing weakness, one that has led to much of the public disenchantment with "the press" as a whole. It is a long-standing fault, so entrenched that many of those in the press accept it, even though resentfully. It is newsroom mismanagement. Although less serious in some news operations, it applies to some degree everywhere. It occurs even where there are highly flexible, intelligent editors, whose talents have helped build important news organizations. Many other good, idealistic editors are trapped in a bureaucratic system that resists change as fiercely as any governmental, industrial, or other professional group.

The simple fact is that much of the news content read in newspapers, heard on radio, or delivered on television is controlled by men and women with limited perspectives of what is or is not "news," who for the most part have received no broadgauged training, and who when challenged react with a defensiveness that astounds and infuriates outsiders. Many of the errors in news handling occur at the primary levels of journalistic gatekeeping. Whether they bear editor, producer, or director titles is of no consequence. They are supervising editors. Above them sit much more influential gatekeepers, the directing editors and their deputies. More than a few of these, unfortunately, have advanced because of technical facility and not because of innovative leadership qualities. Even when some in this latter group are persuaded to try to break out of the standard mold, they face the likelihood of veto coming from a still higher level of gatekeepers, those who represent ownership. The root cause is schizophrenia—the internal war between public purpose and making money.

One of the newspaper profession's heroes, William Allen White, expressed it succinctly in an editorial in his *Emporia Gazette* in 1925. It was about the death of Frank Munsey, one of the early entrepreneurs in chain journalism, both magazines and newspapers, from the 1880s to the mid-1920s. At one time Munsey talked grandly of building a chain of 500 newspapers. He bought, sold, and killed off publications, with profit always the open motivation. When he died, Mr. White wrote: "Frank

Munsey, the great publisher, is dead. Munsey contributed to the journalism of his day the great talent of a meat packer, the morals of a money changer and the manners of an undertaker. He and his kind have about succeeded in transforming a once noble profession into an eight percent security. May he rest in trust."[1]

There were others like Mr. White, who saw journalism as the most essential of all the professions. Their positions were drawn from Jefferson's and Madison's concept of the press as the vital underpinning of a free society, the means by which the electorate could be educated to the issues so that it could vote intelligently. Those like Mr. White read the First Amendment as both protection and obligation. They were a minority, of course. The conduct of the profit seekers was to bring a barb from A. J. Liebling, for many years the most pungent critic of the press, that was quoted perhaps a thousand times: "Freedom of the press is guaranteed only to those who own one."[2] There was evidence to back it up. Payroll studies showed many advertising salesmen and printshop foremen valued well above editors. Much of that gross inequity has now disappeared, but the myopia was to create the dysfunction in newsrooms.

Creating flow patterns to assure that newspapers went to press on time built bureaucracies. Even as new challenges came, the central patterns remained in place. The key gatekeeper positions continued to be filled with those who had some proficiency in marking news copy to be sent to typesetters. Some with talent rose to become editors. More stayed marking copy or became newsroom drifters. A series of revolutions has since remade much of journalism. Radio, the weekly newsmagazines, and the most powerful entry of all, television, have come into being. Salaries and techniques have changed. The system hasn't. And it was the system, not ethical nuances, that brought about Jim Detjen's expensive decision to break loose from the frustrations of working with gatekeepers who were technicians without intellectual breadth, sense of public service, or grasp of professional purpose.

I was to learn that Jim's move was not an isolated one. It appears that each year from six to perhaps a dozen young working newspeople in various parts of the country apply to the four or five top graduate schools. Reviewing his decision in 1984, Jim said, "I was paying off college loans and didn't want to get deeper into debt. I'd written letters of application with no luck. But I felt I had to move and gambled that a year at Columbia would help me land on a bigger paper. Three separate scholarships helped, but I still had to take out some fat loans. Overall, it cost around $7,000, not counting the lost salary."[3] When housing, transportation, books, food, and incidentals are added to lost salaries, the total can run as high as $30,000, a high price to escape from gatekeeper inanity.

In Jim's case it paid off. After graduation he moved to Louisville to be an environmental reporter for the respected *Courier-Journal*. There, he was to win, or share in winning, five national awards. That kind of record always draws attention, and subsequently he moved to the *Philadelphia Inquirer* where he now is science editor. Fortunately for him, both of the papers he has been with since his fresh start are among the roughly thirty in the nation that show a continuing concern for high-quality performance. This automatically signals the presence of senior editors who insist on professional performance and the observance of ethical standards. A number of other equally concerned newspaper editors seek to follow similar standards. But even if one wanted to guess the overall number of truly effective directing editors at 100, it leaves the majority of executives in charge of the roughly 1,650 other dailies in the nation in one of three possible postures: (1) unwilling to believe the polls showing that the press is suffering a major credibility problem with the public at large, (2) convinced that most of the criticisms reflect the old syndrome of wanting to kill the messenger for delivering bad news, or (3), the one I hold the most likely, which is that those in charge are well meaning but either cannot shake off their early training or have always lacked the capacity to impose and maintain firm standards of performance.

What we are discussing is "quality control," and the same general measurement in terms of common-sense professionalism applies equally to TV, which goes into more than 98 percent of the country's homes, with sets per household averaging 1.7.[4] The chasm that divides a newspaper holding to the standards of a *New York Times* from one like the late William Loeb's *Manchester* (N.H.) *Union-Leader* also applies in contrasting the professional tone of the TV networks' news delivery from that prevailing at most of the locally operated stations, where only a tiny number of the 903 commercial stations are under the control of enlightened owners.[5]

Curiously, while journalism's general competence, writing ability, and basic efficiency have never been higher, it has fallen steadily in public trust. This is not simply because of inaccuracy (which is inevitable in any undertaking that places its chief emphasis on speed), but rather because of an arrogance that seems to place journalism's rights above everything else in the society. As James K. Batten, president of the giant Knight-Ridder chain, summarized it, "The truth is, a lot of the American public don't much like us or trust us. They think we're too big for our britches."[6] A study done for the American Society of Newspaper Editors by a team of Michigan State University researchers commented acidly, "In some newsrooms, the public-be-damned attitude reached siege mentality."[7] Wherever this exists, the responsibility lies with those in charge. The chief controllers are the directing editors and the publishers or, in broadcasting, the station managers, news directors, and owners. Any of them who want professional, ethical performance can enforce their demands for it. All gatekeeping begins at the top.

The teaching of ethics in schools of journalism has blossomed since the mid-1970s into what Professor Clifford Christians of the University of Illinois has described as "giving the appearance of a growth industry."[8] He pointed out, however, that of the 92,111 enrolled in journalism schools in 1984, only about 4,000 students actually took such course work. This is not to denigrate the growth in academic interest, which is important if journalism is to win back the confidence of the American citizenry. However, this movement cannot succeed until ethical studies are required, rather than made optional, and unless the profession's gatekeepers are brought into line with the process. As matters stand, many of the 4,000 students who enter journalism with some feeling for ethical approaches run a high risk of facing the same dilemma that tormented Jim Detjen and drove him to take his expensive gamble for a new and better future.

Many in communications see journalism's credibility problems as simply part of the general slide in public displeasure with all of the society's major institutions. Obviously, there is a linkage, but there can be no question about journalism having contributed to its own lower standing, just as lawyers have tarnished their image by their high-fee litigious activity. Some of what has taken place traces to what has happened in education the last two decades. James Billington, director of the Woodrow Wilson International Center for Scholars in Washington, D.C., and who was a noted professor at Princeton, has expressed strong criticism of American universities for ignoring the teaching of values, and their moving to curricula "emancipated from any tradition at all. . . . All this occurred because major research universities became dedicated to specialization somewhat in imitation of the industrial process on the assembly line, where everyone has a specialized function. While you can produce a whole car through specialization, you cannot produce a whole person that way. And without whole people who have strong civic involvement and deep personal convictions and commitments, democracy cannot function."[9] Harvard University's president, Derek Bok, has taken the same position, but was stronger in emphasizing the element I consider vital for journalism when he stressed that the "efforts to teach students about ethical issues are likely to be limited in value and to produce cynicism if the institutions themselves are perceived to be ethically careless or insensitive."[10]

Plainly, that was the perception of CBS held by Fairness in Media, the conservative advocacy group, which announced in January 1985 that it intended to seek control of the network.

Speaking for the group, Senator Jesse Helms (R., N.C.) said the goal was to rid CBS of what he called its "liberal bias." Rather than operating control, it seemed more likely that the drive was intended to try to elect some strong conservatives to the CBS board. However, the campaign was quickly eclipsed when Ted Turner, the flamboyant entrepreneur in cable TV, put in his bid for the $5 billion network. Thwarted by CBS's aggressive billion-dollar buying back of 21 percent of its stock, Mr. Turner withdrew his offer and moved to purchase the Metro-Goldwyn-Mayer/United Artists combine. It promised to give his WTBS-TV Atlanta "superstation" a library of 2,200 films, containing many famous, still-loved old movies.

There was some reason to suspect that Senator Helms and his allies in Fairness in Media had been encouraged in their original moves by their assessment of the antagonism toward journalism not only among members of the public at large, but also among members of the Congress.

The latter was reflected in a *Wall Street Journal* report in February 1985. It depicted major network executives as realizing how deeply legislators in both parties had been alienated on the issue of exit polling, as well as other matters such as children's programming and the stress on violence. Rep. Al Swift (D., Wash.), who formerly was in broadcasting, in addressing executives of independent stations, said, "The networks are perceived the way they are because they're arrogant—not by accident; every day, day in, day out, every day of their lives, they work at it." Before General William Westmoreland announced that he had decided on a negotiated settlement of his $120 million suit against CBS (a case dealt with in chapter 12), House Speaker Thomas P. O'Neill was quoted as saying "Capitol Hill is cheering for Westmoreland."[11] With newspaper and broadcast executives apparently coming closer to acknowledging how dangerous the hostility toward all segments of the press has become, the question is whether intellectual reform in so large and so diverse a quasi-profession is feasible in time enough to restore sufficient balance to forestall serious damage.

Charles Kuralt of CBS News was far from being the comradely commentator one sees on screen when he lectured in mid-1984 at the University of Nevada in Reno.[12] He, too, was thinking of convictions and commitments, and he was scorchingly critical of local television practice. "The most serious of hazards," he told his student and faculty audience, "is the management of TV stations. With few exceptions, the managers came to their present eminence by being good salesmen. They know about sales, they know about revenues, they know about ratings, they understand the bottom line. They don't know anything about news and they don't care. But they make *all* the decisions." Mr. Kuralt deplored the delivery of news "most often by an attractive young person who would not know a news story if it jumped up and mussed his coiffure." He was most indignant, however, about "news consultants," who he described as "a breed of scoundrel . . . giving bad advice." He denounced their urging "staccato pace and the one-sentence interview" and rules "that no story is worth more than 90 seconds. . . . The station managers who employ them [the consultants] eagerly follow their contemptible advice and in city after city . . . the news is cheapened, and the viewer cheated." William Allen White would have applauded Mr. Kuralt's saying, "Since we have only one life to live, I am afraid I must say that television news as it is practiced in most places is not the field in which a serious journalist would like to live his."

All that needs be added is that while the quality of daily newspapers in many of those same cities Mr. Kuralt was talking about also gives serious journalists pause, it is on a far higher level in terms of being comprehensive and useful than what passes for "news content" on most local TV stations. But this observation by no means alters one of the facts of communications life. Critics keep challenging owners of newspapers and broadcasting organizations for giving profits precedence over public service. Owners denounce these views as specious, but the annual earnings records tend to impugn their credibility.

True, only the most immovable idealist will argue that unselfish public service must outweigh the requirements for profitable existence. Walter Lippmann (1899–1974) commented that when there is no prosperous press, "the liberty of publication is precarious."[13] That isn't the issue facing newspaper or broadcast owners in the 1980s. Sir William Haley, the noted British editor, summed it up tartly in 1970 after serving on a Du Pont Survey panel at Columbia. Calling news the lifeblood of democracy, he went on to say about broadcasting: "Lip service is still paid to this ideal. Network presidents are combatively eloquent about it. But there are serious differences between their principles and their practices."[14] Many newspaper editors continue to see TV as so fundamentally tied to entertainment that they do not agree that it has any right to First Amendment protection for its news outreach. For me this is not myopia, but blindness.

How can anyone be working in communications in the mid-1980s and not recognize the enormous effect television has had on virtually all aspects of our lives? The skimpiness of much of TV news reporting is constantly evident to professionals. But there can be no challenging the impact on viewers in instances of major stories. The tragedy of widespread starvation in Africa was proof enough. There had been many stories in newspapers (some papers, at any rate) about the effects of the savage drought, but they made little ripple on the consciousness of people. That changed dramatically when the televised British TV pictures appeared in the United States. TV's impact was even more apparent during the seventeen-day Beirut hostage drama in June 1985. Controversy swirled about the networks going "live" in their drives to be first, thus surrendering editing control to the group holding the hostages. "Our failure to control ownership of the story may have been the problem," said John Chancellor of NBC. Indeed. Not only are the gates untended, but thrown open when editing is bypassed for "live action."

There is no connection, but TV also has problems with political coverage at home. The TV role in 1984s national campaign drew worried criticism from scholars. In a review of three books on this subject, Professor Doris A. Graber raised the thought that the three studies "make readers wonder to what extent televised news, in its current form, is a menace to the effectiveness of America's democratic institutions."[15] There can be no question but that TV's need for dramatic pictures inhibits the freedom of its reporters and editors. It was clear during the 1984 campaign that political managers were to a large extent controlling what was seen and heard.

The most graphic account of the process was published in the *Washington Post* the day before the 1984 election in a study of a CBS producer, Susan Zirinsky. She was described as "a 32-year-old, 5-foot-2 compulsive mother hen who calls colleagues 'pumpkin,' swears like a truck driver and looks like a schoolgirl. . . . Although it is Bill Plante and Lesley Stahl who cover the White House, write the stories, and appear on the air, it is Susan Zirinsky who decides on the pictures as many as 25 million people will see each night in their homes. And as any campaign official will tell you, it's often the pictures that matter most." Howard Stringer, CBS News' executive vice-president, agreed. "On the daily story, with the rush to edit, the pictures dominate," he told the *Post,* "almost despite the narration. The White House—and all great politicians understand that."

The story went on to detail the collaborative roles of the campaign managers, quoting them as to how they tried to arrange events for the best photographic effects, and of how producers warn political managers when they run risks on timing for the evening news. "Let's be honest," Miss Zirinsky said, "part of their job is to get those stories in the air."[16] This is not a put-down of Susan Zirinsky and her fellow producers in the political arena. As will come clear later (in chapter 11), television is the captive of the chase for ratings and the intense scrutiny by money-market managers because of the networks' status as public corporations. How that scrutiny exerts pressure on programming judgments became evident in the months just before ABC made the decision to sell out to Capital Cities Communications, a company one-fourth the size of ABC.

TV's lowest-common-denominator approach galls many able people in television news, but like many of their counterparts in newspaper journalism, they find themselves in straitjackets laced on them by the gatekeepers in the executive suites.

In fairness, the schizophrenic streak these executives have always had over profit vs. duty plainly has been heightened by the new broker-banker focus on communications companies.

An example of how this filters down the line came when Bill Moyers in August 1985 said that he was returning to the CBS Evening News program. "I have concluded," he said, "that serious public affairs reporting in depth isn't going to make it in the entertainment milieu of prime time. I have to be a grown-up fellow and face the fact that reporting on social issues in depth isn't going to be given a fair shot."

I know of no thoroughly trained professional in television who claims domination for TV depth and scope of straight news reporting. They worry openly when any comment is made that millions rely almost exclusively on TV for their news information. John Chancellor held his hands to his head at a luncheon table when this topic was raised one day and exclaimed, "God help all of us if that's all they are going to rely on." Walter Cronkite made similar comments over the years, stressing that everything on a 22-minute newscast (commercials take up the rest of the half hour) cannot possibly compete with a newspaper's space and ability to carry differing points of view at length. Both Messrs. Chancellor and Cronkite are correct about newspapers that work to do the task properly. But it isn't the case where "the system" overpowers rational judgments.

Few editors have been more direct in discussing these aspects than A. M. Rosenthal, executive editor of the *New York Times*. "The trouble is that the vast majority of the country's newspapers contain too much garbage," he said. "They do not print enough news and their sole concern is trashy entertainment. The prime violators are the publishers. Right now, almost anybody can make money publishing newspapers and most have the money to produce good papers. But they won't do the spending. If any newspaper loses the battle for readers' attention to TV, it won't be because of TV, but despite it."[17] A lifetime of immersion in the ocean of news can only produce a compulsive analyst of competence and quality in all of the forms of communications, and I agree fully with Mr. Rosenthal's indictment about newspapers, as well as with Mr. Kuralt's observations about television.

So, too, do growing numbers of the nation's citizens. Many of the country's leading pollsters, and particularly George Gallup and Daniel Yankelovich,[18] have repeatedly delivered warnings to both newspaper and television executives about the downward trend in public attitudes toward the media. One of the other prominent pollsters, Ruth Clark, did a special study for the American Society of Newspaper Editors. Some thoughtful editors surely must have paused to reflect on her finding that "the one big problem is that they [readers who were questioned] don't really trust newspapers to be fair or unbiased or to go out of their way to make sure that they're accurate." Her study also took in TV. Asked about fairness, 38 percent of those queried thought newspapers fair; 50 percent did not; 12 percent were unsure. The same query about TV resulted in 63 percent calling the medium "unfair," 29 percent "fair," and 8 percent not sure.[19]

Of all of journalism's twentieth-century philosopher-thinkers, the mantle of greatness has been bestowed on Walter Lippmann. There can be little question but that he had misgivings most of his life about journalism's course, but certainly he would have been even more troubled had he lived another decade. Fifty-four years ago, he was hoping for a new epoch in the developing American journalism. His mind was caught by "the objective, orderly, and comprehensive presentation of news" which he saw as "a far more successful type of journalism than the dramatic, disorderly, episodic type." He saw it as cumulative, "because it opens the door to the use of trained intelligence in newspaper work. . . . For the ability to present news objectively and to interpret it realistically is not a native instinct in the human species; it is a product of culture which comes only with knowledge of the past and acute awareness of how deceptive is our normal observation and how wishful is our thinking. . . . It has been at times a dignified calling, at others a romantic adventure, and then again a servile trade. But profession it could not begin to be until modern objective journalism was successfully created, and with it the need of men who would consider themselves devoted, as all the professions ideally are, to the service of truth alone."[20]

I was studying Lippmann's thoughts again when the June/July 1984 issue of the editors' monthly magazine came. In it were excerpts from the windup speech of the society's past president. Dealing with TV's "sins and shortcomings," he held that TV "had adopted no standard mechanism for correcting its errors."[21] My mind flashed to three years earlier when this same publisher's newspaper had editorially savaged the National News Council for having the effrontery to accept what it termed a spurious complaint by a Kentucky congressman. No such complaint had been filed, much less accepted. A friendly letter to the publisher pointing out the facts brought no correction. His reply was that the editorial writer was aggrieved because he had not been consulted about the formation of the Council, had opposed the idea, and had felt it his right to condemn it as he saw fit. Reading the publisher contend that TV was still in its adolescence reminded me of the prejudices we all carry, and how too often we abuse the privilege of using printing presses and airwaves to vent private grievances. The distrust voiced to pollsters about journalistic "fairness" shows how astutely the citizens have divined how poorly those editorial gates are tended.

Quite apart from this, however, it is an inescapable fact that the romantic view of newspaper reporters held by many among the public was dramatically changed by the pervasive nature of TV. Until TV became a fixed element in major news coverage, few ever saw reporters in action—that is, in the act of interviewing government officials, or questioning private people, or involving any of the other hundreds of activities that go into the daily gathering of data. As important as any other development was TV's portrayal of the thrust and parry in presidential press conferences. A close second may have been seeing reporters facing grieving families immediately after tragedies. Another came with scenes of wolf pack, or mob, coverage with photographers pushing and shoving to get better positions. What the citizens saw offended them. It was not television's fault that many citizens came to feel that some reporters—identified by name and news organizations—were overly aggressive boors when dealing with the President. It *was* the fault of TV's gatekeepers to have so many TV reporters thrusting microphones into people's faces and asking questions so inane as to have viewers at home cringing. The whole of it was contained in two sets of comments. Ben Bradlee, executive editor of the *Washington Post,* said, "Television has changed the public's vision of the reporter into someone who is petty and disagreeable and who has taken cynicism an unnecessary extra step." Reuven Frank, NBC News president at the time, responded, "The printed press does not show the reporter asking the question. What is peculiar to TV is that intrusiveness is part of the story."

Many newspaper people still seem incapable of recognizing that to the average citizen a reporter is a reporter. If a TV reporter jumps out of a darkened doorway to confront a man walking out of a building (the term used is "sandbagging"), citizens take it as the standard reportorial practice. The finger pointing is juvenile. TV did not invent reporters who are boors, sandbaggers, or who ask stupid questions. One of the oldest newspaper legends is about a New York ship-news reporter who boarded an arriving liner to seek out Albert Einstein, and promptly asked the world's most famous living scientist what kind of doctor he was. In the world of journalism, all the houses are made of glass.

What Walter Lippmann hoped to see developing in journalism in "trained intelligence" has come only at the upper quality level of communications (the magazines of thoughtful analysis have long had it). We see talent at work regularly in both the best newspapers and on the best TV programs. Below that level, the system has worked with a kind of mindless arrogance under individuals who have slavishly followed handed-down conventional wisdoms. One of the better descriptions of this tired old system has come to me from Arnold Rosenfeld, who has moved from the Dayton (Ohio) newspapers to be editor of the *Austin* (Texas) *American Statesman.* He wrote me:

The most crucial level of management at a newspaper, although most of us would hate to admit it, is about at the level of assistant city editor, whatever you might actually call it. These are the people who are more stratospheric management's direct link with the reporters who get the facts and do the work. You can have the highest sounding principles in the world, but unless you have your average, young, hard-working assistant city editor aboard and committed, you'll never actually reach your staff. The problem is that frequently this crucial link with the staff is faced in two directions, not quite sure whether they're management or staff. They are fairly isolated. You think, perhaps, that the city editor is talking to them, but you're never quite sure what the city editor is saying and whether it reflects all those things you've spent hours talking about—tone and fairness and being straight with the reader. If you're an editor, you can say all you want that this paper's major concern is with serving the interests of the reader, but unless someone who is credible to the reporter says that, the language gets lost either in newsroom routine, or worse yet, the hymn-singing of journalism as a religion.

Where does this "average, young, hard-working assistant city editor" come from? In almost every news organization, this new primary-level gatekeeper is plucked from among the staff. "Too frequently," as Mr. Rosenfeld put it, it is

someone who has, for instance, just done a heck of a job on the police beat. That may be one great qualification, but we ought to know more about the people we put in our most important editing jobs. We ought to know what they stand for, what they actually know—or more important, care—about readers before we put them in a position of telling reporters what the paper or the world is all about. Additionally, we ought to be talking to them frequently, and training them. Management training at newspapers has always been viewed more as an art than a craft. We're flattering ourselves and we ought to cut it out.[22]

There is even more here than the words. As is true in all callings, professionals lean on a type of shorthand understanding in which nuances are taken for granted. Only in the most meticulous of news organizations are the choices for assistant city editors or assistant news editor—or in television, assistant directors or assistant producers—made by the directing heads of the staffs. It is not unusual for upper-level gatekeepers to learn long after the act that some individual was chosen for advancement not because he or she had done "a heck of a job," but because the staffer lived in the same neighborhood as the subeditor in charge, or belonged to the same church. There is nothing malicious or nefarious about it. The person selected sometimes is an excellent choice in terms of working diligently. More often, the chosen individual turns out to lack vision or depth. The central point is that the method is so unstructured that it has left more than a few top news executives with personal headaches and a residue of hostility once the damage has been undone.

Stricter rules on employment and promotion have come to newsrooms where union contracts apply. This has brought the inevitable pendulum effect: the swing from high-handed misuse of the power to fire by coldly ruthless editors to the high-handed misuse of power by union leaders to block corrective action by fighting dismissals, even when clear cause is obvious to everyone. I have seen both sides of the coin, and it has tails on both sides. The same equation applies to relationships between directing editors and their publishers and owners. It is one reason why many editors cannot find time to keep close tabs on their subordinate editors who control daily coverage and promotions to primary-level gatekeeping posts. The majority of directing editors never have been given time for thoughtful managerial appraisals. They are captives of a system that obstructs any sound learning process.

To support this strong indictment, I am about to quote from J. Edward Murray's lecture on ethics at the University of Hawaii in February 1984. Mr. Murray began his career as a reporter in Chicago, was a war correspondent in Europe for United Press

International, and after the war became directing editor in Los
Angeles, Detroit, Washington, and Phoenix. He served as president of the American Society of Newspaper Editors, and retired
after being publisher of the *Boulder Camera* in Colorado. These
credentials might mask the fact that he is an intellectual, a type
in too-short supply these days, not only in journalism but in all
of society's undertakings. His kind constitute a national asset
too often overlooked. I have chosen the point in his speech at
which he was discussing news editors, the role on most newspapers just under the managing and executive editors. News
editors basically are those in control of the running news flow—
importance of stories, length, placement, and so on. Many subsequently move up to managing editor posts. Mr. Murray said:

> The average news editor's judgment tends to be shallow
> and uninformed because of a lack of catholic interests. It is
> also beset by the inertia of outdated newspaper traditions,
> of moldy old habits which defraud the reader and hurt the
> newspaper competitively against the electronic media. . . .
> All too many of the news editors I've known, and their
> bosses, the managing editors and executive editors, have
> been figuratively *programmed* with outworn definitions of
> news. In obedience to this programming, the gatekeepers
> seem to function almost like automatons in responding
> only to news that meets at least one of three sets of require-
> ments or preconceptions. First, is it a recent event or devel-
> opment? Second, is it catastrophic, confrontational,
> aberrational, negative, violent, lurid, glamorous or other-
> wise entertaining? Third, does it involve quick, episodic,
> once-over-easy politics, economics, law enforcement or hu-
> man interest novelty of any kind? Unfortunately, all of this
> out-dated programming is guaranteed to miss much of the
> important serious news, which is readily available to news
> desks from their wire services.

Speaking at the 1983 convention of the Associated Press
Managing Editors, I attempted to grade the country's newspapers on qualitative lines and, in doing so, employed the one-

to-four-star pattern many newspapers use in ratings of restaurants. My view was that only four of the 1,688 dailies deserved four stars; a dozen more merited three stars, another dozen two stars, and approximately fifty more one star. Of the other 1,610 dailies, my statement was, "I submit that these run-of-the-mill papers are strangled by budgets that force incredibly tight newsholes and such low salary levels that the editors have no option but to hire the least fit if they are to get their papers out." I was with the managing editors for two more days. Four or five large-city editors said I had it right. There must have been dozens present who had strongly opposing views; not one of them raised any question.

Two score asked for the names of the four- and three-star newspapers, even though this should hardly be any mystery to managing editors. Although any listing is clearly subjective and open to challenge, mine should not surprise anyone. The four-star group takes in the *New York Times,* the *Los Angeles Times,* the *Washington Post,* and the *Wall Street Journal.* Reflecting the fact that there never has been a perfect newspaper and probably never will be, each of these four has individual faults or weaknesses. Their glory is that they are solid, work at trying to be thorough, spend whatever is necessary for quality, and are purposefully deep in talent. Each is owned by parent corporations that rank among the major chains. Put simply, they are world-class newspapers. The three-star group cannot be judged on any basis of evenness of performance. A few rank close to the four-stars in muscle and talent; a few others are coming up fast; a few are close to sliding into the two-star category. Some are occasionally erratic in quality. What they do have is the desire to be quality newspapers, and they strive for it, even when they hurt themselves by cutting corners. At any rate, the fairest way to list them is to divide them in half, as if one were separating large eggs from smaller ones. The six top-drawer three-star papers (named alphabetically) are the *Boston Globe,* the *Chicago Tribune,* the *Miami Herald, Newsday,* the *Philadelphia Inquirer,* and the *San Jose Mercury-News.* The other six take in the *Baltimore Sun,* the Dallas *Morning News,* the *Detroit Free-Press,* the

*Milwaukee Journal,* the *Orlando Sentinel,* and the *St. Peterburg Times.*

The two-star list includes some newspapers once regulars on "top ten" lists. Although still good they have not quite kept up, for varying reasons, including loss of industries for their cities, resulting in fewer jobs and population losses, and strong suburban competition that cuts into advertising revenues. Some have felt the need to curtail spending, which includes tightening news space and inevitably lessens quality. Leadership probably has been a factor in some cases. Lists such as these change constantly. Mine came from steady sampling, and even though checked with neutral professionals, is wholly subjective.

Top-level professionals in television are just as knowledgeable about high-quality performance in news coverage and public service in local TV as are their print counterparts about newspapers. Probably because of their zeal, more TV stations were listed as belonging on the three-star list. In collecting the TV list, I have sought to be faithful gatekeeper, recording what well-placed, widely admired people in the field have given as their judgments. It is interesting that four stations were chosen as belonging in the four-star group and they are listed alphabetically by city: Chicago's WBBM-TV, Minneapolis' WCCO-TV, Salt Lake City's KSL-TV, and Seattle's KING-TV.

The top six among the three-stars are Boston's WCVB-TV, Dallas' WFAA-TV, Houston's KPRC-TV, Louisville's WHAS-TV, Milwaukee's WTMJ-TV, and Nashville's WSMV-TV. The other six are Baton Rouge's WBRZ-TV, Charlotte's WBTV, Kansas City's WDAF-TV, Pittsburgh's KDKA-TV, Raleigh's WRAL-TV, and Washington's WDVM-TV. Others named as meriting three-star calls were Fresno's KFSN-TV, Jacksonville's WJXT-TV, Sioux Falls' KELO-TV, and Yakima's KIMA-TV. One chain, the (Washington) Post-Newsweek group, was praised for its emphasis on news.

Neither any New York City or Los Angeles station drew a single call. One collaborator put it deftly: "They are addicted to personalities. They are innocent of having committed any act of journalism. It's the environment." Another laughed. "Show biz," he said. "The stations in both cities are hooked on celebrity stuff. Looks, lights, talky-talk." He sounded like another Charles Kuralt.

While at this honor-roll tabulation, I am impelled to place in the four-star category the Associated Press, which has to be classed as the Atlas of the world of journalism. Without muscle-flexing or using Madison Avenue techniques to promote itself, it goes about its round-the-clock, 365-days-a-year job of covering wherever it can get to in the world—providing a smorgasbord of news, pictures, features, and all else within its competence, all of it done "straight." AP staff members have won hundreds of awards over the years, including a rather staggering thirty-two Pulitzer Prizes, remarkable since it is not competitive in such classifications as editorial writing, criticism or comment, editorial cartooning, or public service, which is awarded only to individual newspapers.[23] More than 15,000 newspapers, television, and radio stations around the world depend on this immensely able and well-managed cooperative.

Edward Murray's indictment of the ineritia and shallowness of so many news editors can be appreciated more fully when the extent of usage is considered. Countless readers never have seen some of the AP's most honored work because the newspaper editors who scanned the copy decided it wasn't worth printing. How they later can publish the prize lists without giving a thought to their original short-sightedness is proof of their one-day-at-a-time memory—and that of their directing editors and their publishers. To borrow from A. M. Rosenthal's description, these are editors who work in a pattern applied to some computer production: Garbage in, garbage out. The *Times* itself has passed up some of the AP's prize-winning copy, but for a different reason. The *Times* has long stressed its own staff work. AP staffers call it the "NIH syndrome," standing for "not invented here."

John Morton, the country's best-known financial analyst about newspapers, made the point about tight budgeting more forcefully in public comment about a highly successful, smaller-paper chain. "It is basically budget-driven," he said, "and that takes precedence over anything else, sometimes including putting out quality papers."[24]

There is a lot that can be said in criticism of chain ownership, but it has to be acknowledged that a few of the chains started from a high-quality base and their papers reflect it. Of the sixteen papers I have named, twelve belong to big conglomerates. Looking through them, one sees no trace of anything but sound, enterprising, autonomous managements, investing strongly in high-quality content. That is a major concession from one who has been very critical of the sweep into conglomerate communications. There is an inherent danger in the measure of potential central control over the content flowing through the nation's informational pipelines. It has become all the more pertinent with the growing pressures for deregulation. The Federal Communications Commission's decision to end the 32-year-old rule limiting one ownership's holdings of broadcast (AM and FM radio and TV) properties fits into the considerations. Under the new FCC formula, the old rule limiting one ownership to a total of 21 stations (7, 7, and 7), has been changed to 36 (12, 12, and 12) until 1990, and after that there will be no limits of any kind. However it develops, it is clear that the communications industry is acting in precisely the same pattern as every other industry.

*Advertising Age* studies the 100 largest companies involved in communications each year. Its review of 1983 performance noted that 50 of these companies had been buyers of other communications properties and 35 had been sellers in the reshuffling the magazine likened to the "game of musical chairs."[25] In the 1985 issue, editor R. Craig Endicott referred to a "buying craze" in reporting that the top 100 during 1984 and leading into mid-1985 had taken part in "48 purchases involving 207 TV, radio, and cable properties and 32 print purchases consuming 176 properties." The ability of the giants for further outreach was evident in the fact that of 1984's top 100 media companies, 12 had revenues exceeding a billion dollars each. Covering all revenues for the 100 companies—and these do not, by any means, encompass the totality of communications—the figure was $50.2 billion, up 19.1 percent over 1983.[25]

The issue is not the dollar figures, but rather the problem of how the news informational side of the equation is going to be balanced. The United States, after all, is in its thirteenth generation since Jefferson and Madison. There may not have been a greater advance in intellectual breadth since their time, but there has been more technological change than in all of prior history, and the pace picks up constantly. The societal changes, national and international, grow in concert. With them have come high degrees of volatility in public moods. For all the variants that appear, there have been several steady trends. One has been the remarkable loss of faith and trust, on the part of citizens toward society's major institutions. One of the chief losers has been government itself, in substantial part due to the frustrations of the Vietnam War and to the subsequent scandal that forced Richard Nixon to relinquish the presidency. Up-and-down changes in polls of public attitudes may encourage individual participants from time to time, but they do not alter the steadily blinking yellow warning lights.

In his 1981 book, *New Rules,* Mr. Yankelovich compared American attitudes with the constant movement of the giant plates under the earth's surface. He said that his long series of studies showed the national culture to be "shifting relentlessly beneath us."[26] In his preface to the Public Agenda Foundation's 1980 report on *The Speaker and the Listener,* Mr. Yankelovich took note of the press being "in the vortex of highly charged controversy, criticism and debate," and he went on to predict that "general social forces will produce new problems for freedom of the press, and the First Amendment itself may be subjected to reexamination."[27] Only a few among the scores of journalists with whom I have talked agree with that concern and those few are associated, for the most part, with the notable elite organizations.

For my own part, I am as worried as is Mr. Yankelovich. Some of this traces to a personal failure in the 1960s to convince a number of leading editors about the dangers building in a drive for a Constitutional Convention. There will be more examination of this aspect later, but for the moment the following may be said. After Congress declined to approve the late Senator Everett Dirksen's proposal for an amendment calling for voiding the Supreme Court's reapportionment decision (one man/one vote), he joined with the Council of State Governments to campaign for a Constitutional Convention. Under Article V of the Constitution, a convention comes into being with the petitions of two-thirds of the state legislatures. Senator Dirksen's campaign tapped not only opposition to the "one man/one vote" but also to other grievances being nursed among various blocs. The drive moved rapidly, but there was only minimal press coverage nationally. Leading scholars in the field of constitutional law were carrying on extended exchanges with influential lawyers. Having the privilege of reading a number of these papers led to my urging editor friends around the country to examine the points being advanced so that deeper and fuller coverage could be encouraged.

As a would-be modern Paul Revere, I must go down as a miserable failure. Reporters covering legislatures, and their editors, continued to see little news value in resolutions to Congress. Some increase in attention developed when Chief Justice Earl Warren made a series of speeches to bar associations, warning that any such convention could well move to revise some of the basic portions of the Bill of Rights. Basically, however, the attitude of news editors appeared to follow the standard pattern described by Edward Murray. The top-quality newspapers reported what the chief justice had to say, but in general the coverage nationally was in columns of briefs. The central attention was on the usual chase-the-hot-story pattern, and it was only quiet pressure from leaders of the American Bar Association that derailed the Dirksen campaign when it was at victory's edge.

By 1969, only one more petition was needed to fill the required 34. One state was induced to rescind its call, and suits were filed in several other states, challenging the validity of the earlier actions. Yet in almost all of those states it had been unheralded battle. It is too early to say whether history will repeat itself. But as this is written, two major scholarly organizations have joined in study of the deep concerns of those in Congress who live in fear of a "runaway" convention.[28] The fear, of course, is because of a national culture "shifting relentlessly," a culture that has come to believe, among other things, that its press is not fair enough or accurate enough. In that culture are countless individuals who at one time or another tried to register protests about inaccuracies or ineptitude within the press, but were turned away as "crazies" by those who control the gates.

## CHAPTER 2
# The Intellectual Diabetics

*There was a young lady of Kent*
*Who said that she knew what it meant*
*When men asked her to dine,*
*Gave her cocktails and wine,*
*She knew what it meant—but she went.*

SOME ARE SURE to read this old limerick as pure chauvinism, but a bit longer appraisal will show it to be a shrewd depiction of the temptations and vulnerabilities that go on in all human affairs. "All corruption," said the late Senator Paul Douglas of Illinois, "begins with the nickel cigar to the policeman on the corner."[1] He said that the cigar inevitably led to the box, and then to the bottle and on to the case, and from there up the scale. For the press it began with the free meal and free tickets, spawning the widely used "freebie" term. A quip published in the old *Vanity Fair* read, "One answer to the problem of how to treat reporters is to treat them frequently."[2]

In fairness, journalism has made enormous strides in basic ethics since those days. More news organizations than ever have adopted ethical codes for their staffs. It is the rare meeting when the subject is not mentioned, and more conferences are being held focusing exclusively on ethical nuances. Even so, ethics are violated regularly. The "freebie" virus remains alive. In a way, it can be likened to so strong a craving for sugar that even those who know they have an insulin deficiency can no more resist the temptations than could the young lady of Kent. One can apply to them a term contrived from medicine: intellectual diabetics.

Writer-editor Irving Kristol accurately described journalism as "the underdeveloped profession."[3] It will remain so, if only because the nature of the enterprise as a whole defies any standard rules. Cambridge University philosopher A. C. Ewing outlined the ethical problem three decades ago when he wrote that "there seems to be no possibility of validly deducing ethical propositions by some sort of logical argument from the nature of reality without first assuming some ethical propositions to be true; or at least if there is, the way to do so has not yet been discovered by anybody."[4] Saying ethics needed to generalize, Dr. Ewing advanced the theme of *common-sense* ethics," and it is within this kind of framework that journalistic ethics is moving. Unfortunately, this takes an exceedingly long time—which explains journalism's erratic steps in accepting ethical standards.

The first codes for journalism were adopted seventy-five years ago, a span that has astonished all but perhaps a dozen of the hundreds of students I encountered in ethics classes, as well as the many more newsmen and newswomen with whom I have worked over the years. Even the first code adopted by the Kansas Editorial Association in 1910 covered all of the essentials for publishers, editors, reporters, and those in the business offices. A rereading three-quarters of a century later shows it to be bolder, stronger, and more specific in certain ways than many of today's efforts.[5] It is interesting that so many of the ethical drives in journalism sprang up in the Middle West and spread westward. It is not an argument against bigness per se, but I am led to believe that ethics got lost in the intense drives for circulation dominance in the major cities (a subject covered in some detail in chapter 3). At any rate, editors have long disagreed about codes. Journalism went through a long, fallow period, during which standards of fairness slipped, along with a loss of the sense of what Walter Williams, the dean of the first separate school of journalism in the nation (1908) at the University of Missouri, called "the public trust."[6]

In recent years the major journalistic societies have updated codes adopted in the early 1920s in renewed efforts to curb the transgressions that keep occurring. The record is replete with instances of those in sports, entertainment, business, and particularly politics, along with their ubiquitous press agents, working constantly in whatever ways are open to them to influence reporters, editors/producers, and their superiors. It is true that any code, statement of principles, guideline, or whatever term one wishes to employ can be violated by an individual bent on ignoring the rules. But there is a far better chance of holding a sound line on ethical principles with a written code, and all the more so when those who exercise control *want* standards enforced. When those in journalism's gatekeeping roles are determined to keep the news flow free of outside influence, there will come a far more universal acceptance of sensible standards.

The term glacial to describe progress in the field is not hyperbole. I know the record better than most. My first job was on a sports staff run by a sports editor on the "take." It should not be hard to understand the shock of an idealistic youth to suddenly be made aware that all local news, other than coverage of high school and college teams, carried a price tag, with the proceeds going into the sports editor's pocket. I was rescued from that den to work elsewhere honorably. But twenty years later, as managing editor of the *St. Louis Star-Times,* I was to learn that the local wrestling promoter was paying the assistant sports editor $35 a week for printing advance puff stories and that his weekly matches were getting twice the space they deserved. This same desk chief was serving as agent for the then-ambitious Mexican Baseball League, and in our sports office had signed famed Dodger catcher Mickey Owen to a Mexican League contract.[7] I also was to discover that since he also served as chairman of the grievance committee of the Newspaper Guild (the union founded by Heywood Broun in the 1930s), there was no practical way of firing him without taking a strike. That much had to be swallowed.

However, two pluses made up for it. One was to move into command of the sports operation a bright, energetic, totally ethical assistant managing editor who had an affinity for sports. The other plus came out of a talk with the sports editor who, like so many others in his position, was concerned primarily with his daily column. He said that he had never been told about any ethical standards and voluntarily disclosed that he possessed fifty shares of stock in the St. Louis Browns, given free by the team's owners. Does the purpose of the free stock need any explanation? After our talk he turned back the stock, and when the newspaper was sold in 1951 to the *Post-Dispatch* he sat with me and told me that from the hour of our conversation he had accepted no favor of any kind. The way Sid Keener said it showed he was proud of it; and I was for him. He proved that ethics can be implanted, even to a veteran from an editor many years younger.

Framed copies of the American Society of Newspaper Editors' code of ethics hung on the walls of many editors' offices, but year after year came revelations of similar violations all across the country, not only in sports, entertainment, and travel news but also in the wide range of coverage directed to women's interests. In 1953, then in Louisville, I rattled some of these skeletons in public, to the delight of a number of staff members who began to deliver for my files the written and telegraphed blandishments that came their way. In articles and speeches, I pressed the point that news space could be considered for sale whenever writers were allowed to accept gifts and favors for what appeared in a newspaper's columns and, further, that any papers accepting travel and other expenses for covering any news event were taking bribes for the coverage. It was patently open about sports, less well known in other matters. What follows dates back to the 1950s and '60s, but newer incidents will disclose how difficult it still is to keep the news channels clear of tampering. A few tidbits:[8]

• From a public relations firm announcing a "Great Lakes Mink Association Fashion Editor's Award." There were to be awards in a range of circulation categories. The letter said, "Enclosed you will find six pictures with suggested captions, a fact sheet to use as the basis for the story, and a form to accompany your entry. . . . The basis on which entries will be judged is headline (25)%, layout (25%), and story and/or caption copy (50%). . . . The editor who submits the winning entry in each category will receive a beautiful dark ranch mink boa."

• Following a style show, the fashion editor ran a layout of new dresses. The press agent's letter was delicious. The knitting mills' president, it said, "was so pleased with the way his dress looked in your layout that he insisted it be submitted to the jury in our fashion mailing. The jury has voted you a dress as a prize, so please send me the size you would like in a knitted dress and it will be mailed to you. *Should you prefer to have it sent to another address than that of the newspaper please indicate that as well*" (italics mine).

• From an old friend who had been a wire service reporter and had gone into public relations: "If you get to thinking about a new car, and possibly a Buick, let me know and you sure will get the 'preacher's treatment.' "

• Telegram to a movie critic, signed "Jerry Lewis": "Will you please be my personal guest in Chicago . . . (for) the premiere of my production Cinderfella . . . Join me in making it the lushest, plushest, most memorable time in our lives . . . Will send first-class plane tickets . . . A limousine will transport you to deluxe quarters and a well-stocked press room at the Ambassador East . . . You will be my guest at a private champagne dinner . . . and at midnight you are in for a batch of surprises."

• The press agent's letter informing us that on such-and-such a date UPI would transmit a story about his client, plus picture. His claim that she was a local girl could not be verified, leading to the assumption that a hundred other papers had received the same come-on. Story and picture came on schedule— about a would-be starlet whose sole claim for attention appeared to be a 39-inch bust measurement. Policing note: Provided with the file, the late Earl J. Johnson, editor of UPI, exploded in wrath at the Hollywood bureau's culpability.

• The press agent's bait to a movie critic, offering a role in a film to be shot in New York about newspaper life: air travel, hotel, meals, plus a week's pay to be "reporter, rewrite man or copy reader" to provider realism. Later, we learned fifty critics had accepted. Intellectual diabetics.

• The *Wall Street Journal* carried a full-length report, headlined "Many Travel Reporters, Freeloading Off Hosts, Don't Tell Story." The story recounted charges that many travel writers "don't mention the snow, wind and sleet at the 'winter resort' of the French Riviera. They don't mention that fog is likely to foul up flying plans on off-season trips to Europe. They don't mention that some hotels disavow reservations (but not those of travel writers) . . . tend to overlook winter rains in Miami (a city that advertises heavily in travel sections), or Hawaii's commercialism, or excruciating fall traffic in New England as foliage viewers line up bumper to bumper." The article added, "Reporters aren't always to blame for one-sided travel articles . . . Some editors willingly print articles sent free by feature syndicates, some of which are paid for by resorts, airlines or other interests." How little had changed was indicated by the editor's column comment in the July 1981 issue of *Frequent Flyer* magazine. "My associate editor," he wrote, "bristles if anyone even hazards to call him a travel writer."

• CBS's "60 Minutes" made a news splash in 1974 by showing a Pittsburgh newspaper TV critic registering at a New York hotel and being handed an envelope containing two $10 bills. The bills were from CBS for "taxis and miscellaneous." The program went on to report how car manufacturers, airlines, foreign governments, sports teams, and others seek to influence journalists. "With enough stamina," said Mike Wallace on the program, "an enterprising reporter just might be able to keep traveling and eating on someone else's charge account forever." In July 1984, *USA Today* did a fresh report on the networks' hosting of newspaper critics for previews of the fall programs. Standards had improved. For some 115 critics attending the Phoenix and Los Angeles sessions, *Today* said, about 70 percent of the newspapers had paid airfare and hotel bills, but added, "To a degree, it's still a free ride . . . the networks provide the food and liquor. The critics' defense: 'Better to accept a junket than to miss the news.' " Whether it was *news* was challenged by the *Denver Post*'s Clark Secrest, who wrote a memo to his editors suggesting that they not spend $3,000 on this "frivolous event." He told *Today* "After a while you can't remember who you talked to or when and you don't really care." No comment was made about the roughly thirty-five papers that sent critics and paid none of the bills for $120 rooms and what the story described as "gallons of free liquor, bus tours laced with champagne, sumptuous meals that start with strawberry soup."

• In 1950, the *St. Louis Post-Dispatch* and the *Chicago Daily News* shared a Pulitzer Prize for joining in investigating how Illinois state payrolls were being padded, naming a large number of Illinois newsmen on the payrolls. In 1972, *Newsday* undertook a similar investigation and revealed the same tradition existing in the New York area. It named eighteen news people as having held such jobs. "At least seven," *Newsday* reported, "wrote or edited stories for their newspapers about the subjects from whom they were receiving a second salary." It said four of the newsmen had received $10,000 or more a year from the political jobs. One of them told *Newsday* that the abuse of the system "was not what you wrote good about a guy—it was the bad things you knew and never wrote." The head of a political organization was candid. "If we bought a $5,000 advertisement," he said, "it's not as good as one news story from a reporter. A paid political ad, no matter you say, is still a paid political ad."

• As already pointed out, sports has figured regularly in accounts of freeloading and payoffs. So it was not surprising in 1973 to find Nicholas Pileggi reporting in *New York* magazine what had come out of an investigation by the New York attorney general into scalping. Madison Square Garden had a master freebie list. Sports writers and departments on the area's newspapers, broadcast stations, and wire services, in addition to working press tickets, were receiving supplies of extra free seats in preferred locations. The total value of the free tickets to *New York News* staffers, wrote Mr. Pileggi, was $28,635 per season; for *Times* staffers, $24,980; and $10,455 for those at the *Post*. Gilbert Rogin, a senior editor at *Sports Illustrated,* called it "sheer payola." Mr. Pileggi reported that Madison Square Garden publicists felt it would be difficult for the Garden "to get the kind of advance promotion on their less successful events without the kind of access the free tickets permit." He quoted one as saying, "The ego of sports guys for the free ticket is so enormous that it is a trade-wide policy involving the Knicks, Giants, Rangers, Jets and even the circus. . . . The tickets give you access to the newspaper offices. . . . There always have been all kinds of deals floating around the city's sports desks. They are a closed corporation. . . . Even non-sports writers on the same paper are discouraged from hanging around the sports desks. What the hell, you got a good thing, why tell the world?" Mr. Pileggi wrote that A. M. Rosenthal, the *Times'* executive editor, had repeated in surprise, "Forty-two tickets!" He ordered the practice ended immediately.

• How extensive these kinds of arrangements must be could be inferred from a 1977 survey taken by the Professional Standards Committee of the Associated Press Managing Editors Association. It sent questionnaires to nearly 1,000 members and received 287 replies. Of these, 116 said they had tightened policies on freebies. The report said, "A surprising number of managing editors said they didn't know what freebie policies were in their sports departments, but they had policies for the news department. . . . Some managing editors obviously had filled out the entire questionnaire, except for the questions involving sports. They were filled in by another person. One midwest editor wrote about sports, 'No idea what they do.' To one of the questions, an editor replied, 'We don't do that in the newsroom, but the publisher and advertising department will take anything they can get. It is disgusting to us.' To a query about whether he would accept an airline offer of a free 'fun-filled inaugural flight' one editor replied, 'We wouldn't, but my publisher would be first in line at the airline gate.'" Of the standards at the more than 700 newspapers that failed to answer we know nothing.

• The references to publishers recalls the 1963 investigation by the Senate Foreign Relations Committee into the activities of press agents working for foreign governments. Several newspapers, magazines, newsreels, and television stations were found to have been outlets for material subsidized by contracts with foreign governments. Propagandists had even purchased unlabled editorials promoting the interests of their clients. Placed in the record was a letter from the publisher of a South Carolina newspaper.[9] He had joined in a trip to Africa supposedly sponsored by the National Editorial Association. Part of the letter read: "We had five days in Angola and I . . . have never seen such blatant brainwashing. We freeloaded all through it, including terribly expensive lunches, dinners, cocktail parties, etc. One of the American consulate staff told me . . . there was a significant side we weren't seeing. I am disturbed that most of our group seems to have fallen for it, and I am more deeply disturbed that we were not told in advance . . . that Angola businessmen with axes to grind were paying for our visit. What made it worse was that American public relations people staged the whole show with the obvious purpose of changing our national policies." Following the hearings, Congress amended the law to require press agents with such contracts to register as foreign agents. Even so, however, suspicions linger with me that some of the same practices continue, in disguised forms.

● As already noted, news organizations often have been the agencies exposing unethical journalistic conduct. An unusual case came to light in 1979 when the Gannett News Service disclosed that many book editors and reviewers were selling complimentary copies of books sent to their newspapers. Two book editors (at the *Denver Post* and the *Philadelphia Inquirer*) resigned as a result. The owner of the Strand Book Store in New York told the investigating Gannett reporters that some reviewers were making up to $1,000 a month selling books. Ten book editors admitted they had entered into confidential arrangements that their supervising editors were not aware of. Above this kind of embarrasment were the *Courier-Journal* and the *Louisville Times,* which since the early 1970s insisted on paying for all books and records reviewed, and also the *New York Times,* which receives 37,000 review copies a year, sells discards to a secondhand shop, matches the proceeds, and donates the money to the public library. Disclosures like this always bring action, and other newspapers undoubtedly have moved to cut off this lapping at the freebie dish. Unhappily, hundreds of others are still at it.

Much of this seems inconsequential when situations arise such as the one that stunned the *Wall Street Journal* in March 1984 on discovering that a writer for its "Heard on the Street" column, in violation of the newspaper's explicit rules, had sold information about what was going to be published to two brokers for $31,000. One of the brokers, pleading guilty to charges of conspiracy and fraud, agreed to leave the brokerage field and to return $454,437 in illicit profits. One of his clients, a lawyer, also had to leave his practice when it became known he had made illegal profits of $590,000 using the leaked information. The reporter, R. Foster Winans, was convicted in a federal court-trial and sentenced in August 1985 to eighteen months in prison and fined $5,000 for his part in the conspiracy.

Dismaying and discouraging as all this is, one has to be candid and concede that none of all this matches some of the corruptions that have tainted journalism in past years. Two of the most damaging were the Jake Lingle case in 1930 and the Harry J. Karafin episode in 1967. After Lingle, a *Chicago Trib-une* reporter, was murdered in 1930, investigation revealed he had been on the payroll of the most notorious Chicago gangs-ters. Karafin, who in his twenty-nine years on the *Philadelphia Inquirer*, then owned by Walter Annenberg, had become as in-vestigative reporter the best known and most feared newsman in the area. On April 2, 1967, *Philadelphia Magazine* ran a 15-page expose of Karafin as a blackmailing extortionist. Two weeks later, the *Inquirer* took 10 columns of space in its Sunday, April 16, edition to report it had fired Karafin, and denounced him as "shakedown artist and remarkably adept liar." He was tried and convicted. In pronouncing prison sentence, Judge R. C. Nix said, "You have blackened the name of the newspaper industry. . . . A newspaper story can kill an individual and destroy an entire family. . . . You have brought shame to those who have dedi-cated their lives to fair and impartial reporting." Karafin died of cancer in prison in 1973.

Quite apart from this kind of danger, but constantly needing gatekeeping editors trained to protect the public interest, is that flow of news manipulated by public relations people. Much of this has been documented in studies of "pseudo-news," develop-ments or events planned in advance and controlled by private interests. A graduate journalism student at Columbia University decided in 1980 to examine the practice for her master's paper. Discussing the proposal in advance, Viveca Stackig expressed confidence that the leading public relations men would talk freely of their victories. She laughingly called them "war stories." Old editors cannot help but have cynical chauvinism in them, and it was a good guess that her striking blonde good looks and vivacious manner would prove her right. The stories recounted in her thesis were fascinating, with names, stategies, and implementations showing how PR people work their forms of magic in influencing public affairs on behalf of clients paying handsome fees. "The press is the institution PR persons work on most directly," Miss Stackig wrote, "and it is the primary lubricant or tool they use to make things happen. PR people get away with it for two reasons: First, they know how the news business works as well or better than most reporters do and use this expertise to shape their material so that it slides easily into the news system; second, because more than a few journalists are willing to present PR-created or inspired material as the fruit of their own efforts."

Two episodes disclosed that unions also have discovered how to use PR. New York City's transit police wanted more jobs. It needed increased leverage in the negotiations. So the union's PR man, Morty Matz, set himself as a one-man news bureau ("I felt like the city editor of all New York," he boasted) and had policeman call him with every report of subway crime. He relayed these to every paper, radio, and TV station. Mr. Matz's aide told Miss Stackig it was "very successful. News coverage increased several thousand per cent. And the public's concern and the politicians' rose with the news coverage." So, too, with the main police union. Its PR man, George Douris, decided to use TV newscasters' chitchat to promote donations for bullet-proof vests. "We fed them human-interest stories," he said. "We had policemen's families talk to the reporters. We had school children save their pennies to buy a vest for the local cop." Donations rose sharply. A good cause, yet all of it PR-inspired and produced.

On a more sophisticated level was the work of PR man Richard Aurelio, hired by France to help overturn the environmentalist-generated ban on the use of Kennedy Airport by the supersonic Concorde. Mr. Aurelio staged sound-testings for the press in New York's subways and at Studio 54. He did a head-line-grabbing repeat in Paris to test the sound of the organ peal-ing in Notre Dame Cathedral. He told Miss Stackig his firm was helpful in persuading the Federal Department of Transportation to permit the Concorde to land in Houston, and then added, "we had something to use." French President Valery Giscard d'Es-taing was on the first flight of the Concorde into Houston, and that city's mayor made page one of the *New York Times* after he called Houston "the new New York." Ads appeared inviting New York businesses to relocate in Houston. The Aurelio theme was that it now was three hours closer to Europe than New York. The idea did not appeal to New York businessmen. "So we began to pick them up as allies," Mr. Aurelio told Miss Stackig, going on to relate that environmental groups had filed legal actions to have the courts block the plane from using Ken-nedy, but that the Port Authority was then persuaded it could rescind the ban on technical grounds, "thereby giving in," wrote Miss Stackig, "and still maintaining that it tried." News? Sure. Nothing unethical, but nevertheless PR-contrived and managed, helped along by the PR knowledge of how to get through the gates of the news system.

PR planning and skills still seem to be unnecessary in some fields. Take outdoor activity such as hunting and fishing, which consistently involves millions of Americans annually. Coincident with a contentious dismissal episode with an outdoor writer over the use (and publicizing of an outdoor recreational vehicle)—an issue which remains in litigation—Michael J. Davies, then editor of the *Kansas City Star & Times,* and who now is chief executive of the *Hartford Courant,* assigned two reporters to check on the relationships of outdoor writers around the country with equip-ment manufacturers. "Scandalous," wrote Mr. Davies. It in-cluded widespread acceptance by most outdoor writers, from some of the best-known newspapers in the country to smaller regional periodicals, of manufacturers' discounts not available to the general public, of their writing press releases for fees on behalf of hunting lodges and fishing clubs they covered, and a variety of other involvements. Bernard (Lefty) Kreh, outdoor editor of the *Baltimore Sun,* offered the *Star* a pungent comment: "Nothing is free," he said. "People don't give you something because they like you."

The point of all this is to illustrate the trite adage that history's record is two steps forward and one back. Human beings are born vulnerable and open to temptation, with many desires for gratification of the senses. Ethical connotations come with maturity and are either accepted or shrugged off for all kinds of self-serving reasons. It would be comforting to believe that all professions have many in their ranks who strive to serve in the highest ethical traditions of public service. We know it is too much to expect. But each profession includes at least a number of individuals who do put service above reward or applause, and they suffer over the many transgressions that demean their chosen callings.

I know well more than a score of editors who hold such ideals and who anguish over their inability to do more to lift standards. Their inabiity to do more traces, I maintain, to journalism's greatest weakness—the dysfunctional nature of the management of journalism, stripping most editors of the time and funds needed to educate and train staffs properly, as well as limiting their capacity to produce as taint-free as possible the news flow over which they have ultimate responsibility. Mr. Kreh's comment takes me back to the earlier mention of my own newspaper beginnings. But first, I must offer the totally unoriginal observation that morals, attitudes, and ethics grow out of family influences and are expanded by associations with role models. Mix luck with this chemistry and what emerges is the quality we perhaps loosely call "character." This is not an autobiography, but since I am engaged in a critical appraisal of press ethics, a short review of how my own ethical views were shaped seems in order.

A cheerful Englishman, my father was looked upon by his friends as too honest for his own good. He was a liberal who leaned toward what he called "state socialism," under which all natural resources would be publicly owned. Indignant about the

Ku Klux Klan movement in Indiana in the mid-1920s, he became a strong supporter of what now is called civil rights. He loved to debate, arguing one side one week, the reverse the next. With me, he could be moralistic to the point of being a prude. He objected to my leaving school to accept a job offered on the sports staff of one of the three Indianapolis newspapers. I was passionately drawn to journalism and saw it as heaven-sent opportunity. My father quit arguing but kept handing me literary classics he insisted everyone needed to read, and books on public affairs, then quizzing me to be sure I had done the required reading. After he died, it took seven years to pay off the debts he accumulated in the years he helped good causes and underwrote friends down on their luck during the Great Depression.

Obviously, my ethical convictions were shaped in my father's environment. But what he began was nurtured by two mentors of my young adulthood. One was Rowland Allen, who almost literally became my older brother.[10] A Bostonian, he was personnel director of the city's largest department store, a social activist, and a more profound version of my father about ethics. Much later, he had me elected to an organization called the Wranglers Club. It was a replica of a human Noah's Ark, made up of clergymen, two from each of the faiths in the Indianapolis area. Until they accepted me, Rowland had been the only "skeptic." It was the greatest of my learning experiences, an exposure to the great philosophies that accompany all of life's undertakings, absorbed from the monthly dinners at which a member delivered a paper and had to defend his thesis from the challenges of his fellow members.

The other role model was Eddie Ash, who rescued me from a miserable start. As said earlier, my first job was under a sports editor who held to practices prevalent in that period, satirized by Ben Hecht and Charles MacArthur in their play, *The Front Page*.[11] My introduction to the system was an order to leave the advance story of the weekly prize fights out of the Sunday paper because the promoter had not delivered his check. The sympathetic, overworked assistant sports editor understood my dismay and tried to ease my psychic wounds, urging me to keep my attention on my chores and to ignore what was so obvious. I have liked to think he passed on word that I had promise and that this brought the unexpected offer to join sports editor Eddie Ash on one of the other papers. Eddie was widely respected, and few bids were ever accepted so swiftly. Short and powerfully stocky, Eddie had lost his left arm under a train as a boy while playing along railroad tracks. From the aftermath had come a fierce independence. He would accept no physical assistance of any kind. Most important, he was absolutely incorruptible, a rebel against the attitudes of so many of his colleagues. He had a cherub's smile but he was a gruff martinet about accuracy, fairness, balance, and keeping everything on his sports pages "clean." Later it came to me that he was born to be a teacher. The teaching took. His teachings largely seemed to have a basis in his encompassing sense of ethics, of what was right and fair between a news gatherer and his readers, as with, "I'll put up with *you* making a mistake so long as it's your bonehead and no one else had any hand in it." "We've all got a barrel of biases, but it's none of our damned business letting them influence what we print." "I don't give a damn what he said. If you can't get the other guy's side, I'd just as soon lose the story." "I heard that s–o–b try to buy his phony promotion into the paper. I'll try to get him barred from entering the building." Beyond ethics, there were daily lessons about other aspects: "If you don't understand something fully, I don't want you to even think of starting to write about it." "I won't have you writing that tongue-in-cheek stuff. Most people believe what they read in the paper. Don't play games with them." There were hundreds of other counselings, all in terse terms. Eddie not only laid the foundation for my career, he advanced it.

When he decided I was ready, he prompted the managing editor to move me into general news, which meant several years on the beats and various desks. At city hall and the courthouse I refused to join in "syndicating"—the reporting practice of sharing stories so that no one ever got "scooped"—and I repeatedly broke strong exclusives.[12] One of my great delights came later, after I became Eddie's boss. The paper had followed the standard practice of having the baseball team pay all of the coverage costs—travel, hotel, and meals—for spring training and on-the-road games. Eddie resented the position he felt placed in when the team wanted more coverage to promote its ticket sales. Nine years, almost to the day, after starting to work with him, I became managing editor. One early venture was to lobby for a sports budget to pay our own way for such coverage. Honeymoons are often useful in this type of thing, and approval eventually came. Pride in the accomplishment can be understood the morning I walked over to Eddie's desk, leaned over, and said quietly, "When you go South this next time, the tab is on us." The smile was never more cherubic, and his "Good boy!" was reward enough from a man who was no saint, never claimed to be, but who had saintly qualities.

Thus the making of an ethicist—by my father, adopted "brother," and portly little proto-saint. All of them had special reason to be delighted by my new step up. I had become the top news manager of the crusading newspaper that only a few years earlier had won the Pulitzer Prize for distinguished service for exposing and breaking the Ku Klux Klan's power in Indiana (and in the process taking a punishing circulation boycott by Klan supporters and the always timid advertisers).[13]

Half-a-century on journalism's firing lines—33 of them as editor of five newspapers and publisher of a sixth[14]—have left me with a conviction something like Wordsworth's lines about "One in whom persuasion and belief had ripened into faith, and faith become a passionate intuition." Out of my training and exposures to those who saw more in me than I saw in myself was to build the passionate belief that being a journalist meant a compact with those citizens who trusted us. Perhaps overdrawn, it meant construing the role in the sense bestowed by Lord Macaulay's 1828 observation that "the gallery in which the reporters sit has become a fourth estate of the realm." Because it was true, it was galling to read barbs directed at newspapers for condemning gambling on their editorial pages and running racing tips on the sports pages.

While it has no direct connection with news coverage, we confront the image of easy payoffs in 1985 with the revelation of payola (the contraction of "pay" and "Victrola") being back in vogue among radio stations. Banned by Congress in 1960 after disclosures of widespread bribery of disk jockeys, the practice has returned with millions of dollars going surreptiously to program directors and other executives at radio stations who turn over control of popular music programming to record promoters.[15] It is next to impossible to have bribery go on in one department of a communications organization and not have it spread outward and grow with the speed and tenacity of poison ivy.

In my early editing days, I found myself temporizing with the flow of gifts to staff members during the Christmas holidays. The effort was to find a basis for the acceptance of gifts of modest value and draw some sensible lines. What was most troublesome was the awareness of a double standard. If we found a politician accepting favors we would turn into a wolf pack. But if one of our own was found to be on the take, it was a matter to be dealt with internally, meaning privately. We were building our own traps with hypocritical statements that we couldn't be bought with a martini or a ham sandwich. The average journalist didn't buy the argument, as we found out in Louisville when we stipulated that we paid our way for everything, from service-club luncheons on up, and that it was all right to accept a luncheon or dinner provided that there was a next time and the tab was on us. The wave of staff applause was proof of how much they disagreed with the national apologists.

This type of ethical advance comes only when the line staff—the gatekeepers—is an integral part of the rule-making process. Experiencing disappointments firsthand has brought the conviction that the bane of organizational life lies in unmeshed, uncontrolled bureaucracies. There can be no effective control over quality and no rational pattern of ethical conduct without direct and continuous linkage throughout the executive and administrative functions. It is crucial in the journalistic enterprise.[16] Yet in this chapter alone, dealing almost exclusively with what I see as primitive ethics, there are instances of publishers acting in ways that make editors despair, and of editors who either by design, or through higher direction, have cut themselves off from control over sports departments. There are more sophisticated ethical problems that complicate the lives of editors, and these need to be considered also. But for the moment, we deal with simplest of ethical considerations.

The Austin newspapers' editor, Arnold Rosenfeld, has defined how the system begins to operate at the assistant city editor level. The larger an operation, the more editors in training there are, and without top-to-bottom linkage there is certain to come half-a-dozen or more differing policies. No reporter on any news staff of any reasonable size, be it on newspapers or in broadcasting, ever assigns himself or herself to a story without the consent of a desk editor. How that story eventually reads, and what headline goes with it, and where it appears, are matters outside the sphere of the reporter.

A quip depicts the various news departments as being run like leased departments in big department stores. It is painfully true and yet only a part of it can be traced to the spread of modern conglomerate ownership. While a few such chains encourage a large degree of autonomy in management, the general record among chain ownerships has indicated a penchant for standardization, with guidance and control exercised from both regional and national headquarters. As John Morton, the financial analyst, pointed out about one chain, most corporate drives are for bottom-line success, with journalistic quality sacrificed if necessary to achieve the profit objective. Once that becomes the overriding motivation in a journalistic organization, there is little hope of any clear ethical construct emerging, except on the part of individuals who through belief or faith follow through on their own.

My "brother" Rowland advanced a theory I tried checking on my own, concluded he was right, and counseled others to try for themselves. Simply put, it is that all organizations are reflections of their ownerships. There are some notably good ones in journalism. If there were a great many of them books like this would never have to be written. Sir William Haley's comment about there being serious differences between the principles so ardently espoused by network presidents and their practices applies with equal force to those in charge of so many of America's newspaper enterprises. There are too many publishers who give evidence of being exactly like their counterparts in broadcasting—intellectual diabetics more addicted to dollar-sugar than a truly free and independent journalism can survive indefinitely.

## CHAPTER 3

# What the Scoop Hath Begat

"THE TRUTH IS that most American newspaper people are really more interested in dramatic spot news, the splashy story, than in anything else," wrote James B. Reston of the *New York Times* in his 1966 book, *The Artillery of the Press.* "They want to be in on the big blowout, no matter how silly, and would rather write about what happened than whether it made any sense." In developing this theme, Mr. Reston made it clear his emphasis was directed more at editors. "We are fascinated by events," he wrote, "but not by the things that *cause* events. We will send 500 correspondents to Viet Nam after the war breaks out and fill the front pages with their reports, meanwhile ignoring the rest of the world, but we will not send one or two reporters there when the danger of war is developing. Even if we do, their reports of the danger will be minimized by editors and officials alike as 'speculation.' . . . 'Tending the machinery' is the main thing for most editors and this usually means what happened or what somebody said rather than whether it is important in the relationship of today to tomorrow. . . . The conflict of approach and philosophy must be resolved if the newspaper is to attain the level of intellectual excellence it needs in order to compete in the future," and he added, "the dominant role of the technicians in our newspapers is so typical of the crisis in leadership in so many American institutions today."[1]

Mr. Reston was arguing intelligently and forcefully for a more public service orientation on journalism's part, including television's obligations, but he did not openly put enough stress, in my view, on another of journalism's great continuing shortcomings: the passion for the scoop. Confining the assessment to private endeavor, I have been unable to learn of any competition that has been more long-lived and become more ingrained in the psyche of its practitioners than that of journalists.

There is no question about strong competition resulting in a better-informed public. The key question has to be the public importance of the information being sought. From that base we come to the argument of whether the end justifies the means, and it is here that much of journalism over the years has fouled the nest. Mr. Reston's argument for "approach and philosophy . . . to attain . . . intellectual excellence" cannot help but remain the central objective for serious journalists. Yet for all the intrinsic good sense of his appeal, the majority of gatekeepers continues to press for exclusives regardless of whether their being first serves any sensible public purpose.

At times of high-stress straight news coverage, there is justification for news organizations going "all out" to be first. It was particularly noticeable in the Beirut hostage story, and the networks went astray only when zeal led them to broadcast without pausing for editorial oversight. Where justification is strained comes in the insistence on using exit polls to call winners even before vote-counting starts in the states. It smacks of simple lust for the "scoop."

All of it traces directly to journalism's past. The journalism perhaps best exemplified by those like Adolph Ochs, William Allen White, and a number of others was deeply tied to the concept of public service. Making an adequate profit obviously was a vitally important foundation for independent strength. As with all individuals, they were not perfect, but their ethics were sound and from it came broad respect, admiration, and solid rewards. But as in everything else, many more put profits above honor, and they debased the journalistic currency. There is a widely held assumption that television particularly drove many newspapers out of business. The fact is that the great shrinkage in numbers of newspapers happened before TV came on line. The Great Depression and the sharp rises in newsprint costs arising from World War II were the main factors in more than 250 American daily newspapers disappearing in the twenty-year period from 1925 to 1945. What we have had since is the sweep into conglomerate ownership, through which chains now own more than 70 percent of the dailies. Of the national circulation of something like 68 million, four chains control papers adding up to 20 percent of the total daily sales. Of total national newspaper circulation, a reasonable late-1985 estimate is that chains can claim about 80 percent of daily distribution. As David Shaw wrote in his 1984 book, *Press Watch,* "Profits, big profits, are the motive, not public service journalism."[2]

The long history of the "scoop" clearly began with the intense drives by publishers for higher circulations that could induce more advertising revenues. This is not to exempt editors and reporters from culpability. The competitive spirit to be first runs high in egocentric people, and they joined in the chase with fervor. It surely existed earlier, but the first records show that direct, open competition was going on in 1811, when the New York and Boston papers began sending small boats out to meet incoming ships in order to gather the latest information from abroad. The rivalry brought on roughneck violence, the boats became larger, and the competition grew hotter. In 1833 Benjamin H. Day began a new and different approach, gathering police news for his four-page *New York Sun.* The formula was so successful that it was to be copied by printer-editors in other cities. It brought Day a fresh, strong competitor, James Gordon Bennett, one of the most enterprising on record. He used anything to be first: carrier pigeons, steamships, trains, the magnetic telegraph. He was first with sports coverage. His *Herald* became New York's largest paper. His drive to be first led his rivals to organize the first news cooperative.

The next stage was to be far bigger and flashier, provoked by Joseph Pulitzer taking over the losing *New York World* in 1883. So bold was his crusading and sensational approach that by 1887 it passed 250,000 circulation and was the nation's largest newspaper. Stunts came one after another, such as Nellie Bly's 72-day world-girdling trip. "Yellow journalism" owes its name to a comic strip character in the *World.* It was a daub of color on "the Yellow Kid," and the term took on its meaning after William Randolph Hearst invaded New York to challenge

Pulitzer. In their book, *The Press and America*, Edwin Emery and Henry Ladd Smith described it vividly as a "shrieking, gaudy, sensation-loving, devil-may-care journalism which lured the reader by any possible means. . . . It made the high drama of life a cheap melodrama and it twisted the facts of each day into whatever seemed best suited to produce sales for the newsboy."[3] The passion for the scoop became frenetic. In the current purchasing of exclusive rights to sports events, television is simply copying what New York papers were doing before the turn of the century.

The mad scramble was to be climaxed by wildly extravagant reporting from Cuba and Hearst's editorial demands for war with Spain well before the explosion sank the battleship Maine in Havana harbor in 1898. It was to be termed "Hearst's War," in part because of his stridency and in part because of his exchange of telegrams with artist Frederic Remington, commissioned to sketch pictures for Hearst's *Journal* in the period before the Maine went down. As W. A. Swanberg recounts in *Citizen Hearst*,[4] a bored Remington telegraphed:

EVERYTHING IS QUIET. THERE IS NO TROUBLE HERE. THERE WILL BE NO WAR. I WISH TO RETURN. REMINGTON.

Hearst's reply, Swanberg wrote, was Napoleonic:

PLEASE REMAIN. YOU FURNISH THE PICTURES AND I'LL FURNISH THE WAR. W. R. HEARST.

The war was to come and it was to end, but "yellow journalism" had spread and it was to take decades to begin fading. Adolph Ochs played a part in its slide with his success at the *Times,* but so did Pulitzer. His *World* became more respectable. Oswald Garrison Villard, the rival liberal editor of the *Post,* wrote later that Pulitzer, "like many another, deliberately stooped for success and then, having achieved it, slowly put on garments of righteousness."[5] The change, however, did endow Pulitzer with an aura of greatness. Hearst never changed. His several papers nourished the scoop for much of this century. The latest multimillionaire entrepreneur, Rupert Murdoch, clearly believes in the formula and so the scoop pot has been kept not warm, but hot in every country where he owns newspapers.

Even so, some editors of high-quality newspapers echo the old refrain. A touch of ambivalence marked the comment of Eugene Patterson, the *St. Petersburg Times*'s president. "The older I get," he said, "the more I want to be right rather than first, but if someone is going to be first I want it to be us." Eugene Roberts, editor of the *Philadelphia Inquirer,* held that even while he is cognizant of the abuses, "trying to get the story to the reader as fast as possible is an excellent discipline." He argued that in the larger cities, more stories get to the public because the papers are afraid of being embarrassed by their rivals if they don't dig faster and deeper.

William F. Thomas, editor of the *Los Angeles Times,* disagreed. Competition, he contended, breeds irresponsibility.[6] This is my own conviction, flowing out of having witnessed seamy episodes during the "Front Page" period and buttressed by a few judgmental mistakes that brought some personal reappraisals of elemental fairness. The lore is filled with episodes of reporters lying, cheating, stealing private papers, making an art of impersonating public officials, acting as go-betweens for editors in paying bribes for information, and anything else they could get away with, simultaneously being willing to accept bribes for the slanting of news.

A number of large-city publishers share blame for the low ethical tone that marked much of journalism in the 1920s and '30s. They waged superheated campaigns for increased circulations. They approved the hiring of hoodlums who fought rival mobs for control of the best street corners. The publishers were the ones who approved expensive lotteries, such as the one Hearst announced in Chicago in 1921, prompting Robert R. McCormick to put his *Tribune* into the competition and raise the ante. It brought wild scenes in which delivery trucks were overturned by people determined to get their hands on the lottery checks.[7] Publishers in many cities authorized all kinds of premiums for subscriptions, such as pots and pans and sets of dishes, along with lurid promotions like marathon dance contests.

The frantic period was highlighted by the "gasoline war" in Denver in 1927, described with zest by Gene Fowler in *Timber Line*.[8] Trailing the new rival Scripps-Howard *News* in classified ads, the *Post* offered two gallons of gasoline for each want ad put in the Sunday paper. The *News* upped it, and the ante kept rising until Roy Howard decided $3 million was enough to pour into gasoline tanks and worked out a truce with the *Post*'s Frederick Bonfils, who was beginning to fret over his $2 million invested in the absurd competition. To illustrate how much emphasis some papers put on circulation in the 1930s, the *Chicago Tribune*'s circulation manager, Louis Rose, had a $3 million budget and a staff of 462. He got some striking results. After Giuseppe Zangara fired six shots at President-elect Franklin D. Roosevelt in Miami on February 15, 1933, missing him but fatally wounding Chicago's Mayor Anton Cermak, the *Tribune* sold more than 188,000 additional papers.[9] It perhaps is pertinent comment about changing times to reflect that Zangara died in the electric chair on March 20, 1933—33 days after the shooting.

All of it was of a piece—the incessant drives for more and more circulation and thus more advertising, imposing an urgency on news staffs to deliver high-octane "news." Recognizing their natural bent, it was only to be expected that reporters and their editors would have plunged with wanton fervor into the chase to be first. In this maelstrom, it was inevitable that urgings for some ethical restraint would be treated as do-gooder nonsense. Change has come in many ways. But the scoop mentality has spawned several other, equally distasteful by-products.

Before we move to these, one last illustration of how tenacious the scoop virus is. David Shaw, mentioned earlier, for a dozen years has been the *Los Angeles Times'* reporter of what is happening in journalism. In 1977, he chose to concentrate on what was titled, "Scoop: Rush to Judgment in the Newsroom." It was a long, careful report on current problems and practices. Near the end, he began reviewing wire-service competition and quoted a colleague who had wire-service background as saying, "If you're second often enough, they just get someone else to do your job." Mr. Shaw then ended his account with this memoir: "Perhaps that helps explain the following tableau: San Francisco Hilton Hotel. Early 1974. Randolph Hearst has called a press conference to discuss the People-in-Need food program demanded by the Symbionese Liberation Army after the kidnaping of his daughter. Bob Strand of UPI commandeers the closest telephone. An AP reporter demands that he share it. Strand keeps talking to his office. The AP reporter, apparently deciding that if AP can't be first, neither can UPI, produces a pair of scissors and cuts the telephone wire clear through. Strand is left talking into a dead telephone, wire dangling."

Many executive and managing editors deplore this type of kamikaze competition, but they have new and deeper problems with the means reporters employ to gain attention. All are old. All have been troublesome in the past. And all manifest the passion to be first in some manner or another, by any methods open to them. One of the most troubling is the use of the unidentified source, more virulent a journalistic disease now than ever. Another has been the fictional technique drawn from the so-called New Journalism. The third, more dangerous by far, is the outright fiction passed off as news—the hoax. All three are subject to control, providing that the gatekeeping editors are competent enough and well-trained enough to deal firmly with the challenges as they arise. Even the hoax, the most difficult of the problems, is sometimes detectable by editors who have had the benefits of long experience and sound training that prompt them to recognize dangers and, therefore, to keep rechecking every detail of sensitive stories laid before them.

Even with these skills, it is my contention that the task cannot be done successfully without full knowledge of the reporter's sources. Some younger editors believe that reporters they consider reliable merit the liberty to grant confidentiality as issues arise. The record is so flawed as to make the argument specious. Countless reporters hold that when they promise confidentiality, they have pledged not to reveal the source, even to their editors.

It is arrogant nonsense. Trust cuts two ways. If any reporter cannot trust the editor, that reporter needs to go job hunting, immediately. There is only one rational standard that meets the proper test for granting anonymity to a news source. It is that the source must understand from the outset that the reporter must confide in the editor. Not until the top directing editor of the organization has agreed to support the promise can it be valid. No editor can stand by a reporter or a story without thoughtful appraisal of the source reliability and the potential consequences for the news organization.

Any argument that this rule inhibits investigative reporting is absurd. There are a number of news organizations that have enforced such a standard while digging boldly into all types of malfeasance and never have had to face a libel suit. It is a myth that some reporters are born detectives. Some have more nerve than others. Some simply are more persevering. That's all. The truth is that the vast majority of exposes originate with outsiders who have personal reasons for wanting to see chicanery revealed.

Every experienced editor recognizes the vulnerability of some informers. These are people who could face instant discharge or perhaps physical danger if identified. What the reliable "whistle blowers" offer is the knowledge of where necessary documentation can be obtained. The possibility of retribution also applies to people in government. Many have honest concerns about actions and projects being hidden from view and believe they justify exposure. An editor who knows the details is better able to give such stories adequate treatment and be confident not only that the source is protected, but that the publication or broadcast is in the public interest.

A step or two removed from this kind of confidential handling is something not generally practiced. Years ago, I became convinced of the wisdom of having highly able reporters certified as notaries public. Typing or writing out with care what an individual has to say, and having it signed on the spot and instantly notarized, constitutes a piece of evidence valid in any court. How many suits are likely to come when a story carries

the information that the charges being made are supported by
from a dozen to two-score or more affidavits? There will be
vehement denials and expressions of outrage, but legal action is
most unlikely.

The most egregious current practice is the cloaking of
sources for effect. More than a few editors have grumbled that
they suspect reporters prefer to write stories attributed to anonymous sources in the belief that such stories attract more "desk"
attention and get better "news play." Some reporters offer anonymity when it is not asked for and, in the process, offend persons being interviewed. I am among those who have had the
experience. Anonymity is a poor relative to the scoop. There
would be an instant major reduction in the use of unidentified
sources if executive and managing editors imposed a mandate
that all clearance for anonymity had to come personally from
them or their chief deputies.

Cloaking sources grew to grotesque proportions out of
Washington experience. The most forthright denunciation of the
practice came in October 1984 from veteran capital correspondent James McCartney of the Knight-Ridder Newspapers. "The
most salutary thing that could happen in the journalistic community," he said, "would be if every reporter were required to
take an oath that he would walk out of the office of any official
who insisted on talking 'off the record.' The second most salu-
tory," he continued, "by only a small margin, would be if reporters flatly refused to accept routine information on a
'background' basis—not for attribution to anyone, in other
words, by name. And the practice of 'deep background'—in
which the reporter is granted permission to use the information,
providing he use it with no attribution at all—ought to be for-
bidden by constitutional amendment. This is the rule in which
the reporter can write 'on his own authority,' as though the
information dropped from the sky." Mr. McCartney went on to
say glumly that "none of these things is going to happen. . . .
The reason is that we in this business are victims of our own
anarchy and will not work together to stand up to the govern-

ment, and to public officials in general, and say, collectively, that we refuse to play by their rules."[10]

Mr. McCartney was on solid ground. Referring to President Ronald Reagan's off-the-record gaffe during a sound-level test for one of his radio talks—when he said that he had just signed legislation outlawing Russia forever and added, "The bombing begins in five minutes"—Mr. McCartney asked pointedly if a President, or any major public official, is entitled to protection by so-called "ground rules" if he "commits an indiscretion or makes a damn fool of himself?" Excellent question. The only possible excuse that could be offered for President Reagan is that going on and off the record at will has become such a life-style among the press corps, and not only in Washington but all across the country, that it has made unguided missiles of more than one politician. Why does it continue? Because editors are victims of the scoop mentality, too. Many worry over the prospect of not being in on "the know," even if they don't know whether the account has any meaning, or whether the so-called unnamed source is merely grinding a personal or political ax. Further, many are more taken up with their "standing" in the field, rather than with the audiences they serve, lending support to a very old comment that most newspaper people put out their newspapers not for those people who buy them, but to try to impress other newspaper people. It might have been explainable in the days of hot rivalry. It fails all the tests in these days of an almost total lack of print competition in any but the few largest cities.

Much of the spirit is kept fresh by the unwavering journalistic love affair with politics. I confess that mine may be a jaundiced view, brought on by cynicism about the crassness of so much of politics in general, along with suspicions fed by the immense sums candidates spend to win offices that pay a fraction of what is spent. It is clear that the smart politicians have always cast their lines among the press with the skills of master fishermen. Most journalists have been unable to resist the lures because of their unquenchable appetite for anything that eventu-

ally might be seen as resembling a scoop. One side trick of the
political anglers is the automatic usage of first names in dealing
with members of the press. Watch and listen in TV interviews.
The reporter may say, "Senator." The senator will reply, "As
you know, Joe. . . ."

Out of this, journalists have built the shaky premise of a
"symbiotic" relationship existing between public officials and
reporters. For the most part, it is purely the angling of baited
hooks, with the fingers of politicians firmly on the rods and
lines. They swiftly learn the difference between the educable
dolphins and the predator sharks. The implied quid pro quo in
the bait-and-reel-in game in that the reporter either will get
preferred treatment (a scoop) or, at least, be protected from
being scooped if a major story develops. Ben Bradlee of the
*Washington Post* tried, years ago, to break the "off-the-record"
dependency, but was forced to retreat when the political games-
men happily siphoned their most important leaks to the *New
York Times*. Mr. Bradlee had to recognize that he had too few
fingers to deal with all the leaks in the dikes. At least he had the
courage to try.

Emphasis on the scoop has been most evident in recent years
in television's focus on exit polls and election-night reporting. In
the truest sense, it is a modern, more sophisticated replay of
what went on in the old newspaper circulation wars. In 1980,
NBC drew a barrage of criticism for declaring Mr. Reagan the
winner. Charges were made that the early call discouraged West
Coast voting and affected some close races in that zone. In 1984,
the networks issued pious statements that no races would be
called in any states until polls had closed there. But simply on
that basis, Dan Rather of CBS called the election, to use *Time*
magazine's words, "officially over at 8 p.m. E.S.T., when little
more than 1% of the votes had been tallied. At ABC, which had
vowed in advance to practice 'good citizenship' and restraint,
Peter Jennings announced a Reagan victory 13 minutes after
Rather. NBC, which transformed the rules of political reporting
four years ago . . . responded to critics by delaying Tom Bro-
kaw's victory decree until 8:30 p.m. . . . As it turned out, the

networks called the race for Reagan before the polls closed in New York."

Television's executives were struggling with some ethical confusions well before election day about exit polls, and they now have appeared to unite in holding that their making calls on the basis of exit polls is not the problem, that the real fault lies in the nation not having a unified time span for opening and closing all of the country's polling places. Most of TV's spokespeople appear not to have done their homework. What they advance was laid out in comprehensive form twenty years ago by Frank Stanton, one of the few statesmen in electronic communications.[11] Then president of CBS, Dr. Stanton checked off almost all of the nation's primitive registration and voting procedures. He called "the whole system a hodgepodge of irrationalities, inconsistencies, anachronisms and harassments." He called for interstate, permanent registration "making full use of modern electronic equipment," and for computer ballots that could be tabulated in seconds. Dr. Stanton pointed out the savings already being made by districts where machines had taken the place of paper balloting, and that they had minimized the possibilities of fraud. Most important, he advocated a 24-hour uniform-time voting day—"a common opening time everywhere, regardless of the clock hour in any one place, and a common closing time." He also recommended that "the national uniform voting day should also be a national legal holiday . . . to free thousands to vote at their convenience, rather than attempting to squeeze it in before work or at lunch time or on the way home." Dr. Stanton added, "We should be moving beyond that to thoughts of nationwide electronic plebescites on grave questions of public policy for the guidance of our government." This latter could work properly only with a journalism doing an outstanding job of objective reporting in depth of the issues at hand. There can be little argument, however, with the worth of the basic proposal he laid out on registration and uniform-time voting. Exit polling has its value in providing information for studious assessment of voter attitudes, but it is no substitute for computerized returns coming swiftly from the states. While it would not curb election-night punditry by the stars, it might serve as a shock treatment for the mania that grips so many journalists every election night.

It will be no cure-all for other aspects of the scoop thrust. The New Journalism, for instance, is more complex, an outgrowth of the magazine freedoms Clay Felker encouraged during his brilliant record as editor of *New York* from 1967 to 1977. Tom Wolfe is credited with being one of the first artists in the new form. Mr. Wolfe made a case for the practice in a 1973 book titled *The New Journalism*.[12] The essence of his argument was that the standard practices in reporting and editing stripped atmosphere, color, and flavor out of stories, and that sensitive journalistic observers could more readily convey the thoughts and feelings of individuals involved in events by the use of fictional techniques. An example cited by ardent supporters of the Wolfe thesis is the late Truman Capote's *In Cold Blood*, which appeared in 1965. A fact the advocates glide over is that Mr. Capote was not a part of daily journalism. *In Cold Blood* came out of long, deep research and writing of a high order. As Professor John Hulteng commented in his book, *The Messenger's Motives*, once the reporter "begins dipping into the novelist's paint pots, how true will his colors remain to the journalistic ethic? How is the reader to know which 'facts' are reality and which are semifiction."[13]

More disturbing were reports of some younger gatekeepers expressing an affinity for the new technique, with older editors openly expressing uneasiness over assertions that a generational gap was blocking progress. The fact is that depicting atmosphere, color, and flavor is an art not at all lacking among gifted journalists, and that having to keep to "the facts" has never hindered them. Mr. Felker's experimenting came when the campus protests of the '60s had burst into revolt. The new form appealed greatly to those in campus journalism and some excesses in academic newspapers were, literally, sophomoric. Many were to get jobs in standard journalism. By '69 and '70, the battle was joined. Eric Sevareid, who won his television honors deservedly, spoke up in strong terms in 1970, writing:

Militant young men and women, in both newspapers and broadcasting, argue that even the quest for objectivity is a myth, that the prime purpose of the press is not to report the world but to reform it, and in the direction of their ideas. We have all read the learned articles that tell us objective news accounts deceive the reader or hearer, obscure inner truths that the reporter perceives. He must therefore personalize the news, infuse it with his own truth. They would not leave this to the editorial writer, columnist or commentary writer, whose work is clearly marked away from the hard news. They believe that this will give a true integrity to the news columns and news broadcasts. I believe it will ruin them.[14]

Mr. Sevareid is not a seer, and his final sentence may read to some like massive overstatement. Most students of modern polling would agree, however, that his arrow landed close to the bull's-eye. Mr. Felker himself is critical of the excesses. "It takes very talented writers to be able to combine the reporting and the literary techniques," he said. "That's why you get a lot of half-baked young reporters using these techniques claiming to be practicing New Journalism when all they're doing is inventing things," adding the patently critical factor: "Editors have lost control of their writers."[15] Mr. Felker may have been reinforced by polls. One, for instance, taken by Gallup for *Newsweek* showed a third of those responding saying that they believed "reporters often make things up."

The issue was to arise anew in June 1984 when a staff writer for the *New Yorker* since 1959 admitted that for years he had been embroidering nonfiction reports by renaming characters, rearranging events, and composing conversations so that he could produce "a larger reality." The magazine's editor, William Shawn, was slightly defensive about the disclosure at first, then took a firmer position.[16] Newspaper editors reacted much more strongly. "It is an indulgence we cannot afford in this business," said Leonard Downie, the new managing editor of the *Washington Post*.

Michael Gartner, then the president of the *Des Moines Reg-*

*ister,* was tart. "Anybody can be a good writer if you don't have to deal with the facts," he said, So, on some of the better papers the New Journalism has come under tighter rein. However, the long record proves that it will continue to reappear unless most of those holding the top corporate responsibilities in news organizations recognize that this type of ethical dilemma is not going to disappear by trusting to the evolutionary processes. Without strong investment in the education and training of all who are assigned to direct reporters, and edit and check their copy with knowing care, there will continue to be extraordinary risk in allowing reporters to take liberties with "reconstructions" about news events and individuals.

Mention "hoax" in the presence of any group of professional news executives and the predictable reaction could be likened to someone at a church meeting suddenly mentioning the subject of herpes. "Hoax" is a code word in journalism that chills editors instantly. Perhaps the most deliberately planned hoax in recent times was perpetrated by Janet Cooke on the *Washington Post.* That is a story in itself and is treated in the chapter to follow. It was an aberration. But if anyone thinks it was the only one in that period, some education will be useful. The fifteen months starting September 21, 1980, was a journalistic nightmare. That was a week before Miss Cooke's fabricated story appeared. Preceding it was the first of two stories in the *Portland Oregonian* reporting what had been an exclusive interview with Washington's Governor Dixy Lee Ray. A week earlier she had been defeated for renomination in the state's Democratic primary and the interview with Wayne Thompson was her first extended comment. He had a tape recorder going. So did the governor. But when he sat down to write his exclusive, Mr. Thompson found his tape inaudible. He then made one of the classic journalistic mistakes. He wrote from memory and from scrawled notes.

The moment she read it, and the following day's story, Governor Ray protested vehemently. She called a press conference and produced a transcript of the interview as taken from her office taping. She asserted that she had been "victimized by a deeply biased press that opposed me from the day I filed for office and never let up." Both major wire services carried stories. The transcript disclosed that most of the statements attributed to Governor Ray had been things said by Mr. Thompson and not by her. The *Oregonian* moved rapidly to check the matter thoroughly. It ran a front-page story, apologizing to the governor, and retracting material it considered "false and distorted." It ran lengthy excerpts from the transcript to pinpoint each mistake. It carried a separate apology from Mr. Thompson, who said he was "devastated" to learn his memory had failed him and he attributed his mistake to overstrain. He was suspended for two months. Governor Ray wrote to J. Richard Nokes, editor of the *Oregonian*, commending the corrective action. Later, on television, she called it "the only honest paper in the Pacific Northwest." Just ahead lay the fields Miss Cooke and others had mined.

One exploded at the *Post* two weeks after Miss Cooke left the newspaper. This was not a hoax, but surely a distant cousin. It was failing to verify. The correction on April 30 simply said, "An article in the April 5 editions of the *Washington Post* presented an inaccurate depiction of Texas Tech University and the city in which the university is located, Lubbock. Texas Tech students do not carry guns to class, as the article stated, and the city itself is a quiet town with orderly and law-abiding citizens. There is no 'pistol-packing' tradition in Lubbock, as the article inaccurately implied." The *Post* had published a 10,000-word report by a team of reporters checking on the movements of John Hinckley, who attempted to assassinate President Reagan. The inaccurate material consisted of thirty-two words saying, "A penchant for guns hardly strikes anyone as ominous in free-wheeling Lubbock, where some university students carry guns to class and the pistol-packing tradition runs deep and long." One of the *Post* reporters picked up this information in reading a first edition of the *Philadelphia Inquirer*. Had he picked up the phone to check with Texas Tech officials he would have received a more balanced account. Indeed, an alert copy editor at the *Inquirer* quickly noted that such clarifying passages in its story had been sliced out in the composing room for space reasons. He had them restored in all later editions. Eugene Roberts, the *Inquirer* editor, estimated the full story reached 750,000 of the paper's 800,000 readers. To illustrate how many things can go wrong in the process, the National News Council also went astray in its review of the episode. It asked the *Inquirer* to send a copy of the published account and received a clipping from the first edition! As the Council wrote in later apology, "None of this makes excusable [our] failure to call the *Inquirer* before we referred to the episode in our book on 'Jimmy's World.'" All said, what surely happens more often than most news people want to concede was contained in the Council's report about the reaction of the Texas official who had been quoted. According to colleagues, said the Council, he had said, "I don't want to have anything to do with the news media ever again."

Ten days after that the scene shifted to New York. Michael Daly, a columnist for the *Daily News* resigned. A week earlier Columbia's School of Journalism had given him the Meyer Berger Award for distinguished reporting. His resignation was triggered by a column he had written from Northern Ireland, highly critical of British troops. The London *Daily Mail* called it "a work of pure imagination." Summoned to New York, Mr. Daly maintained his column was authentic, but admitted making up the name of a British soldier he had quoted, and he was unable to verify other elements in the account. He argued that his techniques were the same he had used in 300 other columns he had written for the *News*. Michael J. O'Neill, then the newspaper's editor, said candidly that he and his aides had been "too permissive" in supervising young writers.

The ink had barely dried when, on May 23, WABC-TV in New York broadcast a statement that its executive producer, program director, a reporter, and two others had resigned "or were terminated" for faking letters to an advice-to-viewers program. The whistle-blower had been a viewer who complained that a letter attributed to him had been written by a neighbor who worked on the program. A check disclosed letters had been fabricated on two other WABC programs.

The next mine went off late in May in the offices of the New York Times Company. Through a subsidiary sales corporation, it ran a service distributing articles taken both from the *Times* and from free-lancers. The wire carried free-lance stories from Poland purporting to describe underground Solidarity activities. A number of papers, including the *Times of London* ran them. Solidarity was quick to call them part fraud and part gross distortion. Walter E. Mattson, president of the Times Company, acknowledged that the articles "appear to be of questionable accuracy," adding that the service "will no longer handle such free-lance material."

Worse luck was to befall the *Times* itself. On December 20, 1981, its Sunday magazine carried a free-lancer's article about a trip to Cambodia. In mid-January 1982, Alexander Cockburn wrote in the *Village Voice* that a closing passage in the article, written by Christopher Jones, 24, who lives in Spain, was strikingly similar to a passage in a novel by Andre Malraux. That prompted a letter from the *Times* to Mr. Jones. It escalated to full investigation after the *Washington Post* on February 18 reported that Khmer Rouge officials in Bangkok had denied Mr. Jones had ever visited the rebel strongholds mentioned. The *Times'* Sunday editor and its Rome bureau chief who had formerly been correspondent in Southeast Asia were flown to Spain to join Madrid bureau chief James Markham to quiz Mr. Jones. Result: A confession of fabrication, concocted in a Spanish seaside villa, using maps and other material, relying on some background drawn from an article he had written for the Asian edition of *Time* in October 1980, and with the added flourish of a plagiarized passage from Malraux. He called it "a gamble—that was it." A. M. Rosenthal, the executive editor, recited all the steps that had been taken—prechecks on the writer's prior record and work, close scrutiny of the copy, and so on. He wasn't satisfied. "We do not feel that the fact the writer was a liar and a hoaxer removes our reponsibility," he wrote. "It is our job to uncover any falsehoods or errors. The major mistake we made is in not following our customary procedures in showing an article in a specialized subject by any writer without outstanding credentials to one of our own specialists."

There are episodes of hoaxes at other good papers, some that can be looked on with sardonic humor, some still painful in the memory. That is why I see the scoop so dourly. There are too many who crave it to the point that if they cannot come up with one legitimately, they are perfectly willing to invent one. And if it can happen in the best and proudest of news organizations, I shudder to think of what gets through the gates in so many less-skilled newsrooms, where pride is never even discussed.

## CHAPTER 4

# "I Don't Want To Know"

"SHE WAS STUNNING: A tall, dark-skinned woman in designer fashion clothes and looking lean, fit and ultra-professional. I shook hands for the first time with Janet Cooke, still not making the connection with the remark about an 8-year-old heroin addict. . . . It was hard to imagine someone hitting the streets in clothes such as those. . . . One thing kept bugging me that day and into the next Sunday when I read the story. I kept seeing those designer shoes and that designer handbag and trying to fit them into the streets I knew. They just didn't fit. That I knew for sure."

These words were written to me by Robert C. Maynard, whose present role was described crisply by *Newsweek* in May 1983: "As a successful black journalist in a profession dominated by whites, former *Washington Post* writer Robert Maynard has grown used to setting precedents." Mr. Maynard had just bought the *Oakland Tribune* for $22.5 million, making him, *Newsweek* added, "the first big-city editor within memory to buy out his own paper, and the first black proprietor of a metropolitan daily." Before he left the *Post,* Mr. Maynard had been considerably more than a writer. From a "street reporter" he had moved up steadily—to White House correspondent, member of the editorial board, assistant managing editor, ombudsman. The afternoon he met Janet Cooke and heard her story he was a visiting West Coast editor who had stopped by to see old colleagues at the *Post* and was urged to stay to hear about the story being worked on.

Few episodes better illuminate the immense importance of his kind of perceptive gatekeeping skills than his reactions to Janet Cooke's before-publication recital of her fabricated scenario of seeing an 8-year-old boy being injected with a shot of heroin, and how a wide range of standard newsroom assumptions up and down the line led one of the best newspapers in the United States into publishing a fanciful hoax contrived by an overly ambitious 25-year-old reporter. Truth was of no consequence to her. It was a weakness that was to cost her a Pulitzer Prize and damage not only her newspaper but all of journalism. She got as far as she did with her fiction presented as "news" because she had been listening, watching, asking questions. One has to conclude that she recognized the holes in the gatekeeping system and gambled that she could sneak through the gates. She did, indeed, but had set a trap for herself that she could not escape because she was unable to control her penchant for embroidering facts.

In a sense, it was this latter miscalculation that was a lucky break for the *Post* and for the rest of journalism. If her entry had not been chosen for a prize, she might still be a walking time bomb within the staff. It might also have hidden still another unguarded set of gates, those in the meeting room of the Pulitzer Prize board, where an equally unquestioning set of editors, elders in the calling, had refused to listen to challenges raised about the entry. Start to finish, it might be likened to the government's series of failures to properly install adequate gates at its Marine post and embassies in Lebanon.

Before moving into some of the detail of judgmental mishaps at the *Post*, four things ought to be made clear. One is that hoaxes in journalism are aberrations. More happen than we know about, of that I am sure. Even so, my estimate puts outright fakery on the scale of highly unusual. Point two is that it is more likely to be attempted in large operations because they inevitably tend toward becoming bureaucracies. The news organization's interests sometimes become subordinated to departmental gamesmanship. Point three is that, by happenstance, everything that could go awry in a situation such as the one Janet Cooke contrived went wrong at one time at the *Post*. There was slippage in double checking and assumptions that the essential detail was known to the subeditors in charge. In all, blind faith in the "system" took control. There was no direct rundown of a check list, such as airplane crews go through before takeoff. Point four is that the *Post* learned from its anguish over the episode. The question is whether other news organizations studied the record and also learned from it. If not, other time bombs are waiting to go off under them.

How did, and does, Robert Maynard fit into all this? He and I are warm friends, and he confided his experience at the *Post* to me after the paper learned it had been the victim of a hoax. We had served on the Pulitzer Prize juries in March 1981. He was on the features writing panel. Janet Cooke's story had been entered in general reporting, and therefore, no one on the features jury saw it, or knew it had been chosen as the features winner by the prize board until the announcement in May. The Pulitzer judging procedure has often been criticized, and the selection of Miss Cooke's story richly deserved the caustic criticism that came from many quarters.

What the prize board had done was to arbitrarily move the Cooke entry from general reporting, where the jury had *not* recommended it as the top choice, to features, *where it had not been seen.* One member of the board, Eugene Patterson, chairman of the *St. Petersburg Times,* objected. He told his colleagues that the story was an aberration, and should never have been published, much less nominated. The board declined to go along with him. It might have saved itself the extra embarrassment that came later if only it had paused to check with the chairmen of the two juries involved. Since Mr. Maynard had been on the features jury, his insights could well have brought some reflection into the procedure. Why are many of the nation's leading editors asked to serve as jurors and then treated as subordinate screeners who are never consulted about the reasoning behind their recommendations?

After *The Post* learned it had been hoaxed, and declined the prize, the board then hastily barged into another arbitrary mistake. It chose the alternate in the feature writing category to receive the prize, but picked a story the jury, chaired by Judith Crist, the film critic, had tried to "shut out" (Miss Crist's description) in favor of one the same writer had produced and that the panel had chosen. There was another *Washington Post* alumnus on the features jury, Joel Dreyfuss, then managing editor of *Black Enterprise,* who now is an editor at *Fortune* magazine. Mr. Dreyfuss also had heard of internal misgivings at the *Post*. The Pulitzer board simply had locked itself behind its own gates and, like the *Post,* boobytrapped itself.

It was in this context that Bob Maynard shared his Washington experience with me. Hence, it was natural that I would ask him if he would feel free to put his memory into writing for this book as a potential service for editors young and old. He agreed. He had gone to Washington in September for a publisher's association committee meeting on government affairs. He wrote:

Late that Thursday afternoon, I took a stroll through downtown, savoring the place I lived in and loved for so long. I decided to make a nostalgic trip back to the *Post,* to the newsroom where I grew up. When I reached the fifth floor, I was stunned by how much the place had expanded. Many faces were familiar, but the newsroom had grown to the size of three football fields. I stopped to say hello to Bradlee and after a few minutes of light chatter about the news business in Oakland and Washington, I wandered deeper into the maze of desks and VDTs. Way in the back, standing at his desk in a glass cage, Bob Woodward waved to me. I walked in to find Bob and Milton Coleman in conversation. We exchanged greetings and I took the usual jokes about transcending the gravitational pull of the reporter's orbit for life in the stratosphere of editing one's own paper. It was growing late and I moved to leave, explaining that I didn't want to clog up the works at deadline. "Oh, no, stay," said Woodward. "You'll be interested in this. One of our reporters has just come up with one hell of a story about an 8-year-old heroin addict." I was sickened at the thought. As any father would do, my mind flashed to my own 8-year-old and I cringed at the image of a child his age on heroin.

Only a few seconds later I looked away from Woodward's desk and saw a young woman waiting for a signal to enter. She was stunning: a tall, dark-skinned woman in designer fashion clothes and looking lean, fit and ultra-professional. I shook hands for the first time with Janet Cooke, still not making the connection with the remark about an 8-year-old heroin addict. Coleman asked Janet how the story was developing, saying. "We were just telling Bob Maynard about it." As she began to speak about "Jimmy," my mind began to reel with questions. I had been thrown off balance because of one overriding question from the instant I saw her. I could not connect this elegantly tailored young woman with the kind of street reporting that would turn up any kind of heroin addict. I listened to a recitation of the now familiar details. My eyes fixed on her handbag and shoes. I recognized them as expensive, designer products. It was hard to imagine someone hitting the streets in clothes such as those. There are things about the streets you learn as a street reporter. One is how you dress. A woman dressed as she was would set off a 57-decibel alarm on the streets where addicts live. People dressed as she was would be presumed to be from the law and nobody in their right mind would get within 100 yards of her. She said something to indicate she had just returned from the neighborhood. Something in my gut was churning with questions I simply could not ask. These were editors of the *Washington Post* doing their jobs. I once lived there, but now I was the editor of the *Oakland Tribune* and a guest. I could only listen.

I wanted to ask how she had come into contact with the people she described. Why had they chosen to take her into their confidence? If such blatantly antisocial activities were taking place, why would they talk with a reporter about them? What would be the motive for anyone pumping heroin into an 8-year-old? What do you know about the paradoxical effect? This is important. You remember that I broke the story on the use of ritalin and speed to "modify" the behavior of hyperactive children in Omaha public schools. I learned then that there is a paradoxical, or reverse, effect of speed on prepuberty children. While speed hops up an adult, scientists think it calms children. In the case of heroin, what happens? These were all questions I hoped would be answered in the story in the *Post*. For me to jump into the role of editor in somebody else's news organization seemed wholly inappropriate, but as I listened to Miss Cooke, her tale seemed to me curiouser and curiouser. I suppose I would have wanted to go over those details with a fine-toothed comb if I were her editor. There were so many elements that did not fit with what I thought I once knew about street life in Washington. I reminded myself that whatever I knew was from a period long ago and I now lived far away. When I left, the sun had gone down. There was a chill in the air as I walked back to the hotel, turning over and over in my mind what I had just heard. I cannot tell you I disbelieved the story. I just didn't know what to think. But one thing kept bugging me that day and into the next Sunday, when I read the story. I kept seeing those designer shoes and that designer handbag and trying to fit them into the streets I knew. They just didn't fit. That I knew for sure.

Half a year later Bob Maynard was to discover that a lot of other things hadn't fit, either. Janet Cooke had lied about her record in her application to the *Post* and had not been caught because the paper's checking was so casual as to be useless. Asked to update her biography when the "Jimmy" story was being submitted for prize consideration, she did more doctoring. The Pulitzer Prize office always attaches the submitted personal data to its press release of the winners. The *Toledo Blade*, where Miss Cooke had worked before being employed by the *Post*, told the Associated Press that its report on her academic record did not match the facts. Applying to the *Post*, she said she graduated from Vassar with Phi Beta Kappa honors, that she had won an award from the Ohio Newspaperwomen's Association, and could read two languages. Her update for the Pulitzer entry said she graduated from Vassar magna cum laude, had received a master's degree from the University of Toledo, had attended the Sorbonne, had won six prizes from the Ohio Newspaperwomen's Association, and could read four languages. Too late for the *Post,* it was learned that Miss Cooke had *not* graduated from Vassar. The master's degree also was invention, because there was no graduate program at Toledo.

The *Post* moved into intensive examination. It had the attorney's office deliver her 145 pages of notes and the tape recordings she said contained interviews. These had been delivered to the lawyers when city officials had threatened to subpoena the records. The *Post's* counsel had said they fell under First Amendment protection. This was the *first* examination of Miss Cooke's source data by *any* of the senior editors. City Editor Coleman was told to accompany her to have her identify the house where "Jimmy" lived. She was unable to do so. Mr. Woodward already had decided she had lied and Mr. Coleman agreed. Miss Cooke's attitude had changed somewhat, but she continued to hold that the story was correct. The decision was made to let her talk alone with David Maraniss, editor of the Maryland staff, who had befriended her in her early days at the paper. He quoted her as saying: "I was afraid I was going to be left alone with you. The first time I saw you today I thought, 'Oh boy, he knows, and I'm going to have to tell him.' I couldn't lie to you. I couldn't tell them. I would never tell Woodward." She resigned, giving Mr. Maraniss a short written confession, and the *Post* took two immediate steps. It notified the Pulitzer Prize office the award could not be accepted, and it "invited" the paper's ombudsman, Bill Green, to prepare a full report for publication—"invited" him because he had been assured of autonomy when he took the position, one Robert Maynard had held a few years earlier.

The *Post* had been the second newspaper to adopt the ombudsman function in 1965. After several years of naming top senior staff members to the position, Mr. Bradlee decided to reach outside the staff and to sign specific-term contracts, granting full autonomy to those who took the job. The first outsider was Charles Seib, former managing editor of the *Washington Star.* Mr. Seib extended his role into becoming a syndicated columnist and his work appeared in a number of newspapers. When his contract expired, Mr. Bradlee tapped Mr. Green, who had been an editor on three North Carolina papers, had served with the U.S. Information Agency as press officer in South Africa and in Bangladesh, and "for one glorious year" served as the USIA deputy to Edward R. Murrow in 1963–64. He had returned home to be Duke University's public relations officer and was granted leave to accept the ombudsman post. He now is back at Duke serving as a vice-president.

Within hours of Miss Cooke's resignation, he began interviewing everyone on the staff who had known her or had dealt with her. Forty-six hours later Mr. Green sat down before a typewriter and, with only short breaks, wrote steadily for 24½ hours. A research aide and an editor moved his copy into the electronic system. His 18,000 words occupied three-and-a-half pages in the Sunday *Post*. Mr. Green's report made it clear there had been many protests from readers immediately after the story appeared. As he wrote, "Readers were outraged. The story was described as racist and criminal. The concern was for Jimmy. 'What about the boy?' was the central question. It was repeated for the next four days in as many versions as the human mind can invent. . . . The *Post*'s telephones never stopped ringing." Much of the most bitter remonstrance came from public officials.

There undoubtedly are many in Washington who to this day still do not accept Mr. Green's report as full truth. I am one willing to testify to my conviction that the *Post* laid out every fact it could uncover. In that period, I was chairman of the National News Council and personally accepted a complaint tendered by ten members of Howard University's journalism faculty. Several *Post* executives were upset by my action at the time, but later recognized the News Council had done a service by its reexamining of every phase of Mr. Green's report, and more. The leading figure in drafting the complaint had been on the staff of the *Post*-owned *Newsweek* magazine, had been discharged, and had conducted a long, losing court battle all the way up to the Supreme Court.

In the preface to the Council report, I wrote that the complaint was flawed because it was overstated and suppositive:

But a flawed complaint is no more unusual than flawed journalistic products. If the News Council study served a purpose, it was to verify the integrity of the *Post*'s efforts to make a clean breast of the entire episode, even while at the same time finding some of the editing defenses during the original process to have gone wrong and seriously so. At a lesser news organization, there probably would have been some bland excuse for the overstatement of academic achievements and a basic defense of the story. A reporter would have kept a Pulitzer Prize and the issue would have been forgotten. No news organization to my knowledge has ever gone so far and so fully into public accountability.

The Council's two associate directors did the on-the-scene reexamination and were given full freedom to question everyone from publisher on down. Richard P. Cunningham formerly had been ombudsman for the *Minneapolis Tribune* and A. H. Raskin was known throughout the profession as having been the top labor reporter and analyst in the field, and later deputy editorial page editor of the *New York Times*. Totally unlike the caricature-image of newsmen as abrasive cynics, Dick Cunningham and Abe Raskin are men of intellect and grace, skilled in eliciting answers from even the most suspicious and resistant individuals.

In his book, *The Kingdom and the Power,* Gay Talese described the high-tension rivalry and competition that existed within the *Times.* Mr. Green had already discovered the same patterns to be flourishing at the *Post,* and Mr. Cunningham and Mr. Raskin were to discover it for themselves. Neither newsroom is unique in this regard. Nor, for that matter, is any other enterprise that I have heard about, or read about. Journalism may be more subject to the strains because it attracts a large number of intense, innately ego-centered and highly ambitious individuals. Almost all news operations give birth to cliques which vie for both attention and position.

At the News Council I became the principal editor of the Cunningham-Raskin report and raised many questions. Both men answered with names, dates, and precise notes. From their interviews what came forth was a staff view of a newsroom "in

which temptations are strong to court editors' favor by stretching every story to the ultimate" and that "a great number . . .
[had held] doubts about Miss Cooke's story they either did not
communicate or did so weakly that their suspicions were dis-
counted." Among these was Mr. Maraniss, who felt the story did
not ring true and had urged Mr. Woodward to reread it before
submitting it for a prize. Mr. Maraniss was candid in telling Mr.
Green he had been pushing a series by a member of his own staff
and had not been as explicit as he should have been for fear of
appearing to be lobbying for his own staffer. At least, Mr. Maraniss was not tainted by the customary political knife-play that
comes from the burning desire to win prizes.

I have gone through the Cunningham-Raskin and the Green
reports repeatedly, weighing all the things that went on. Each
reexamination has persuaded me that few episodes provide
stronger reinforcement for my conviction that journalism's
weakest link is the dysfunctional nature of the gatekeeping system. There are certain to be those who will contend that I am
making judgments based on hindsight. Agreed, hindsight has
always been the only perfect science. But without hindsight, how
can any of us ever learn?

Take Bob Woodward and Milton Coleman, two of the *Post*'s
brightest individuals. The record indicates clearly that they were
the victims of one of journalism's oldest blind spots, that of
moving people into managerial positions without giving them
meticulous advance training for their new roles. The worst place
to rely on the learn-by-doing method is in news staff management. At one stage in my career I took the gamble that brains
and character were enough to assure success in running a newsroom. That theory was exploded with one spectacular miscalculation. Yes, brains and character are essential, but they won't do
without the vital added ingredient of advance preparation.

Mr. Coleman joined the *Post* when he was 30, assigned to
cover Montgomery County and later city hall. At 34, he was
named assistant city editor and only two months later promoted
to city editor. His immediate supervisor was Mr. Woodward, 37,
famous for his reporting role in the Watergate exposures. He had

become an assistant managing editor supervising the more than 100 members of the metropolitan staff and it was his first managerial role. Bright and sharp as they were, why did not the same kind of questions that occurred to Robert Maynard occur to them? Part, to be sure, lies in the plot designed by Janet Cooke to achieve stardom. So astute was she that she created a situation worthy of the most talented mystery writer. Mr. Woodward certainly was a successful reporter. But sitting in an editor's chair demands a different state of mind. Neither of them was prepared for a reporter who would lie to them. Granted, not many do. But old hands at editing discover that there are a few sinners in the flock and they learn ways and means to get backstop checking without giving any hint of disbelief. If anyone at the *Post* ever raised such a suggestion, it has not come to light.

Mr. Coleman consulted often with Howard Simons, 52, then managing editor, and who now is curator of the Nieman Fellowships at Harvard. One of the ablest of science writers, Mr. Simons joined the *Post* in 1961 after a year as a Nieman Fellow and became managing editor ten years later, also without having had prior managerial experience.

This aside, what was said in some of the meetings remains hazy to this moment. Mr. Simons disagrees with my emphasis on this point, but thorough understanding and agreement among members of a line staff has long seemed to me crucial in newsroom operations.

After Janet Cooke confessed to Mr. Maraniss, she told him she thought she could carry off the hoax for three reasons: (1) the police could not find a boy who did not exist; (2) she was not afraid of city officials who had denounced the story; and (3) Mr. Simons had told her he was not going to ask for the name of the boy or his mother. In Mr. Green's report, a quote attributed to Mr. Coleman was, "Howard said she should deal with me and tell me the child's identity. 'I don't want to know,' he said, somewhat jokingly." Mr. Coleman told the two news council appraisers that this made his memory appear more concrete than it was. Mr. Simons could not recall saying it, but he added that it conformed with his belief that the managing editor did not have to know, but that the subeditor in charge should know. On one aspect of this, Mr. Simons is quite correct in holding that an editor given a name and address of a source means nothing unless the editor has some familiarity with the individuals. Several experiences taught me there are other ways of checking, but none was pursued at the *Post*. More than a few people knew about the story and many had doubts. But the linkage was weak and the doubters were reticent to speak up. The "I don't want to know" posture, or its variant, "I don't need to know," has been a factor in the excessive growth of anonymous sources. Mr. Simons' point about subeditors needing to know clearly is in order, and he holds that when they are not sure they ought not to publish. Yet, in the "Jimmy" hoax, Mr. Coleman says that at no point did anyone at the *Post* ever ask him the key questions directly. "I don't want to know" ought to disappear forever and be replaced with "I've got to know everything."

Two things threw Mr. Coleman off stride. One was that Miss Cooke had been assigned to follow up a tip about a child heroin addict. She reported she could not find the child, but had heard about another boy and asked for time to track it down. The second was a memorandum she wrote. It was pure invention, but it was enough to give Mr. Coleman pause about checking deeper. In the memorandum, she wrote that the drug pusher who was injecting the 8-year-old boy with heroin had said to her, "If I see any police, Miss Lady, or if any police come to see me, we"—and he glanced at a knife in his hand—"will be around to see you." Mr. Coleman told Mr. Green he raised this with Mr. Simons, who agreed with his concerns and had added it would show distrust in the reporter for someone else to visit the family.

After the story appeared, misgivings started to arise within the *Post* newsroom. A surge of reader protest centered on a perception of indifference at the *Post* about saving the 8-year-old boy from the situation Miss Cooke had contrived. Mr. Coleman assigned several reporters to follow up various aspects of the story. Courtland Milloy, a black reporter, went with Miss Cooke to seek a second child addict. He returned to tell Mr.

Coleman that Miss Cooke did not know the area she had described. "I voiced my concerns to Howard," Mr. Coleman told Mr. Green, "and he said in so many words that they were legitimate. But he urged me to find the most creative way to examine them, stressing that I, more than anyone else, had to stand by my reporter. At the point that I even began to hint that I thought she had not been truthful, her trust in me could be destroyed."

Three weeks after publication, Mr. Simons told Mr. Coleman, "That kid's still out there . . . let's find him. Take Janet with you." Mr. Coleman informed Miss Cooke but before they could make a date to go to the house, she reported there was no point in going—that she had gone and found the family had moved to Baltimore. Mr. Coleman expressed anger to Mr. Simons, who said it raised a doubt in his mind for the first time. "But all I had to go on was a hunch," he said, "and the fact she had ducked the visit. How do you prove a negative?"

Mr. Green wrote in his report that *before* publication:

> None of the *Post*'s senior editors subjected Cooke's story to close questioning. Simons was on vacation in Florida the week before it appeared. . . . Ben Bradlee read the story that week and thought it was "a helluva job." Are they satisfied with the preliminary screening? . . . Simons answered: "Yes, there was no reason to disbelieve the story." Bradlee said, "I am not satisfied now—but I was then." Coleman, who was editing Cooke's copy, reflects on this: "Much of my attention was concentrated on the story and formulating it. Subconsciously, I think I firmly believed that the extra eyes of the backup system would catch anything I missed."

Later to Mr. Cunningham and Mr. Raskin, Mr. Coleman said he had come to believe other editors were relying on him. "We never really debated whether or not it was true," he said. "I think—if I can gore my own ox—they kind of took it for granted that Coleman should know."

In the light of all that had transpired in the weeks after publication—Courtland Milloy's report that Miss Cooke did not know the area where she had described "Jimmy" to be living, her quick dodging out of any trip with Milton Coleman to find the boy to help him, and questionings within the staff, even if put forward gingerly—why was the story placed in nomination for a Pulitzer Prize? Mr. Green's report listed several reasons: a statement by the mayor soon after the story appeared that the authorities knew who "Jimmy" was; a letter from a psychiatrist that seemed to say he knew of many "Jimmys"; attribution of some internal doubts to staff jealousy; the failure of staff members to press their individual doubts; and taking what Mr. Woodward described as "our Watergate mode: Protect the source and back the reporter." Mr. Coleman said pride also contributed. "We had published the story in the first place," he said, "and stood by it. We probably put too much faith in the hope that maybe things were not the way so many indicators suggested they might be." So it was that he moved to recommend it for a prize, calling it readable, accurate, and complete, and lauding the reporter for resourcefulness and enterprise.

In Mr. Green's report, Jonathan Neumann, a past winner of a Pulitzer Prize, was quoted as saying, "A number of people felt strongly that it should not be nominated because it could disgrace us. I think we felt that it wouldn't be fair to put her on the carpet when we couldn't prove anything." Mr. Woodward decided to plump for nominating the story, referring to his decision as "in for a dime, in for a dollar." Mr. Simons said, "I didn't know of any staff doubts, but I had some of my own. I had reason to doubt, but no reason to disbelieve." In this context, it is easy to understand Mr. Bradlee's later discomfiture. "Nobody ever came into this room and said, 'I have doubts about the story' before or after publication, and nobody said someone else has misgivings about the story," he said.

Mr. Bradlee had not collected himself when he spoke to the convention of the American Society of Newspaper Editors the week after Miss Cooke had confessed. He said he had placed an extra trust in Miss Cooke and Mr. Coleman because they were black, and he considered them to be experts on the poor, black section of the city where "Jimmy" and his mother had been portrayed as living—an area about which Robert Maynard had experienced instant confusion in trying to equate someone like Janet Cooke working as a reporter dealing with heroin users. As brilliant and intuitive as he is, at that moment with the nation's top-ranking editors, Benjamin Bradlee was being defensive. He was saying about himself some things that had let the whole episode happen, the failings so many of his editors had exhibited all during the handling of the fabricated story—*Assuming. Taking things for granted.* I was present when he said it. The thought crossed my mind that he had spoken hastily. Having read about Miss Cooke's background, and from what Bob Maynard had told me, it seemed implausible that she could be an "expert" on poor, black zones. No, that was the kind of momentary slip on Ben Bradlee's part that all of us have been guilty of too many times in our lives.

There was, of course, an immense amount of soul-searching inside the *Post*. Bob Woodward said the affair had "driven a spike in my head." He had gone along for ten years taking it for granted that reporters always tell the truth and government officials always lie. "That's not a good mode to be in," he said. Ken Ringle, a reporter and former assistant city editor, who had been on leave for more than a year, returned to attend a meeting called to discuss the incident and said, "the real villain is glamor journalism, the cult of personality."

What bothered many of the *Post* people was the original posture of refusing to give information to the police. Mr. Woodward said it had put the *Post* in a "morally untenable position" of having witnessed a crime and saying "to hell with" the 8-year-old victim. Former ombudsman Charles Seib wrote an article for *Presstime,* the American Newspaper Publishers Association magazine, saying that the lack of concern for the child before the story was published "spotlighted a blind spot that the news business had better do something about." Mr. Seib said that one *Post* editor had suggested to him that the newspaper could have urged the mother to get the child into treatment with the paper paying the costs. "The irony here, of course," wrote Mr. Seib, "is that if he had done that—if he had allowed a humanitarian instinct to rise above the enthusiasm for a smashing story—there is a good possibility that he would have uncovered the deception and the story would have died aborning." Quite right. On balance, however, the *Post*'s gatekeepers were like their counterparts almost everywhere in journalism. They were more caught up in what looked like "one helluva story" than in the many societal nuances it posed.

Several reforms went into effect rapidly at the *Post*. One was a mandate that editors had to know the identity of confidential sources and accept the responsibility for granting anonymity. Another was to apply firm rules on checking applicants' claims. Still another was a program to increase training for both reporters and editors. It is doubtful that the *Post* will fall victim soon again to having a general reporter go it alone on a story of this type of impact.

What it needed desperately at the moment of decision was the perceptive, specialist skills of a Robert Maynard. Born in Brooklyn to a Barbadian family tied to education, he went "west" in 1961 to go to work at the sprightly *York Gazette* in Pennsylvania. His reporting was so strikingly effective that it was to win him a Nieman Fellowship at Harvard, and, subsequently, an offer to join the *Post*. His reporting for the *Gazette* was to remain so well remembered that in May 1984, York College invited him back to award him an honorary doctorate of humane letters. In his days in York, Mr. Maynard says, "I had an editor by the name of Jim Higgins, an Irishman with a twinkle in his eye and an awesome sense of humanity and decency. He and I sat down in 1961 and began to talk about how to cover the poor. . . . I wanted to meet the actual people behind the statistics and write about their life circumstances in a concrete way. . . . With Jim Higgins' help, I went around the country to look at how other cities were dealing with the problem. I discovered I had to write about housing, education and transportation and how they fit into people's ability to get work. What came out of it was a body of work that described the evolution of the cycle of poverty, of how people got to be poor."

After joining the *Post,* Mr. Maynard covered the cities and the riots of the late '60s, producing one series used by newspapers all across the country. He moved on to cover politics and, before joining the White House press corps, he criss-crossed the country on an assignment he said "gave me some of my greatest exposure of what this country was all about. It was during those trips that I discovered the Bay Area and how poor newspapers were here. Everyone agreed the area needed a good newspaper and I began to feel I would love to come back here some day as a newspaper editor." He achieved it, of course, and it was that kind of sensitivity and his ability to look beyond "one helluva story" to see all manner of unanswered questions when he sat as a visitor in September 1980 and listened in awkward silence as Janet Cooke outlined her fanciful story.

I do not blame Howard Simons, or Bob Woodward, or Milton Coleman. In varying ways, they fell victim to newsroom mythology. That mythology casts a protective screen over all that journalists do. Long years ago, one senior editor cautioned me, "Don't believe anything you hear and damned little of what you see." He was right, but I was to make countless mistakes before fully learning how true his counsel was. Check, double-check, triple-check. It still bothers me that none of them got a car, climbed into it with Janet Cooke and took a tour of the "poor black area" she claimed to know, had her point out the house, and then sat down to figure how they might set up a stakeout to look for "Jimmy" coming and going. As Charles Seib wrote, any kind of on-site check would have flushed Janet Cooke out of the protective cover she had contrived. Bill Green and Bob Maynard and I have since talked about it and they agree fully. My newsroom sermonizing included one persistent theme, born out of sleepless nights of retracing steps on scores of fouled-up stories. It was that mistakes in journalism are inevitable, but that the test was whether we learned from them—that if we made the same mistake a third time we were in deep trouble. Obviously it is impossible to check out everything. But the priorities change abruptly with each different story, and caution lights start flash-

ing the moment there are stories of importance, sensitivity, or
societal interlocks. The "one helluva story" impulse has to be
challenged instantly. There has to be someone in the gatekeeper
ranks who pulls back and says, in effect: "Wait a minute. We
need to check this one out from hell to breakfast. Let's sit down
and talk through what we need to do to make this one stand up."
As Bill Green reported, none of this took place with Janet
Cooke's story. The most revealing sentence may have been
Milton Coleman's. "We never really debated whether or not it
was true. I think . . . they kind of took it for granted that Coleman should know." Journalistic mythology was too rooted in
the 1980 *Post* newsroom for the challenges crying out to be
voiced.

My guess is that Milton Coleman is likely to become one of
journalism's stars. He has brains and character. He left the city
editor's role to take on political coverage in the 1984 campaign.
He was the one who reported on the Rev. Jesse Jackson's references to Jews as "Hymie." Other black journalists vented bitter
criticism at him, and he was given rough treatment at the convention of the National Association of Black Journalists in August 1984. He was, fortunately, to receive more than adequate
support when Lem Tucker, the CBS News correspondent, arrived on the scene in Atlanta to address the meeting. Like Robert
Maynard, Mr. Tucker is a role model of some consequence.
From a beginning as a copyboy at NBC News, he rose to be in on
the Vietnam coverage, to presidential campaigns, the Iranian
hostage crisis, Biafra's civil war, and many other major stories.
He won an Emmy for his "Hunger in America" series, and he is
not one to run from a challenge. "Excellence," he told the convention group in Atlanta, "is color blind. There is no such nonsense as black journalism and white journalism. There is good
and bad journalism. And merely asking the question, 'Are you
black first or a journalist first' is bad journalism. . . . For
months now, black people who call themselves journalists have
assailed a black journalist who did his job—with excellence—
calling him a traitor, saying he violated some sort of unspoken
covenant among his race. Well, I am black, I am a journalist and

I stand . . . with Milton Coleman, because he stands for excellence. My covenant and yours should be with the questions 'Who?' 'What?' 'When?' 'Where?' 'Why?' It should be with truth, with honor and with yourself and the public—black and white. . . . We must watch our priorities. . . . Never forget that your color still plays a role in your getting a job in this industry. Once you are in, you are there to be a journalist."

Change Mr. Tucker's word "black" to anything else—land of family origin, religion, sex, political bent, *any* link of any kind—and his arrow quivers in the heart of the bullseye. The prejudices that torment society everywhere are not soon to melt away. Journalism has done its share in helping to reduce the mindless cruelties of bias. Unhappily, it also has fallen victim too often to maintaining stereotypes, as it has permitted itself to become sterotyped as uncaring, insensitive, and arrogant. Almost all of that blame I lay to the weaknesses in the gatekeeping system, as the Janet Cooke hoax demonstrated. But as said earlier, the *Washington Post* set an example for all of journalism with its decision to recount all of its many mistakes in judgment and to open itself further to outside, independent review. It would be a great plus to see that become an embedded journalistic ethic.

## CHAPTER 5
# "How Do You Make an Editor?"

THE TRAUMA that goes with publishing a hoax was still haunting the charismatic and dynamic Ben Bradlee of the *Washington Post* in the spring of 1981 as he sat in his office, reviewing once again the failures in oversight that had led to the publications of Janet Cooke's invented account of a child heroin addict. Mr. Bradlee's customary self-assurance had been shaken. There was more than a touch of frustration in two questions he voiced, obviously not expecting his visitor to offer any answers. "How do you make an editor?" he asked. "Do we bring them along too fast?"[1] At that moment, his mind was not on journalistic history, but he was echoing the same questions that preoccupied publishers when they were building great American newspapers. They are questions that now have come into consideration in the executive offices of the giant television networks.

There are many kinds of editors, but the ones Mr. Bradlee was thinking about, and this book is focused upon, are those who deserve to be "in charge" and those who do not. We are not talking about that group of essential editors whose interests center on the use of language: words and their precise meanings, syntax, style, form, and flow. There may be some writers so gifted they do not need such editing. I have known only one in my lifetime.[2] Such writers and editors are even rarer than those few editors who seem born for command over everything in a news operation. There is, of course, still another kind of leading editor, those who concentrate on voicing opinion. There have been, and are now, many who have exercised significant influence upon public thought by force of coherent good sense and eloquence. However admirable these editors, they also do not fit into this appraisal, even though it deserves noting that conflicts between the news and opinion editors arise often over differing judgments on the importance of issues or emphases perceived by one or the other. The functions under examination can be likened to those of field marshals and their aides selected to carry out an unending war of deciding where the main battle lines of the moment are, and more important, where they may be tomorrow, next week, next month. They move their forces as they assess each situational change. The outstanding ones may seem ideal for their roles, but the records are of many testings on the way, and as in all things, for each success story, there are hundreds of untold failures.

"Executive editor" is a relatively new title. It came into use in the early 1950s as evolutionary necessity. Consolidations had brought many competing morning and evening newspapers under single ownerships, but the desire for separate news staffs gave birth to a fresh strain of the "front page" virus. It was almost as if the staffs taken over by new managements regarded themselves as sold into bondage and were determined to "show 'em." Antogonisms grew, and feverish competition spread to theft of the rival staffs' advance work and to following radically different standards. Their patience frayed, publishers chose executive editors to coordinate general policies and end the fratricidal caterwauling. The idea also appealed to publishers in whose operations there had grown Sunday departments responsible for many sections and exercising such stubborn independence as to constitute open rivalry with the main news force.

I became an executive editor in 1962 to supervise morning, evening, and Sunday operations. It was to become the most productive eight-year period of my professional life. The function actually is that of super managing editor. It calls for more hours devoted to the undertaking, whether in the office or not. But it provides a blessing every editor desperately needs: Time to think. Time to plan. Time to try to train the next generation of leaders. Time for innovative testings. It has become an essential in large operations, because no editor can effectively deal in depth with more than about seven deputies. Military leaders discovered that practicality long ago. No matter how it is measured, however, the task remains essentially that created in the last century—an editor in charge of all the news operations, a managing editor. Significantly, it was the title chosen by Walter Cronkite of CBS and continued by his successor, Dan Rather.

Are there any great managing editors in current journalism? I don't know. There are some outstanding ones, but only when their records are examined from the distance of time can there come any rational appraisals. What will be studied, I suppose, will be whether they advanced the quality of journalism, raised ethical performance, selected people for advancement properly, trained them, broadened their sights and instilled a sense of mission. Just as journalism is history in the raw, so it is in appraising those now in the command posts. What I do know is that it is a task that calls for people curious about everything that goes on, who learn to sublimate their prejudices to achieve a cold professionalism in judgment, who have the capacity for quick, decisive action, are so engrossed in the importance of the undertaking hours mean nothing to them, and who possess a capacity few individuals like to admit to. The late John Fischer, the noted editor of *Harper's* magazine, made perceptive comment about the editing craft twenty years ago in "An Editor's Easy Chair" essay.[3] "Happy is he," he wrote, "who is born cruel, for if not he will have to school himself in cruelty. Without it, he is unfit for his job, because the kindly editor soon finds his columns filled with junk." Or, it can be added in terms of daily journalism, he finds himself deferring too often to strongly advanced, but unwise, counsel from subordinates, or postponing the prospect of unpleasant confrontation with a rebellious staff member in the hope of finding a more gentlemanly solution. There are none.

There has been only one unquestioned giant as a managing editor in this century—Carr Van Anda, for the *New York Times* from 1904 to 1932; and, I suspect, only one near-giant, Oliver Kirby Bovard at the *St. Louis Post-Dispatch* from 1910 to 1938. How significant it is that both were chosen by and worked under two owner-publishers who left their own indelible marks on American journalism, Adolph Ochs and Joseph Pulitzer. The Pulitzer archives at Columbia University hold fascinating insights into the first Pulitzer's absorption in the selection of editors. The eccentric autocrat who was the driving force behind the *New York World* in 1900 was just as wrapped up and demanding that same year in deciding who would be city editor of his *Post-Dispatch* in St. Louis. Ochs and Pulitzer were true gatekeepers.

All manner of speculation offers itself. Perhaps it was the time in which they lived. Who knows? But Van Anda and Bovard shared so many of the same traits that it seems a bit uncanny. Neither of them finished schooling in the current sense, Bovard going only through the eighth grade, but both were superbly self-educated, Van Anda particularly so. His range of interests casts present editors as appearing to be parochial and slow-witted.[4] He knew enough about physics and astronomy to merit comparison with scholars. Both men worked hours current executives would consider unthinkable. They shunned public attention. They had the "simple ruthlessness" John Fischer described. Bovard was to fascinate me for understandable reasons. One was that I arrived in St. Louis to be managing editor of the *Star-Times* shortly after Bovard had died in retirement. I was to be exposed for several years to the legends about him, as well as compete with the impressive news staff and tradition he built, although the paper was beginning to show the first signs of an arrogance Bovard would have squelched instantly. Arrogance begets carelessness, and we were able to make enough inroads to win respect at the top levels of the *Post-Dispatch*.

One story about Bovard was so intriguing that I often used it in speeches, seeking to jar editors out of their complacency. There are several versions of the story.[5] Mine came from the late Ben H. Reese, who succeeded Bovard both as city editor and managing editor. As a reporter, Bovard was known familiarly as "Jack," and he was a regular among colleagues in after-work imbibing. He had been an interim assistant city editor for a time under the talented martinet, Charles Chapin, who was to be transferred to the *World* in New York. Chapin went to prison in 1918 for killing his wife. On the morning of his appointment as city editor, Bovard took over the chair and a companion of the evening before strode up, hand thrust out. "Congratulations, Jack," he said. Bovard did not extend his hand. "From now on," he said with a quiet firmness, "it's *Mister* Bovard to you." And that was the way it was until he left in 1938. Like Van Anda, he was hated and yet respected to the point of awe. I agreed with Ben Reese's interpretation of the Bovard gambit. It was that Bovard knew he had crossed the line. He no longer was one of the crowd. He was the boss and no one was to forget it.

Malcolm L. Mallette, who, as former director of the American Press Institute, saw thousands of subeditors at seminars, has called the pattern of recent years as reflecting one of editors being "too genteel," of wanting to be popular with their staffs.[6] Few if any possess what *Times* staff members termed Van Anda's disapproving look—"the Van Anda death ray."[7] Van Anda had been night editor of the *Sun* before going to the *Times*. For twenty years as managing editor he arrived at the office daily at 1 p.m., went home for dinner at 6 and was back at 10 p.m. to stay until 5 a.m., twelve hours a day, seven days a week. Bovard came in before 7 a.m. and still was at work when everyone else had left. Each was remembered as being a one-man school of journalism. Each, in his way, built astonishing records.

Bovard's strength was in investigative reporting. One of his insights was about Teapot Dome, until Watergate the nation's greatest governmental scandal.[8] Among Van Anda's many strengths was his prescience, demonstrated at the time of the Japanese-Russo War and later about the sinking of the *Titanic*. It was Van Anda who recognized the importance of British testing of Albert Einstein's then-obscure relativity theory and who broke the story of the confirmation of it. He saw the importance of the discovery of the tomb of Tutankhamen and got exclusive American rights to the story. There is no question about Van Anda's drives to be first in everything, but the towering difference in his approach and that of the "scoop-happy" was that Van Anda's interest was in stories of national and international substance, and never in trivia. Bovard, no trivia man, either, was engaged in one major crusade after another, fighting corruption and venality in both government and business. When Van Anda was honored in 1929 on the twenty-fifth anniversary of his being managing editor, Louis Wiley, the noted business manager, said, "It is well known that The Times prints only advertising for which Mr. Van Anda's news leaves room, in a paper of the size determined by him."[9] That was Adolph Ochs' doing. Gerald W. Johnson's biography of Ochs bore an ideal title, one few publishers have matched, *An Honorable Titan.*"[10] Although leagues from being qualified to carry Van Anda's or Bovard's pencils or notepads, I may have been one of the last beneficiaries of the freedom and power those two greats exercised so brilliantly.

The examples of Ochs and Pulitzer were to have a ripple effect through American journalism. Some publishers tried to emulate them and regional newspapers flourished under owners of conscience until the 1929 crash and the Depression. They started to recover, but were hit by depression again in 1937, which started the first big wave of mergers and closings. There was to come a lot of publisher posturing, but the dominance of newspapers, begun in 1690 in colonial America, had begun to erode under a number of pressures, principally the rise of wireless and then electronic transmission. The first warning had come on election night in 1920 over KDKA, Pittsburgh. *Time,* the first weekly newsmagazine, appeared in March 1923. Television came on line in 1947, and the pace became like that of aviation's sweep from the twin-engined DC-3 to the 747 and the supersonics. In fewer than forty years television was to rocket from a marriage of newsreels and motion pictures to the colossus in capturing audience. Nothing could illustrate it more than ABC's investment of $400 million in television rights and production of the 1984 summer Olympic Games. The telecasts often may have seemed like "one long commercial," as critic Edwin Diamond complained, but the audience ratings showed that 180 million people watched all or part of the newscasts.

Of far more significance was the national political experience of 1984, when television's outreach, featuring personalities and scenes, all but buried the essential arguments of central issues and governance. Preceding all this, however, had come a revolution. Just as locally owned department and specialty stores and factories became part of growing chains, so, too, did newspapers. One reason was the inheritance tax law. Many publishers sold out for a combination of cash and stock in the chains, plus continued, if meaningless, roles under their old titles. Their editors were either retired or given new positions as vice-presidents for public affairs, and new, younger editors were moved in. The days of strong editor autonomy were all but ended.

There was overwhelming evidence of this in one of 1983's best-read newspaper reports, titled *Editors and Stress*.[11] The report contained the results of a study in which 544 members of the Associated Press Managing Editors Association and 358 spouses had responded to a lengthy questionnaire about their feelings and attitudes about their work. The editor of the report, who also directed the study, was Robert H. Giles, editor of the *Democrat & Chronicle* and the *Times-Union* in Rochester, N.Y. In a frank opening commentary, Mr. Giles wrote:

> For years we have accepted the idea that stress is a part of the newspaper life. It is, but not in the ways we imagined. The adrenaline that flows when we are on deadline or in the grip of a big story works like an injection, giving us a burst of energy to focus on the day's news. That stress is what we love about newspapers—the *editor* role, directing the staff and shaping the newspaper. The adrenaline also flows when we confront the frustrations of the *manager* role, when duty compels us to act for the *company* in ways that seem to be not in the best interests of *readers*. That stress bores into your pride and strips us of the sense that we are in control. In can leave us dispirited and vulnerable.

The scope of the study can be judged from the fact that there were 942 possible responses to the series of questions posed: 77 percent of the editors said there was more work than they could complete in a normal day and 64 percent said their jobs cut into evenings and weekends. The difference between the Bovard/Van Anda work loads was that men in their positions could select what they wanted to concentrate upon. Today's editors are the victims of the paper deluge that came with photocopying, the torrent of memoranda and reports from management along with the added flow of correspondence and reports flowing out of the often highly useful committee work in which editors' organizations have become increasingly involved. It is clear that almost all of today's managing editors urgently need able assistants, a function that has proved highly effective, but which most managements have not seen fit to approve. One result of this lack of competent aides was revealed when 61 percent of the editors agreed that they were compelled to make news judgments "without as much information as I would like to have."

Nowhere in the study was the shift of gatekeeping authority over the news columns more pronounced than in that part of Mr. Giles' study when questions were asked about editor relationships with "The Boss and The Company": 71 percent of the managing editors reported that their work involved "implementing decisions with which I disagree"; 49 percent reported receiving assignments "without sufficient people and resources to carry them out"; 53 percent said that spending for such items as travel, conferences, and training had been cut. Most revealing of all, 48 percent answered that they agreed with the statement: "The newspaper does not back up its public commitment to journalistic excellence with the resources necessary to attain it." Equally striking was that 37 percent said that when they became editors they had received no training to prepare them for the responsibilities they were about to undertake and that they had received little thereafter. In terms only of the size of the study, it meant that at least 200 daily newspapers had given less thought to the appointment of those individuals chosen to serve as chief gatekeepers over the news and feature content of the newspapers than to assessing advertising and circulation managers, something I know from direct personal knowledge of practices within the industry.

John Fischer, in the same *Harper's* essay about the editing craft, mentioned earlier, had also made sharp comment about this trend. One of the essentials for good editing, he had said, was enthusiasm. Lack of it, he said, would "show on every page—in the uncombed syntax, the jaded idea, the unweeded cliche, the routine caption, the perfunctory proofreading. Such dispirited editing has become commonplace among American newspapers during the past generation, as competition has disappeared from one city after another. When all the papers in town, plus the broadcasting stations, are owned by one firm—and especially when that firm is dominated by businessmen who have no vocation for journalism and regard their media simply as money-machines—then most of the incentive for good editing and writing is likely to evaporate."[12]

When John Fischer wrote that, the chain-ownership avalanche was just beginning to pick up the momentum that was to thunder down on both large and small newspapers and transform the industry. The new system was to further reduce the freedom and authority of directing editors from what might have been called second-class status in the executive chain of command to third class and, in some cases, fourth class. Headquarters came first, of course, regional executives second, local publishers third. A few of the giants—Knight cum Knight-Ridder and Times-Mirror notably among them—accorded publishers and editors a high degree of autonomy. In general, however, the observable pattern was to release seasoned local executives and install younger, lower-salaried officers from smaller newspapers in the chain organizations, to adopt standard typographic patterns, and to transmit computerized budgets from the central headquarters. Many publishers and editors were to be "moved about like pawns,"[13] a phrase used by Malcolm Mallette, who has become the American Press Institute's director of development. It is hardly a system one can call dedicated to consistent and continuing service in the public interest.

One other facet showed up in the *Editors and Stress* study, but it is beyond cure. Almost 240 of the editors (44 percent) said that decisions about their future were based not simply on their abilities, but on their relationships with their publishers, company politics, and "my ability to play the game." It is admittedly a cynical observation, but this is true in everything in organizational life, no matter what the field. Other than with the rare exceptions of securely confident chief executives, there comes executive staff reshuffling with each top-level change in managements. Personal chemistry has always been a dominant factor in organizational life and, I assume, will remain so unless there comes a miraculous change in human nature. One of the changes that has come in journalistic practice is that of placing the search process for new news executives in the hands of "head-hunters," the term for professional organizations that keep extensive files on editors grown uncomfortable with uncertainties about their current positions. The "head-hunter" pattern can be applauded for its broad reach. The professionals know what type of individual the news organization is seeking, the preferred age range, intended salary, and other such essentials. They are good at checking the countless details. They provide a candidate list, and it is up to the company to do its own final appraisals and hiring. Under all this trapping, however, is confession of internal training failure. Even some of the best of newspapers have failed the organizational litmus test of rigorous training of the next generation of leaders.

My career happens to have been a case in point, as it was for my two oldest friends in the editing craft, Lee Hills, who rose to be Knight-Ridder's chief executive, and succeeded the late, famed John S. Knight as editorial chairman, and William P. Steven, now semiretired after years as editor in Tulsa, Minneapolis, Houston, and Chicago. We were "firemen." Every position that came after my leaving the old *Indianapolis Times* was in the nature of having to put out a fire and then rebuilding and refurnishing the house. Even the great Louisville newspapers fell victim in the 1950s to a serious case of procrastination. It had a managing editor who had been in the position too long, was too trapped in the thought patterns of his young days, was distrustful of and resistant to every suggestion for improvement, and who had picked as his coterie of gatekeepers those willing to follow his ways without argument. It was a situation not unfamiliar in other organizations. Change was essential, but every one of the six senior subeditors lacked the flexibility to readjust their judgment patterns. A quiet search was underway when the

*Star-Times* folded in 1951. Barry Bingham, Sr., the owner-editor, and Mark Ethridge, the publisher, were taking meticulous care in canvassing the field. Four offers had come my way, all declined. Two were from newspapers where control seemed too firmly vested in families with deep ties to the business life of their communities; one was from a magazine, a field about which I felt a lack of competence; and one was from Hearst, where the "fit" seemed implausible. There was not the slightest question about the fit when the call from Louisville came. Later, Mark Ethridge, who was one of the outstanding newspaper executives of his time, revealed quietly that they had checked enough to know more about me than I then knew about myself, and well knew all the strengths and weaknesses. Another case of careful gatekeeping.

There seems little left of the management philosophy that built the highly successful independent newspapers and television stations. Two stories out of Louisville illustrate the kinds of freedoms given editors in those years. The afternoon *Times* was a typographical hodgepodge. Seeking to bring some order to it, I experimented with all the headline typefaces in the composing room, finally decided nothing there would do, and went to talk it over with Mark Ethridge. He nodded. "Figured that's where you'd come out," he said. "What kind of head face would you and Barry like?" I asked him. Surprised look. "You're the managing editor, aren't you?" he said crisply. Incredulity must have been showing in the short response: "Hells bells, Mark, what I'm thinking of is having a new face cut for us." "Well," he said in his Southern drawl, "what's stopping you?" The instant retort was, "I'm talking a lot of money." "Anybody say anything to you about money?" he asked. A long minute's silence while we looked at each other. One last effort: "Don't you want *anything* to say about what I might pick?" He twinkled, saying again, "I'm not the managing editor, am I?" With strong support from the papers' talented art director, Louis Dey, and the design staff of the Merganthaler company, came "Spartan," the type face still in use on many afternoon papers. It is hard to imagine sweeping freedom of that kind being granted so readily to any editor now working.

The other story has to do with the Louisville papers' decision in 1965 to abandon the old narrow-width eight columns on a page and adopt the six-column format. It was taken to improve readability, not to save money. The idea was broached by me, but it could never have been implemented without the talent of another of the unusual executives in those newspapers' history, Lisle Baker, Jr., one-time banker who also had been studied with care before being invited into the fold to become general manager. Lisle Baker was a Kentuckian of intellectual depth and an innovative turn of mind, and he had a sense of ethics few on the news side could match. He had been a pioneer in exploring automation when others in the industry were trying to pretend it was light-years away. During lunch one day he asked in high good humor whether any great new ideas were being nursed about improving the papers. The equally good-humored reply was that in younger days, a fanciful dream had been for only one edition of each paper: an afternoon paper printed at 5 p.m. and delivered to every front door at 5:30 p.m., and the same cycle for a morning paper. "The new one is for a six-column paper," he was told. "The shrinkage in newsprint rolls has made eight columns a headache. Crummy headlines. Cramped pictures. Nuts maybe, but it's a dream." Lisle said nothing and we went on to other matters. But it became obvious his quick mind had been going through the possibilities when he suddenly said, "I'm not so sure that six-column idea is far-out. I'm going to look into it." He did—from every angle.

Finally, we decided on a full trial run, resetting all the ads to fit, and set a date for both papers to test reaction. Two days before the trial, I stopped by Lisle's office to say we seemed to be in good order and he asked, "What was Barry's reaction to it?" It was instantly apparent neither of us had mentioned it to the owner-publisher-editor. We sprinted down the hall to burst in on that estimable gentleman to tell him what we were doing. He leaned back in his chair and laughed. "Good thing you told me," he said. "I certainly would have been confounded. I love the idea. Let's see how it works." Readers applauded. So did local store owners. Chain stores balked. Their advertising copy came from regional offices in standard-sized matrices. Some said they would cancel contracts and print and distribute their own ads.

We conferred with Barry Bingham. There were two plus factors, easier reading and the probability of substantial cost-savings in composition. The minus factor was chain advertiser resistance with a potentially substantial loss in the first six months. Barry thought it over for a minute, then said, "It's the right thing to do. This happens to be a time when we can afford the risk. Let's go." It was to enhance the papers' reputation for innovation, it delighted readers, and drew industrywide attention. The chain stores gave in.

Yet it was to take ten years to take hold nationally, and then only because publishers saw big savings in new, narrower newsprint rolls, and this could be achieved only by going to six columns. The story is appropriate here because it demonstrates that innovation in the interest of improved service to readers comes only when the stance of the chief gatekeepers—the owners—is not constrained by a preoccupation with the amount on the profit line. It ties in with the caustic comment of the *New York Times'* A. M. Rosenthal that "the prime violators" in lessened newspaper quality are the many publishers who make money, but "won't do the spending."

On balance, however, it must be conceded that willingness to spend does not necessarily make an editor. Every news executive who has had long experience has failures to point to in this endeavor. Failures can come from the constitutional inability of many highly intelligent, dedicated, and talented people to manage others. They fail the John Fischer test, which was not intended to put cruelty per se on a high level, but rather to emphasize the necessity of being capable of *demanding* high-quality performance through the exercise of personal authority when it becomes necessary. Robert Townsend, the Avis executive who wrote *Up the Organization,*[14] held that "a good way to tell a line from a staff man is to find out how many people he has personally fired." He has a point, but it sounds too glib. The issue is not "how many." It is the *capacity* to fire when necessary. In a sense, every firing represents some kind of supervisory failure. It can come inevitably from failures in following through adequately at the time of employment. It can come from casual or too-rapid indoctrination. It can come from bending over backwards to be kind when a new reporter shows signs of carelessness. There can be no end to the educational procedure of instilling habits of discipline. The most unsettling element in newsrooms is what is known as latrine gossip. A staff writer who is bearing a grudge against a subeditor who has been sharply critical of reporting flaws can be likened to a poisoned well. The sensitive individual who can be wounded easily by latrine gossip is one who can be classified as a staff rather than line person. Writers, like all artists, tend to be wrathful about criticism. An editor has to understand this, or must be moved out in his or her own behalf. I have contributed a fair share of managing editors to the ranks and smile over the often-used phrase that amounts to "Let me show you my scars." Immodestly, I take it as a tribute due a good teacher.

No wonder, then, to experience semishock in reading *Editors and Stress* and learning that some 200 managing editors reported they had received no training to prepare them for their jobs and little thereafter. This is gross managerial negligence. It may be worse at the majority of locally operated TV stations. A survey done in 1982 by the Radio and Television News Directors Association (RTNDA) disclosed that the average tenure of news directors at such stations was from one-and-a-half to two years. A follow-up study in 1983 showed marginal improvement, up to two-and-a-half years. What continuity of knowledge about local and regional affairs can there be with this kind of constant turnover? It is dysfunctional not only in the economic costs to news organizations, but even more so in that each change inevitably brings a period of fumbling news judgments applied to local and regional affairs, or at least highly tentative judgments, until there is time to gain some familiarity with the new territory.

Television executives who properly can claim to have

gatekeepers of long experience on their staffs do not question the accuracy of the RTNDA findings,[15] but they do not hide their disgust over the irresponsible, bottom-line preoccupation of so many station owners. The disparity between network investment in news and that of local station owners is immediately apparent in the RTNDA report's finding that many commercial TV stations are operated without news staffs and, more shocking, that most of these "are independents located in the top 50 markets." The figures on staffing make it clear why some critics of the Federal Communications Commission's deregulation decision have sound reasons to raise challenges on the grounds that deregulation in broadcasting contravenes the original concept of channel assignments based on adequate public service. The networks, with their big, expensive news staffs, are as many light years ahead of the vast majority of the approximately 1,580 television stations as are the handful of four-star newspapers when compared to the 1,500 or so uninspired and pedestrian dailies operating across the country. There are at least two dozen high-quality TV stations in the nation, but besides them the spectrum appears to hold an agglomeration of incompetent signal-senders, run along the lines described so viscerally by Charles Kuralt in his Nevada speech.

If anything has come clear in journalism over the experience of the last 100 years, and more particularly the last 25, it is that journalism in all its forms has become too powerful an instrument to have its content controls be turned over to the undereducated and untrained, to those untutored in or uncaring about ethical nuances, or to those whose driving instincts are for excitement rather than seeking substance in the best interests of an informed citizenry.

Speaking of nuances, I confess to being despondent over the blindness of so many editors in not recognizing how they have helped debase the level of civility by abandoning nominal courtesy titles, and in the process, I am convinced, have contributed materially to the steady fall in journalism's credibility. They continue to fret openly about their credibility, as the Society of Newspaper Editors did in its May 1985 *Bulletin*, devoting the entire issue to the subject. Yet no mention was made of the widespread public dissatisfaction with their current practices. Mrs. George Bush, wife of the Vice-President, may have put it best in a *Washington Post* story. "It always gives her a shock," it said, "to be reading along and come across, 'Bush says . . .' only to realize that the reference is to her."[16]

It is not simply coincidental, I hold, that the two newspapers in the United States held in highest respect—the *New York Times* and the *Wall Street Journal*—have held resolutely to the policy of using courtesy titles. A Roper poll in 1981 was fascinating. Women asked about titles in newspapers opted strongly for Mrs. or Miss. By far the largest number (65 percent) for using titles were non-high school graduates, with high school graduates not far behind. College graduates divided equally.[17] Personal experience with women expressing antagonism for current practice has convinced me that editors who have acquiesced in eliminating courtesy titles have stripped millions of citizens of a sense of dignity. I lack evidence to support the assertion, but am driven to the conclusion that the greatest psychic damage probably has come to those citizens classed as being among the minorities.

What print and broadcast people offer to the young in society is a picture of a culture in which there is no trace of the civility that existed in their own youthful days. No reporter will face a banker or other business executive and deal on a basis of other than "Mr." Yet in print or on the air, the courtesy is wiped out without thought. A number of editors who do think in broader terms have been reflecting about this issue and one can keep hoping that many more will come to see the matter in the larger terms of building self-respect among the citizens whose names merit use in print or broadcast. They may well discover that credibility begins with respect for those they presume to serve.[18]

Closing his year as president of the American Society of Newspaper Editors in 1982, Michael J. O'Neill, who later stepped out as editor of New York's *Daily News,* made one of the most powerful appeals in many years to the nation's directing editors. He called the power of the press a problem for the republic. "Our assignment," he said, "is to report and explain issues, not decide them. . . . We should cure ourselves of our adversarial mindset. The adversarial culture is a disease attacking the nation's vital organs. . . . Editors need to be ruthless in ferreting out the subtle biases—cultural, visceral and ideological—that still slip into copy, into political stories mostly, but also into the coverage of emotional issues like nuclear power and abortion. Lingering traces of advocacy are less obvious than Janet Cooke's fiction, but, for that reason, are more worrisome. Editors—myself included—have simply not exercised enough control over subeditors and reporters reared in the age of the new journalism." That comes close to answering Ben Bradlee's questions about the making of editors. It means careful and taxing training, maturity, a constant interplay of thought and intent, and the "eternal vigilance" John Philpot Curran raised in his 1790 speech as being the price of liberty. In the journalism of the 1980s, "eternal vigilance" is the prime duty for those holding the highest gatekeeping roles in American journalism. Translated into a direct obligation, it means editors in both newspapering and in broadcasting accepting the ethical duty to *insist* that all staff members reach constantly for professional excellence, even if this should mean having to emulate Carr Van Anda's "death ray" when a situation demands it. It means they must understand and accept the fact that their roles and intentions are precisely the same as *Mister* Bovard recognized them to be the day he "crossed the line."

## CHAPTER 6

# The Seed Bed of Heresy

THE NATIONAL NEWS COUNCIL lived for ten years, seven months, and twenty-one days, visible proof of actual sin to the great majority of those in communications. Those who served as midwives at the Council's birth, and those from journalism who worked with it, were constantly aware that they had fallen from grace for having had the temerity to embrace a cause that challenged the most sacred cow in journalism's holy credo—its self-proclaimed right to reject any type of examination of its performance. With a few exceptions, those in the press shuddered over the heresy. The remarkable aspect is that the Council was able to survive as long as it did and to do enough sound work to convince more than a few in the craft that it deserved a place in the communications firmament before it finally surrendered (a record examined in chapter 7). A number of thoughtful journalists who took part in the endeavor are convinced it eventually will be revived in remodeled form. These individuals became well aware of the weaknesses built into the News Council as it existed and are in general agreement as to how an improved oversight agency could be constructed. Whatever develops, the move will not rely solely on the decade of experience, but on what had preceded the effort.

In a speech at Washington and Lee University in 1981,[1] as part of its program in applied ethics, I said that if journalists under 40 or 45 were asked for their thoughts about "the Hutchins report," the chances were about 50 to 1 that the answers probably would be something like, "the *what* report?" There was double intent to the oratorical ploy: (a) the too-frequent experience of having to fend with an astonishing lack of knowledge of history, even journalistic history, on the part of so many in the field, and (b) a need to impel some attention to the intellectual seedbed out of which grew over the ensuing four decades the several continuing campaigns for higher ethical standards in journalism. Although the Hutchins report was issued at the time when television was still part novelty, its vast potential was recognized and the report remains the most important assessment yet made of modern communications and its obligations.

It apparently began in December 1942 with a dinner table conversation between Henry Luce of *Time* and Dr. Robert Maynard Hutchins, colorful chancellor of the University of Chicago. Mr. Luce suggested a study about press freedom and offered $200,000 to fund it. The *Encyclopedia Britannica* added $25,000, making a total perhaps equivalent to $2 million in current terms. No shrinking violet, Dr. Hutchins chose twelve great intellects to serve with him and grandly titled the venture, "The Commission on Freedom of the Press." By press was meant communications in its totality.

Work began late in 1943 with final drafts coming late in 1946. Many of us later wished we could have sat as observers in those years and listened to the discussions between people like Reinhold Niebuhr of the Union Theological Seminary and the three giants from Harvard—historian Arthur Schlesinger, Sr., philosopher William Hocking, and lawyer Zechariah Chafee, Jr.; Chicago's pair, anthropologist Robert Redfield and political scientist Charles Merriam; Columbia's economist John Clark; Yale Law's Harold Lasswell; John Dickinson of Pennsylvania Law; Hunter's President George Shuster; Beardsley Ruml, chairman of the New York Federal Reserve Bank; and Archibald MacLeish, the poet who also served in the government. Why there were no journalists is not known. It has seemed curious that Dr. Hutchins did not invite Walter Lippmann since in 1938 he had sought to entice Lippmann to accept an endowed chair at the University of Chicago and teach only a few months a year.[2] This aside, the venture was far from a series of pedantic "ivory tower" exchanges. Six important books came out of the study,[3] as well as the final *A Free and Responsible Press*.

The distinguished group was unanimous that without a free press there could be no free nation. There also was unanimity that free press was in danger because it was not providing "a service adequate to the society's needs," and because it was "engaged in practices, which, if continued, society will inevitably undertake to regulate or control." The report not only was strong but also remarkably eloquent, and it is no surprise that some of us in the trenches were stirred. We were, however, an all-but-silenced minority. The movers and shakers in communications were contemptuous of the report and brought forth their heaviest artillery to bombard the commission on every possible front.

What did this so-controversial report say? It conceded that the goals it was advancing probably could never be met completely. It rejected government action as a greater evil than the failings of the press. It wanted high standards of truth, fairness, and accuracy in news. It wanted the widest latitude for opinion, even to calling for repeal of laws prohibiting expressions for revolutionary change when there was no clear and present danger. It urged full First Amendment rights for broadcasting and for films. It can be called the first freedom of information committee report, since it called on the government to provide full information to the media.

It wanted the widest possible open discussion of public issues. "We need," said the report, "to reproduce on a gigantic scale the open argument which characterized the village gathering two centuries ago." The bill of particulars brought outraged denunciations from the overwhelming majority of publishers. They saw it properly—a frontal attack on all their proclaimed rights. But, oh, how close to the mark were these arrows:

● The commission said the nation's general law applied to the press. "The First Amendment," it said, "was intended to guarantee free expression, not to create a privileged industry."

● It said concentration of ownership could become so powerful it could constitute a threat to democracy; that the big chains had to control themselves or be controlled; and that the government should not hesitate to use the antitrust laws to maintain competition.

- It said there wasn't evidence to justify complaints that advertisers influenced newspapers, but it was critical about radio. It said big advertising agencies placed contracts, wrote, directed, and produced programs. "The great consumer industries," it wrote, "determine what the American people shall hear on the air."

- It challenged the news judgment criteria of recency or firstness, proximity, combat, human interest, and novelty as limiting accuracy and significance. It called for comprehensive coverage of events in a context that gave meaning.

- It termed identification of sources in news necessary in a free society. "The names and characters of the participants must not be hidden from view," it said.

- It expressed scorn about keyhole gossip, rumor, lies, and character assassination.

- It sharply criticized stereotyped portrayals of social groups, saying carelessness perverted judgment.

- As an alternative to libel suits, it urged opportunity for reply, or for legislation to compel retraction or restatement.

- It said trying to turn journalism into a profession was not possible, but held that professional ideals and attitudes should be demanded. In this connection, it said the schools of journalism had focused on vocational training and had failed to accept the obligation of providing professional attitudes and in pushing for the broadest liberal education.

- It called for self-regulation by the press, including a new independent agency to appraise and report on performance.

As almost all compaction does, this recitation strips the report of its flavor. I submit this passage as one indicator:

> The great agencies of the modern press can facilitate thought and discussion. They can stifle it. They can advance the progress of civilization or they can thwart it. They can debase and vulgarize mankind. They can endanger the peace of the world. They can do so accidentally,

in a fit of absence of mind. They can play up or down the
news and its significance, foster and feed emotions, create
complacent fictions and blind spots, misuse the great
words, and uphold empty slogans. Their scope and power
are increasing every day as new instruments become available to them. These instruments can spread lies faster and
farther than our forefathers dreamed when they enshrined
freedom of the press in the First Amendment.

Almost forty years ago, when that was written, it was too
much for the already frightened newspaper publishers to appraise with thoughtful detachment. Radio and newsmagazines
had challenged their fiefdom. Television had come on line, excitement about it building rapidly. The many newspapers without broadcast properties were in a state of near panic. Thus, the
visceral reaction of so many owners in 1947 and of many of their
veteran editors, even though the small book that contained the
report lifted the spirits of some younger editors. As example, I
wrote an applauding column in the *St. Louis Star-Times* and had
to endure an explosive argument with my ascerbic publisher,
Elzey Roberts, who had not read the report and refused to look
at it. He insisted on relying on the wisdom of publishers with
whom he had discussed the report by telephone. The best account of the temper of the period came from the late Herbert
Brucker, an admired educator who had become editor of the
*Hartford Courant:*

> I shall never forget the reaction that followed at that
> year's American Society of Newspaper Editors convention.
> As a new member I sat on the back benches as my betters
> howled and growled at the commission and all its works. In
> those days the society spent the Saturday afternoons of its
> three-day sessions debating resolutions. The 1947 tran-
> script reveals twenty-four pages of disputation over how to
> phrase the anathema to be pronounced upon the Hutchins
> report.[4]

By the vagary of coincidence, that choleric session came at
almost the same time the British government was appointing the

Royal Commission to study the press that the House of Commons had voted for six months earlier.[4] Two members of the House, both journalists, had introduced the motion calling for examination of the financing, control, management and ownership of the press. The stated object was to further "the free expression of opinion through the press and the greatest practicable accuracy in the presentation of news." The supporting argument was "increasing public concern at the growth of monopolistic tendencies in the control of the press." It was to take two years for the Royal Commission to complete its study, recommending that the press itself create a central organization to be called the General Council of the Press. There were to be long discussions within the press, but no sign of action. That, however, came swiftly when a motion was introduced in Commons in November 1952 to establish a press council by legislation. By February 1953 the press had reached an agreement on a draft constitution, and it was to be formally created on July 1, 1953.[5]

Neither the records of the Hutchins commission's work nor those dealing with the British movement disclose any mention of even so much as polite inquiry crossing the Atlantic, although the two journalist members of Commons, Haydn Davis and Michael Foot, might well have heard some report of an American study being under way. It seems more likely that the only relationship was independent concern over the number of newspapers either failing or passing into combination ownership, along with a sense of frustration over gatekeeper responsibility. In the House of Commons debate, Mr. Foot had asserted there had been a serious decline in the quality of British journalism, and he attributed it to the decline in editor's authority, due to the encroachments of owners. Many editors had become, he charged, little more than "stooges, ciphers and sycophants."

I have heard *A Free and Responsible Press* likened to a roman candle that sent up brilliant flares and then sputtered out in a figurative moment of history, and have steadfastly disagreed. Any study of the many drives for upgraded standards and ethics will reveal direct relationships to that 1947 report. By 1949 and '50, some editors began raising strong protests about the spread of off-the-record statements from government into business life.

One offshoot came immediately after the 1952 presidential election in which Dwight Eisenhower was swept to victory over Adlai Stevenson. There were enough episodes of clear slanting to impel Sigma Delta Chi, the journalistic fraternity, to take up the "one-party press" charge and vote for an examination of press performance during the 1956 campaign. It was not to come about because the formal, carefully drafted proposal by a team of the best-known academic and professional research experts was rejected overwhelmingly by the nation's editors and owners.[6] One interesting aspect was that the publishers and editors this time were fighting off an approach by the largest professional and academic society in journalism. One small, but significant, breakthrough came in 1959 when the New England Society of Newspaper Editors voted for an experimental study of objectivity in the news columns of all of the region's daily newspapers during the 1960 presidential campaign, in which John F. Kennedy defeated Richard Nixon.[7] Two stories were chosen by the three-man panel delegated to do the study. Each posed potential embarrassments to the two candidates. One was the move by the Roman Catholic bishops in Puerto Rico to influence the election there in Mr. Kennedy's behalf. The other concerned a $250,000 loan made to Mr. Nixon's brother, Donald, by Howard Hughes and his Hughes Tool Company. What the panel concluded was that while it could not find proof of bias on the part of the New England newspapers studied, it had been dismayed and confounded by the evidences of such erratic, mindless gatekeeping performance as to have been incomprehensible. "It is compelled to report, and sadly," it said, "that the New England Society's next objective might well be directed toward a raising of professional standards." The best of the newspapers in the area had covered the news with efficiency and fairness. But the rest looked as if they had been thrown together without any of the editors seeming to have understood even the basic elements of news interest. It took fourteen years for another New England competency study. Led by Loren Ghiglione, editor-publisher of the *Southbridge* (Mass.) *Daily News,* and helped by a Markle Foundation grant, the study found many newspapers in the area still operating on "don't-rock-the-boat" policies.

On the broad national scene there were varied efforts to improve ethical practice and text accountability, all of them drawn from the philosophy contained in the Hutchins studies. What began in the 1950s picked up momentum in the 1960s and brought major press council activity in the 1970s. One of the innovations was journalism reviews, the most effective being the *Columbia Journalism Review,* founded by Edward W. Barrett, then the dean of Columbia's Graduate School of Journalism. Its first editorial (Autumn 1961) spoke to the Hutchins origins:

> To assess the performance of journalism in all its forms, to call attention to its shortcomings and strengths, and to help define—or redefine—standards of honest, responsible service . . . to help stimulate continuing improvement in the profession and to speak out for what is right, fair and decent.

On balance, the reviews have provided an effective role in challenging the profession's conventional wisdoms, even though they have not always evidenced the care and balance promised, sometimes because they have relied on freelance work, or because their own staff work contained its own biases. Nevertheless, the reviews have focused frequently on shoddy practices that would not have come to attention otherwise. The Columbia review, in particular, built an admirable record under its first two editors, James Boylan and Alfred Balk, but in recent years has appeared less certain of its goals. One of its rivals has been the *Washington Journalism Review,* which often has tended to cuteness, but has seemed quicker to grasp and respond to some of the issues bedeviling journalists. Some of the best continuing series of reports and assessments on journalism have come from the *Wall Street Journal* and David-Shaw's well-focused articles in the *Los Angeles Times.*

But of all the Hutchins' fires none got more devoted stoking than the one which sent up the signal for "the establishment of a new and independent agency to appraise and report annually upon the performance of the press." Some exploratory efforts were undertaken by two smaller-city California papers in the late 1940s and into the early '50s to set up advisory councils with citizens, but they were later abandoned. Connecticut's late Senator William Benton in 1951 proposed an oversight agency for radio and television, but it failed to win support and died. In 1961, John Lofton of Stanford University advanced the idea of an institute to monitor and report on press performance. Again, no action. In 1963, Professor J. Edward Gerald of the University of Minnesota urged a national council to be supported by journalism's professional and educational associations. Result: More foot-dragging. That year, Barry Bingham, Sr., owner of the Louisville papers and their radio and TV stations, spoke out for local press councils. A strong effort was made to find citizens of probity and ability in Louisville to help take up the challenge, but with that news organization's long record of openness it was perhaps inevitable that there would be no takers. Further, there was no way to finance such a move other than the suspect one of having the newspaper and its broadcast affiliates underwrite it.

However, some experiments with local press councils did come in 1967, as the result of a $40,000 bequest from the Mellett Fund for a Free and Responsible Press. Administered by the Newspaper Guild, four small-city councils were established in Bend (Ore.), Redwood City (Calif.), and Sparta and Cairo (Ill.), with two advisory councils set up in St. Louis and Seattle.[8] The results were mixed, but there were enough constructive aspects to sharpen the appetites of the idea's supporters, and two much larger efforts were to surface and succeed. The most important was in Minnesota, where Robert Shaw, the manager of the state newspaper association, was the chief architect and was influental in persuading the organization to adopt a procedure for the hearing of complaints by its Goals and Ethics Committee.

What was to help galvanize this into a press council was a speech given in Minnesota in October 1970 by Dean Elie Abel of Columbia's Graduate School of Journalism:

It is my sober—and sobering opinion that if we do not make the effort to police our own ranks, to label and expose malpractice where we know it exists, to raise and then maintain ethical standards, to deal honestly with the most vulnerable elements in the community, then others, less qualified and less kindly disposed, will move in and do this for us.

It had double effect because Dean Abel not only headed the most prestigious of journalism schools, but had a long, brilliant record as *New York Times* and later NBC correspondent.

First, the job must be done by journalists sitting in judgment on their peers, not by outsiders. Second, when fault is to be found it must be specific, naming names, so the public at large may know what is happening. . . . And I have a modest proposal to put before you. It is that these Twin Cities might show the way for the rest of us by setting up a Twin Cities Press Council. . . . The press council idea has not, till now, had a trial run in any metropolitan area of the United States. The Twin Cities strike me as perhaps the best place to determine whether it is an idea of value for the rest of the country.

Two months later the news association board approved the idea not simply for the metropolitan zone, but for the state as a whole. So it came into being, and is still going. One of the secrets of its success was strong, collaborative support by the state's largest newspapers.

The other large effort was in Hawaii, where an impelling reason was a continuing bitter disagreement between Mayor Frank F. Fasi and the two Honolulu newspapers, so tendentious that Mayor Fasi had imposed blackouts on news information. National organizations tried to serve as intermediaries, but Mayor Fasi was adamant and concerned civic leaders then sought other ways to deal with the problem. What they quickly discovered was that George Chaplin, the editor-in-chief of the *Advertiser,* and A. A. Smyser, editor of the *Star-Bulletin,* favored discussions of the possibility of a press council. Explorations among leading citizens resulted in Harlan Cleveland, president of the University of Hawaii, becoming the chairman of a steering committee. In November 1970 the state's Community-Media Council held its first meeting. It has not had as many issues to examine as has been the case in Minnesota, but it continues, and its periodic public meetings draw large crowds of interested citizens.

There had been another important development in this same area of public accountability three years earlier, when the Louisville newspapers had seized upon a proposal made by A. H. Raskin in the *New York Times Sunday Magazine*. This was for internal ombudsmen (a subject covered in detail in chapter 8). A flashback to the *Washington Post*'s experience in the Janet Cooke incident is one illustration of ombudsmen effectiveness.

The two state press councils' timing happened to coincide with the evidences of a worrisome growth of the credibility gap between the public and the press. The Associated Press Managing Editors had confirmed it in 1969, and more proof came with the torrent of abuse from the so-called "silent majority" supporting Vice-President Spiro Agnew's attacks on major Eastern newspapers and the three TV networks. The tenor of the times was such that I mistakenly believed that, as president of the American Society of Newspaper Editors (ASNE), I might be successful in inducing the membership to add a grievance committee to the society's functions. It would have been empowered to consider complaints of substance against member newspapers when readers could demonstrate they had been unable to gain adequate responses from editors to protests about inaccuracy or unfairness. The 1969 fall meeting of the board of directors was held in London so that all could assess the work of the British Press Council and meet with the top figures in journalism there to ascertain their views. The British press extended itself with hospitable warmth. Every publisher and editor interviewed left no doubt they believed that the Press Council had proved its value, and particularly so in the reduction of the previously burdensome and expensive round of legal suits the leading newspapers had been experiencing. This had come about as the result of a waiver clause introduced by Lord Patrick Devlin, chairman of the Press Council, and a former chief justice of Britain's high court. The waiver was two-sided. Those who complained to the Council agreed not to pursue their grievances in court procedures, and the editors agreed to publish the findings entered by the Council.

When we left, the strong impression was that most members of the ASNE board had been impressed and that some of the doubters had changed their minds. It was to prove an illusion. What resulted was something like a playback of the Hutchins experience. There was no expectation that anyone could sway some of the publishers who had proclaimed bitter opposition over the years, but the hope was that enough of the editors could be persuaded to give the proposal a working trial. What we encountered was a two-pronged attack. One came from some of the same publishers who had pilloried the Hutchins group so vociferously twenty years earlier, along with some younger inheritors of the tradition of resistance. Those of us trying to keep the movement on track learned that a few of the old publishers were practically spending their days on the telephone, exhorting others around the country to hold their organization's position and urging them to do what they could to keep their editors "in line." That alone became a major problem. Several editor friends confided candidly that they were in favor of the grievance committee plan, but that their owners had expressed themselves so forcefully that they would not be able to openly support it. Several such editors felt that the board of directors ought to adopt the proposal on a one- or two-year trial basis to avoid a bad-tempered floor fight, and most specifically to sidestep any open vote. This, however, was the central thrust of the other prong of the attack. It came from within the group known in similar professions as "elder statesmen," principally a number of former presidents of the society.

The most vigorous antagonist was an old friend, the late Turner Catledge, the former executive editor of the *New York Times*. A man of immense Southern charm, one of the great raconteurs of his time, he was widely popular among fellow editors. Hence, in both the personal sense and his newspaper connection, he wielded extensive influence. One of his arguments was greatly persuasive with many members. Journalism, he maintained, was not a profession like law and medicine and no editor had the right to pass judgment on what other papers did; editors had to be responsible to themselves for what was published and how, and the editors' society was threatening to impugn the integrity of editors by imposing a committee to pass judgment on whatever decisions they made in good faith. He let all know that he intended to rise on the floor and to move for a hand-counted open vote.

The strongest supporter of a trial run was Vincent S. Jones, the Gannett newspapers' vice-president for news, and the immediate past president of the society. Supporting the Catledge position was Newbold Noyes, editor of the *Washington Star,* and who was in line to succeed to the presidency. The proposal had burgeoned into the most divisive issue to torment the society in its modern years, and a check made it clear the board of directors would vote against recommending it to the membership. The only alternative was to agree to the appointment of a special committee made up of a number of the society's most prominent former leaders to weigh all the nuances and issue its report. It included several of those who had been most vocal over the years in criticizing inferior press performance, but the outcome was foreordained. No matter how important editors may be in their roles, the ultimate decisions are made by the publishers, and this was an issue a majority of the publishers of the country had decided against.

The special committee's study was to come to naught and the proposal was to be summarily shelved by the board of directors in the administration that followed without further discussion. To his credit, it needs reporting that at a later convention Newbold Noyes said candidly and publicly that he had been wrong in taking the position of opposing the proposal. The one editor in the group for whom I hold the most admiration is Vincent Jones, who to the very end tried to convince his colleagues that it was unworthy of a calling claiming to be at the cutting edge of a steadily changing society to refuse even to try experimentally a new and challenging idea. In sum, it was another lance broken in the long duel, but the issue was to be taken up by the Twentieth Century Fund. It appointed a task force of fourteen, nine drawn from the field of communications and five from the public at large. Significantly, the small book published in 1973 containing the task force report bore a title taken directly from the Hutchins study. It was called *A Free and Responsive Press*.[9] From that study and report was to arise from the ashes, at least for the decade to follow, another phoenix with new and very different feathers.

## CHAPTER 7

# The Eagle-Hearted Kiwi

THERE WAS a curious hop-skip-and-jump byplay in 1970 on the way to the National News Council. It was well intended but it backfired, and in hindsight it takes on major importance in that it blocked a chance of the Council's getting a decent start and going on to succeed. People wrapped up in causes lose perspective, and I was no exception. It is easier in retrospect to recognize that everything in organizational life is affected by the interplay of personalities, professional rivalries, and the institutions that the organizations serve. All three elements operate in how ideas are judged. Many well-motivated undertakings have become losing labors of love when they have either cut across the grain of conventional patterns or have directly involved individuals caught in strong disagreements over both ideas and the exercise of power. By happenstance the News Council ran into both entanglements.

Two institutions were directly involved in the 1970 byplay, the Twentieth Century Fund and the *New York Times,* and two strong individuals, A. M. Rosenthal, then managing editor of the *Times,* and Lester Markel, the newspaper's former Sunday editor. The real power rested with the *Times* because of its preeminent position in American journalism. What happened in 1970 was to hang over everything that was to unfold in the next fourteen years. Unworthy of discussion is the idea that any news organization is monolithic in thought. Like all others, the *Times* shelters dozens of points of view under its roof on all conceivable subjects. As far as the News Council idea was concerned, the range ran from ardent support to unbending opposition. The essential factor in the equation was that what Adolph Ochs created had become the nation's most important daily, and the majority of publishers and editors gave it deferential respect. In most matters, how the *Times* reacted to journalistic matters carried great weight in a quasi profession which, despite much posturing, was not generally noted for independent thought.

Internally, the *Times* was like all other news organizations, churning with personal rivalries and disagreements over policies.[1] Of all rivalries, few ran deeper than the one between Turner Catledge, first as managing, then as executive editor, and Lester Markel, as Sunday editor. Even though his political skills were remarkably good, and he was close to Arthur Hays Sulzberger, who was publisher from 1935 to 1961, Mr. Catledge was unable to exert any influence over Mr. Markel's Sunday empire. It continued to be treated as much a powerful separate domain as the editorial page operation.

That was to change after Arthur Ochs Sulzberger became publisher in 1963. It can fairly be said that "Punch" Sulzberger was a graduate of the Catledge School of Journalism, and I do not fault this. The two became even closer friends than Mr. Catledge had been with the father. And there was no questioning Turner Catledge's knowledge of journalistic practice. I do not know why he came to hold the press council concept in disdain. Curiously, in 1953, when the nation's publishers overwhelmingly rejected the Sigma Delta Chi's proposal to study press coverage during the 1956 election campaign, the *Times* chose to be one of the corporal's guard of seventeen newspapers voting approval—and Mr. Catledge agreed with the decision.[2] If there is a seeming contradiction here to my point about the *Times'* positions, let it be noted that on having its political coverage examined, the paper had nothing to fear. Many others certainly did. It may be that the long national feud with bar associations over press/bar relations changed Mr. Catledge's views about access, but certainly by 1969 he was strongly antipress council. Sufficient on that for the moment.

Early in 1970, when it was becoming known that the grievance committee plan within the editors' society was in trouble, Murray Rossant, director of the Twentieth Century Fund, suggested we meet. Like many others, he was intensely interested in what was going on and out of this grew a series of meetings. At one, Barbara Ward, the British journalist, gave an assessment of public reaction there to the press council. At another, Mr. Markel was present. In September 1964, he had been abruptly shifted out of his Sunday editor's role as Mr. Catledge was named executive editor to control all the news operations. Six years had passed but Mr. Markel still bore resentments. He had begun work on a book under the Twentieth Century Fund's auspices. At our luncheon he was the crusty Olympian of old, scornful of the ASNE roster of "elder statesmen" and most specifically of Mr. Catledge. It was Mr. Markel who called to ask me to participate in a New York meeting with other editors to talk about press councils, share views and offer counsel.

On the day chosen, Mr. Rosenthal and I were the first arrivals. We had been friends ever since meeting in India in 1958. He knew no more than I did about the meeting to take place, but he was in a good mood. He had been a great reporter and there were reasons to believe he would be an outstanding editor. He was perceptive, bold, innovative in spirit. Later I claimed to understand him because we shared some of each other's worst faults, one being a lack of subtlety, another our being equipped with terribly short fuses. We were joined by five others: Stanford Smith, the American Newspaper Publishers Association's general manager, and representatives of the AP, UPI, *Daily News,* and the Dorothy Schiff-owned *Post.*

The start of the meeting was delayed because Mr. Markel had not arrived. After a time, Mr. Rossant decided to begin without him. He began by putting emphasis on the Fund's interest in protecting the press's rights and then moved to what was tantamount to an announcement. It was that the Fund's trustees had decided a press council could be helpful as a buffer against the many attacks being made on the press, and that they had voted for a council to operate in the coastal zone from Boston to Washington. He was talking without notes and there was an unfortunate slip in construction when, to stress that they were not going through a charade, he said that even though there might be great opposition, the decision was an "irrevocable" one. All of it came as total surprise. It had never been mentioned in any prior discussion. It had one obvious plus. Such a council would cover the major bloc of Eastern newspapers, the headquarters of the big press associations, as well as of the giant television networks and the weekly newsmagazines. Nothing was said of the thrust of any such operation, and there were a number of questions begging to be asked.

A glance across the table showed the storm clouds gathering. Mr. Rosenthal's face had flushed and the look he had fixed on Mr. Rossant was almost baleful. Mr. Rossant finished by saying he and the trustees hoped for our candid reactions and suggestions. Words began to tumble out of Mr. Rosenthal and almost at that moment, Mr. Markel rushed in, apologizing for being late. He took the empty chair only one removed from where Mr. Rosenthal sat. Mr. Rosenthal turned to look directly at him. In acid tones, he began all over again, and in almost these words, said: "I have been brought here under false pretenses. I was told my counsel was to be sought. Instead, I am presented with an announcement." Never moving his eyes from Mr. Markel's, he continued; "You know as well as I do that this is directed at the *Times*. There is no other target. Why did you dare to invite me under the pretense that my counsel was to be sought?" He ended by repeating, "How dare you?"

In the moment of silence that followed, Mr. Rossant looked stunned. It was far from the normally combative Lester Markel who offered soothing comment about what he said must have been a misunderstanding. Moved to speak, I reported also understanding the meeting to have been a sharing discussion, with our counsel being sought. Stanford Smith promptly followed with the same reaction. Mr. Rossant took over again, saying he deplored any misunderstandings, adding that while the decision was a firm one, nothing was graven in stone, and that he and the trustees wanted as much professional input as possible. Mr. Rosenthal's outburst had ended any chance of that, and after another couple of attempts to get some discussion going, Mr. Rossant felt obliged to end the meeting. Mr. Rosenthal got up, still angry, and walked out of the building without another word. It was pure disaster.

Part of Mr. Rosenthal's indignation, certainly, involved pride. Top-rank newspapers exercise a strange mastery over those who move up into positions of responsibility, and those who rise become intensely protective of their newspapers. Of all the people I have known, no one has ever matched Abe Rosenthal's commitment to his paper. He has made more than a few enemies by placing loyalty to the *Times* above everything else. Later, I decided the suspicion that Mr. Markel might have had a hand in the planning might have been enough to blow the fuse. Whatever it was, I should have recognized—and did not at the time—that any idea of a press council without the *Times*, in at least a neutral position, was hallucination. It was the last mention of a seaboard press council—or what Mr. Rossant thought of in terms of a "metropolitan area" council. The idea was quietly abandoned.

During the year that followed, Mr. Markel's association with the Fund ended. The report was that there had been disagreement about his book, but a year before his death Mr. Markel indicated it went deeper than that. He was a brilliant and imperious man and totally open in saying he should have been chosen the News Council chairman. I suspect his book began to take second place to his interest in planning a council. About the time of our last conversation I saw a letter Mr. Rosenthal had written opposing press councils. It included the comment that "the sponsors of the idea blithely disregard the opinion of editors and publishers as if they were of no account. They have made it clear from the beginning they intend to go ahead with this whether the press likes it or not." Since the plan was abandoned, it seems clear the "irrevocable" usage was unintended hyperbole. Yet in essence, Mr. Rosenthal was correct. The Fund was going ahead.

The new thrust surfaced a year later with the appointment by the Fund of a special task force "to examine the feasibility of establishing a press council—or councils—in the United States." The task force had fifteen members, nine of them well-known journalists, and five nonjournalists.[3] Among the journalists were Barry Bingham, chairman of the Louisville newspapers, my publisher over two decades; John Oakes, editor of the *Times*' editorial page; and Richard Salant, the president of CBS News. Two judges were among the public members: C. Donald Peterson, justice of the Minnesota Supreme Court, who also chaired that state's press council, and Justice Paul Reardon of the Supreme Judicial Court in Boston. Judge Reardon had been chairman of an American Bar Association special committee and had endured a firestorm of bitter Hutchins-type press criticism after his panel's report was issued in 1966. As was true of Robert Hutchins, Paul Reardon was a victim of the vast majority of the press being unwilling to give careful study to a thoughtfully crafted body of work designed to curb police, prosecutorial, and courtroom abuse of basic rights of defendants.[4]

The task force studied the problem for just over a year. What finally emerged as outline for the National News Council turned out to be too limiting in practice, but it was to be remembered that the models that existed (principally Britain's) all had smaller spheres to deal with. It was one thing for the United Kingdom with its 110 newspapers, including all the nationals and weeklies, and entirely another for the press in the United States, which encompassed 1,750 daily newspapers, some 8,000 magazines, and the huge broadcasting enterprise. The task force finally came to agreement when a proposal was made for a press council that would review "news reporting by the principal national suppliers of news," defined as the wire services, news magazines, syndicates, the big broadcasting networks, and any national newspapers. It eliminated the worry about a deluge of complaints from all parts of the country descending on a small staff unlikely to have the resources to properly assess all of them. Further, it had the illusory appeal of creating an agency to meet an issue that worried many thoughtful people—the cacophony that had arisen from Vice-President Spiro Agnew's *un*-"silent majority" supporting his attacks on what he had called the "liberal eastern establishment."

This limitation was to hamper the new council in its early work and draw criticisms that it had been established to monitor the best in American journalism and ignore the worst. It was a burden the council was prompted to shed three years after its beginning. It changed the bylaw to include "news reporting in all media, whether national or local in initial circulation, if the matter in question is of national significance as news or for journalism and the Council has available to it the necessary resources." That last clause was direct reflection of the underfunding that greeted the council's inception. In announcing on November 30, 1972, the Fund's plan to create the news council, based on the task force report, Mr. Rossant referred to an agency with an annual budget of $400,000. He said the Fund was seeking financing from a consortium of foundations, including Ford. The hope of getting Ford proved fruitless. McGeorge Bundy, president of the giant foundation, and his communications adviser, Fred W. Friendly, felt that encouraging state councils, like Minnesota's, made more sense. Privately, they took soundings of a few state press groups, offering start-up funding if any were interested.[5] None were. More, the Ford executives, like others, were aware that six months earlier Mr. Sulzberger, in a commencement speech at Montclair (N.J.) State College, had stressed the dangers of government regulation of the press and had said press councils "would simply be regulation in another form."

Reading this, I had two automatic flashbacks—one to that 1970 meeting, the other to Gay Talese's description in *The Kingdom and the Power* of the close ties Turner Catledge had built with the young man who was to become publisher in 1963, and who would soon after give Mr. Catledge "unquestioned authority over Lester Markel's Sunday department."[6] Since Mr. Catledge had so vigorously opposed my ASNE proposal, it is understandable why Mr. Sulzberger's remarks could be construed as a reprise. Ford had poured millions into public TV and into a training program for minority journalists, and I recognize why Mr. Bundy could see no reason to court disfavor with the country's leading newspaper over a venture about which he held honest doubts. So it was that when the council began work in August 1973, there was no $400,000 budget. Twentieth Century put up $100,000 and the John and Mary R. Markle Foundation matched it.

William B. Arthur, the council's first and only executive director, found himself with $250,000. This was to be the budget line for three years and would then begin to grow mainly through the council's own efforts. Mr. Arthur, a former president of Sigma Delta Chi, had been the last editor of *Look* magazine. More than anyone else, he kept the News Council afloat during its first trying years. Conscientious, dedicated, and tenacious, this quiet and modest man went foraging for furniture and equipment and kept "the faith," no matter how many discouragements. The task force chose California's highly respected former chief justice, Roger Traynor, as chairman. This was a direct copy of British practice. Interested as he was, Judge Traynor lived 3,000 miles away. Vice-Chairman Robert B. McKay, former dean of law at New York University, had joined Aspen Institute, so Mr. Arthur operated, in effect, as unofficial chief executive. A year later, Judge Traynor accepted a chair in legal science at Cambridge in England. Stanley H. Fuld, former chief judge of New York State, was named chairman, and served until late 1976, when I was elected and held the post until 1982 (the two three-year terms of eligibility).

The first two years of the Council's life were fascinating in how boldly it sought to make its way against bitter resistance. In his formal comments in July 1975, Judge Fuld noted discouragement about the *Times*'s unyielding opposition, saying that it was a newspaper's prerogative, but that the paper's "refusal to sit down and discuss the Council's operations hardly befits a newspaper of such stature."[7] All was not bleak, however. An ASNE monitoring team lauded the Council's approach as "deliberate, thorough and judicious" and several publications, noting the general lack of cooperation, praised its starting efforts. While the fledgling Council had come forth as something akin to a flightless New Zealand kiwi, it was to be a bold little bird that, to put it in fanciful terms, frequently evidenced the heart of an eagle.

In October 1973, during a White House press conference dealing with Watergate break-in events, President Richard Nixon, referring to network newscasts, said, "I have never heard or seen such outrageous, vicious, distorted reporting in 27 years of public life."[8] The kiwi took up the issue, issuing a statement saying the charges warranted investigation and a public airing. Over three months, Mr. Arthur tried everything (trips to Washington, telegrams, repeated telephone calls) to get the White House's specifics as to what episodes of distortion could be cited. In December, the White House said that it would be "unable to join in any cooperative research . . . because we simply don't have the staff or time."[9] The Council persisted. It got abstracts of network newscasts and commentaries from the Vanderbilt Television News Archives in Nashville and submitted them to Press Secretary Ronald Ziegler. The Council kept at it without success, surrendering only when Mr. Nixon resigned.

On other fronts the young Council raised questions with CBS News about paying former White House aide H. R. Haldeman $50,000 for his appearing on two hour-long programs, and offered a guideline calling for disclosure of payment beyond actual expense so that the public could draw its own conclusions.[10] It upheld an Accuracy in Media complaint against columnist Jack Anderson. It also upheld ABC News' right to "robust opinion journalism" but criticized the network for telling viewers its documentary was "a primer on oil and oil policy . . . designed to help understand the current crisis." Interestingly, while the *Times* declined to provide any information on a request filed by an Ohio congressman for investigation of protests made by the U.S. Ambassador to South Vietnam about "inaccuracies and half-truths" in an article, *Times* reporter David Shipler wanted to cooperate. He submitted not only background information supporting his article, but also a detailed response to the ambassador's cable. The information convinced the Council majority the article was not inaccurate. In that two-year period, of the 59 complaints filed, 33 were held unwarranted, 5 were upheld, and 21 were dismissed on a variety of grounds.

Despite a rather general "blacking out" of Council actions on the part of wire desks around the country—even though coverage was being provided by both the Associated Press and the United Press International—there was a substantial increase in complaints during 1976 and 1977, along with added activity taken by the Council on its own initiative. One of the most encouraging developments came from a report early in 1976 made by a special evaluation committee set up by the Twentieth Century Fund and the Markle Foundation.[11] It was the committee's unanimous view that "there does exist a positive need for a national news council." It went on to say that the Council "has made a sound if not spectacular beginning. It has handled the complaints submitted to it in workmanlike fashion. It has assumed jurisdiction over several difficult problems. It has conducted its own inquiries with skill and insight. In all of its work it has been guided by high professional standards and care." It added that "it is more than clear [its] work will continue to be handicapped by the opposition of media elements and personalities" and went on to say there was "little likelihood of news media financing." The committee was the first to urge the expanding of jurisdiction "to cover the entire nation and all media whether national or local in initial circulation." It saw no reason to disqualify as Council members individuals "because they are active employees of national media." The committee called the Council's financial resources "inadequate" and yet concluded it deserved a minimum period of ten years "before a sound evaluation of its permanent usefulness can be made." What it added was strong, indeed: "The task of the Council is a complex and difficult one. But its importance to the body politic is such that the Committee feels every effort should be made not only to continue the Council but actively to seek to deepen and broaden the opening pathway which it has hewed out." In the light of that, it is not difficult to understand why I accepted the urgings later in that year to become its new chairman and its first working chief executive.

The evaluation committee was mistaken about one aspect—that there was little likelihood of news media financing. Media support picked up in 1977 and continued to grow, along with many favorable comments. Every one who served on the Council naturally has certain "key" issues uppermost in memory. There

are a dozen important ones that come to mind quickly, but Bill
Arthur and I remain convinced that the high mark of what the
News Council was all about came in what was not a complaint,
but a Council statement prompted by wire stories in early July
1976 reporting an explosive conflict within the Panax chain,
which published eight daily and some forty weekly newspapers.
The chain employed as New York correspondent a former
*National Enquirer* reporter. He wrote two questionable stories
about President Carter. These were sent to the Panax newspapers with a memo from the chain's headquarters to "run the
attached stories as soon as possible" and asked for page-one
placement if possible. Two Michigan editors objected. David A.
Rood of the *Escanaba Daily Press* refused to run the two stories.
Robert Skuggen of the *Marquette Mining Journal* refused to run
one of them, rewrote the other.

After meeting with executives of the chain, Mr. Skuggen's
verbal resignation was accepted. Mr. Rood refused to resign and
was discharged for insubordination. Panax's headquarters then
sent all editors a new code description of copy coming from
corporate headquarters. The principal code was listed: "No. 1.
MG—means McGoff, or Must Go!" A Panax public statement
said, "John P. McGoff not only has the privilege but the right as
principal stockholder, president and chief executive officer of
Panax, to distribute whatever news copy he deems appropriate
and to demand, if necessary, that such copy be printed." Thirteen Council members were reached by phone. The vote was 12
to 1 for issuing a statement saying, "the central issue is the relationship of chain ownership to news control. Mr. McGoff has
highlighted one of the great underlying public fears about newspaper chains—that what the public reads is directed from afar by
autocratic ownership. Either Mr. McGoff and his executive associates are unaware of the difference between *editorial opinion*
policy and *news content,* or they are determined to ignore the
principle espoused by most chain groups that news judgments
are delegated to the resident editors. . . . The News Council
finds Mr. McGoff's policy regressive—a throwback to the crass

episodes that marked the journalism of a by-gone era—and brands it a gross disservice to accepted American journalistic standards."[12]

What followed was a bizarre melange, and we were to learn over the ensuing months that Mr. McGoff was an international entrepreneur as difficult to keep pace with as a legendary whirling dervish. He demanded a public hearing by the Council. It was set. At almost the last minute he refused to attend if the two editors and community representatives also were allowed to participate. A fresh hearing date was set. He boycotted it, but the meeting went on and the Council reaffirmed its position. The incident stirred new interest in his many activities. In 1975 he had failed in an attempt to buy the *Washington Star;* had then bought a half-interest in UPITN, a newsfilm business, then owned by UPI; and had bought an interest in the West Coast *Sacramento Union.* In December 1977 *MORE* magazine, then a New York-based journalism review, devoted a page to Mr. McGoff's many ties with South African officials. He had told a progovernment South African newsweekly that "South Africa needs to tell its story and through something like UPITN we can do it." He delivered in part by having his newspapers publish pro-South African material. Early in 1978, Panax vice-president Ralph Kaziateck admitted in a public hearing that Panax newspaper reports on Mr. Rood's firing had been inaccurate.[13] The hearing was on Mr. Rood's claim for unemployment compensation; Panax opposed it, asserting he had been discharged for misconduct. During his testimony, Mr. Kaziateck said an entire paragraph in which Mr. McGoff was quoted did not match the facts.

By a strong majority, the Council held its ground all the way. And several rewards followed. One was a series of advertisements by the big chains, stressing their commitment to editorial autonomy. Another was visibly heightened approval of the Council's bold stand. Most important was an increase in media corporate giving. By 1980, 26 percent of the funding was coming from news organizations, and if all the units involved in the chain ownerships were counted the total approximated 10 percent of the nation's newspapers. The kiwi was still trying. But it couldn't flap much when the clipping services continued to have a hard time finding many traces of the stories the wire services had sent out, and it was hard to keep up with New York's ever-escalating rents and other costs. If it hadn't been for the tender loving care given by the big lessee at the Children's Television Workshop (president, Joan Cooney, a founding member of the Council), it would have been even harder to meet the monthly bills.

Back to the McGoff case. Three Council members joined in arguing that the stories ought to be examined and not the policy. Henry Geller, just-retiring as adviser because he was about to become an assistant secretary of commerce for communications, wrote to say he disagreed. The policy *was* the central factor, he held. "The concept of local autonomy is not the answer to the difficult problem of increased chain ownership, but at least it alleviates the problem . . . and on that basis I urge affirmance of the ruling."[14]

On November 19, 1984, the *Washington Post* reported that Federal prosecutors had recommended that Mr. McGoff be indicted for failing to register as a foreign agent. The story said, "The recommendation, in a 700-page prosecution memorandum . . . brings to a head a five-year investigation of McGoff's alleged acceptance of $13.5 million from the South African government."[15]

Earlier, in September 1980, Panax stockholders liquidated the assets of the company, at the same time selling three of the daily papers in Michigan and two weeklies to Thomson Newspapers of Toronto for a reported $21.5 million. Both the Escanaba and Marquette papers were among the dailies sold.[16]

Bill Arthur is not likely to forget *United Press International* v. *Synanon*. Synanon was in the headlines often beginning in 1971, largely as a movement that had taken on cultist trappings. It became all the more prominent after a 1978 incident when Paul Morantz, a Los Angeles attorney who had been involved in a successful $300,000 default legal action against Synanon, was bitten on the hand by a 4½-foot rattlesnake when he reached into the mailbox at his home. Two Synanon members were arrested, and Charles Dederich, the founder of Synanon, also was arrested on charges of conspiracy and solicitation to commit murder. That was the time Synanon embarked on what it called its "Retraction Project." UPI's complaint was that Synanon had undertaken systematic efforts "to threaten UPI's reputation and relationships with subscribers and, generally, object to any news coverage which reflects unfavorably on Synanon." UPI said that even reports on the Pulitzer Prize award to the *Point Reyes Light* for its expose of Synanon drew retraction demands on pain of suit.

Investigations like that took money and nerve. Money, because the Council lived up to the ethic of paying its own way. On this particular aspect, it needs to be recorded that from the day it began, the Council process was a costless one for anyone who filed a complaint. Some of the investigations ran into the thousands of dollars in working hours, travel, and related costs, as well as all the other functions that keep an organization going. Several of us always felt that some moves to enter complaints with the Council were withdrawn on the advice of lawyers; this may seem an uncharitable view, since it presumes that so many lawyers see no virtue in costless undertakings. The news organizations that contributed to the Council's funding knew full well that their subscriptions provided no protection.

As for the nerve, in the Synanon instance, it was provided by Bill Arthur. It meant his going into Synanon to see and ask all manner of questions. He got instructions on where to drive his rented car, park it, and wait to be picked up by another car. As Bill cheerfully admitted later, at moments like this, you get to wondering if you chose the right business. Anyway, he got there to find a legal department of 65 at work on the letters that poured out regularly to newspapers, magazines, and broadcasters all across the country. Bill learned that this was the direct result of a clause—inserted into the California Civil Code at the urgings of publishers and broadcasters seeking added protection against libel actions—that had come back to bite, and bite hard. The paragraph read:

1. In any action for the publication of libel in a newspaper, or of a slander by radio broadcast, plaintiff shall recover no more than special damages unless a correction be demanded and not be published or broadcast, as hereinafter provided. Plaintiff shall serve upon the publisher, at the place of publication or broadcaster at the place of broadcast a written notice specifying the statements claimed to be libelous and demanding that the same be corrected. Said notice and demand must be served within 20 days after the knowledge of the publication or broadcast of statements claimed to be libelous.

Synanon reported candidly it had sent 960 letters during 1978 and 1979. There had been 144 lawsuits over the decade, some of them claiming astonishingly high damage claims (such as a $76.75 million suit against *Time* magazine, later withdrawn). Mr. Arthur's report, crowded with detail, ran the length of a small book.[17] In its finding The Council decided the free flow of information had been cut off by Synanon's campaign, adding: "The history of press freedom makes it plain that there is no substitute for courage in such cases" and praised the position taken by the *Berkeley Independent and Gazette*. To ten Synanon letters it had routinely replied by inviting the organization to join with the paper's staff for a full exploration of Synanon's views and attitudes. Not once had Synanon taken up the invitation. Courage. Perhaps the clipping service was incompetent, but even though UPI had naturally filed a full story on the Council's decision, we could find coverage in only the largest of the California papers.

It was a life of pluses and minuses. Elie Abel, chairman of Stanford University's communications department, was vice-chairman of the Council its last few years. In a speech to the California Newspaper Editors in July 1984, he said that CBS cooperated with the Council and contributed to its financial support. "But CBS did something even more important," he said.

"When one of its programs drew fire from the council for lapses in fairness or accuracy, CBS made no secret of the adverse finding. It reported the finding as news on the same program. That is how the news council idea is supposed to work. When it does, it's a beautiful thing to behold.

Here's an example: CBS News put on an hour-long documentary called *Gay Power, Gay Politics*. It started with the thesis that San Francisco politics has been profoundly changed by the emergence of a new political force: a gay rights voting bloc. Had the program stuck with that legitimate theme and expanded it, *Gay Power, Gay Politics* would in all probability never have come to the Council's attention. Unfortunately, the program degenerated into a peep-show treatment of glory holes and sadomasochistic sex facilities, which had little to do with the announced theme of the program. The Council had harsh things to say about that treatment, but CBS made no dirty little secret of the finding. Every bit as heartening was the fact that both the *San Francisco Chronicle* and the *San Francisco Examiner* put the Council story on the front page. The front page was where it belonged, at least in San Francisco.

Would that this kind of action-reaction cycle became routine [Dean Abel went on.] It did not. CBS's conduct regarding the finding against it remained a shining exception. Far more typical was a recent case, one of the last to be dealt with by the Council, that directly involved the *New York Times*. On December 1, 1983, the Council upheld a complaint against the *Times*. In the Council's judgment, the *Times* had 'committed factual errors and presented information selectively, inappropriately, producing a distorted perspective' in a story about the use of dioxin by Arkansas rice growers. Not a word of that finding did the editors of the *Times* see fit to share with their readers. Not many days later, the *Times* printed a report that the British Press Council had reprimanded a London newspaper for its exuberant treatment of the Prince Andrew/Koo Stark affair. The story of royal high jinks obviously must have passed the *Times'* time-honored test: All the news that's fit to print. A 'complaint warranted' verdict against the *Times* itself, just as obviously, flunked. That's accountability for you.[18]

He brought to mind the dismaying love/hate memory about our *Columbia Journalism Review* experience. Just as important in the early days as anything was the move by Edward W. Barrett, the *CJR*'s publisher, to work out an arrangement with the Greve Foundation to underwrite regular publication of the Council's findings. It was intended to give legitimacy to the effort and it became doubly rewarding because the reports became widely used in journalism schools. Many of the invitations for the Council to meet in university settings grew out of those reports in the *CJR*. The reverse side of the coin came a few years later. Enrique Durand, who had been editor in charge of UPI's Latin-American department in New York for seven years, complained in 1980 that an article in the *CJR* criticizing his department's work was a biased report. It had been written by one of the *CJR*'s editors and the Council upheld the complaint, citing "several serious departures from sound journalistic standards." These were adjudged to include factual errors, unacceptable reliance on unnamed sources, and sensational descriptives, along with what the Council called a distressing "defensiveness, lack of care and lack of analysis" in *CJR*'s response.[19] It was painful to have the magazine's top policy board vote 3 to 2 a year later to cease publishing the Council's reports, and to know that one of the votes was cast by the author of the article. More shocking was to learn from David Shaw of the *Los Angeles Times* that *CJR* editor Spencer Klaw had told him that one of the principal factors in the decision was a considerable degree of lingering unhappiness over the finding for Mr. Durand. I could wince over that kind of act by a third- or fourth-rate newspaper, but to have it come from a magazine established to "stimulate . . . improvement in the profession" was a brutal reminder of how deep defensiveness can run even in the reviews founded to promote accountability.

Was all the travail worth it? Was anything meaningful learned? Can a press council work in a journalism so often disagreeing about so many matters? The answer to the first question is a firm yes. Like several others, I have no regrets over the countless hours of trying to make the impossible work. And yes, it was a tremendous learning experience. After all, it was built out of the dreams of conscientious, earnest people. Put to the tests, the concept was flawed in several ways. With each adjustment it worked better. A working blueprint now exists. As to whether journalism is going to be adult enough to recognize a council's virtues, there is no way of knowing. Fundamentally, I subscribe to Dean Abel's view that, "Sooner, rather than later, in one form or another, the News Council will be reinvented. It may be a long wait, though."[20]

Simple lists of "how-to-do-it" are totally subjective. Each participant has his or her own formula. For what it is worth, I present the following: Any new undertaking ought not to be sponsored by a single organization. It should come out of journalism itself—assessed, debated, and charted by the top representatives of all the major organizations in all branches of communications, along with the top educators. If it sounds like a convention, so be it. My hope would be for a smaller council— say, twelve in total, with nine drawn from the press side, and the other three being public figures of recognized accomplishment. None of the twelve should have any strong political inclinations; that is, all ought to be people of breadth of mind, independent in spirit, objective in approach. The ten-year experience brought many brilliant individuals into the process, but there were too many awkward left-right standoffs, and too many episodes of having to explain journalistic processes to the public members. Every member ought to have unquestionable credentials. The original thought put too much emphasis on what can be called a populist base.

Too much has been said about journalism being too important to be left to the journalists. It is a catchy phrase (I have been guilty of sometimes using it, and hereby eat the words), but it is as much nonsense as saying the same thing about medicine. Journalism needs to open its mind to all the inputs it can get from everyone in the general public. But the work to be done is journalistic, and only thoroughly trained journalists can properly analyze the problems and decide good judgment from bad. When the leaders of American journalism get enough confidence in themselves to stop relying on the "full-speed-ahead" counsel of so many First Amendment lawyers, they will find themselves willing to sit together and talk about the utility of an American news council that can provide a costless service to both press and public with skill and dignity, and draw respect from all sides. When and if they sit down to talk, before every one of them there should be a copy of the short poem Arthur Hays Sulzberger wrote in 1950 for his son, Punch:

> The careless doctor may poison and kill a patient.
> The careless newspaperman has the power
> To poison the minds of vast multitudes.[21]

The whole News Council record is now in the hands of the School of Journalism at the University of Minnesota. It is a rich lode for all the researchers and believers in the dream.

Finally, the unpleasant truth is that while the News Council, for all the reasons recounted, undoubtedly had almost no chance of surviving for any extended period in the form it had, it had a good deal more life than it allowed itself. For the record is that quite suddenly late in 1983, its leaders decided that in an age of bigness it had to be big, too. They seemed to take little cognizance of the fact that the big foundation support had run its course (led all through the ten years with the Markle Foundation's $100,000 a year). They called for a $750,000 budget, hired fund raisers, and charged off on an "emergency campaign." The Council simply spent itself out of business in the effort. An odd ending. If I can be forgiven temptation, an odd literary maxim too: Brave little kiwi, pretending so often to being a great soaring eagle, and then charging off into the sea just like a lemming.

## CHAPTER 8
# Fighting Intellectual Herpes

ABRAHAM HENRY RASKIN may be as erudite as an Oxford don, and certainly anyone's equal in the command of both the spoken and written language. What one notices first about him are his eyes, sparkling, alert, intense. Second, his hair, a flowing shock instantly reminiscent of pictures of the great Albert Einstein. More, Abe Raskin's courtliness is unusual for one with more than half a century in journalism, and particularly so for a man who built a brilliant record as a specialist in labor relations. His eloquence is accompanied by hands in motion just as constantly as are Zubin Mehta's or Leonard Bernstein's when they are leading an orchestra. Matching the Raskin eloquence is a thought pattern that is precise and forceful. When I was in Louisville, my attention was riveted by an article in the *New York Times Magazine* of June 11, 1967. Then assistant editor of the *Times'* editorial page, Abe Raskin had written an article bound to excite any editor involved in fighting for "public accountability" by the press. The article described the press as "addicted to self-righteousness, self-satisfaction and self-congratulation" and went on to say that what threat there might be to the press was in "the unshattering smugness of their editors, including myself." None of that was new. What was different and exciting was a proposal by which the problem could be attacked:

> I feel there is a need in every paper for a Department of Internal Criticism to put all its standards under re-examination and to serve as a public protector in its day-to-day operations. . . . The department head ought to be given enough independence to serve as an *ombudsman* for the readers, armed with authority to get something done about

complaints and to propose methods for more effective performance of all the paper's services to the community, particularly the patrol it keeps on the frontiers of thought and
action.

We moved to take the challenge. Eight days later, the
*Courier-Journal* and the *Louisville Times* announced the appointment of the first newspaper ombudsman in the United
States. In 1977, while at the University of Texas, Fred V. Bales
studied the sequence and perceptively noted that, while it might
seem romantic to envisage rapid-fire action on the heels of sud-
den conversion, "a reservoir of frustrated good intentions lay
behind the move implemented in such short order."[1] He was
right. Louisville was very close to being a journalists' paradise in
the '50s and '60s. On many occasions, I have said that if the
ideal publisher had to be invented, someone like Barry Bingham,
Sr., probably would come forth. His forte was in making editorial policy and writing editorials. I have long felt that he and
Vermont Royster of *Wall Street Journal* fame were the two best
essayists among newspapermen of my generation. During most
of my years in Louisville, the title of publisher was held by Mark
F. Ethridge, a topflight editor in his own right, but just as capable in business affairs. Barry Bingham, a strikingly handsome
and militarily erect six-footer, is my senior by two years. He has
all of the famed Southern charm and has always been a liberal in
the truest sense of the word. Long before the movement took
firm shape, his newspapers had been in the forefront in editorial
support for civil rights.

It was a delight to be teamed with an owner whose views
about journalism matched the Hutchins Commission theme and
who aspired to have newspapers that reached for greatness. He
has been the first owner to advocate local press councils, and at
one time he had sought to sell his television and radio stations,
feeling that it was not in the highest public interest for the newspaper to also be involved in broadcasting. The Federal Communications Commission rejected his move, holding his stations'
public service record was too good for him to be permitted to
cast them off. Reflecting on journalism's present pattern, it may

be remarkable for an editor to say that over the two decades of working with him, there was never a mention of any budget, and never a discussion of money—except in the instances of our gaining his approval for a major capital investment, or in appraising the area's financial trends. He was greatly supportive of a series of provocative speeches I made in various places around the country. Mark Ethridge liked to tell of his experience at a meeting of the publishers association, an annual gathering Barry would not attend. One publisher approached Mark and raised questions about the tenor of my comments. Mark said he had replied, "Didn't it ever occur to you that he might be saying a lot of things Barry and I happen to agree with?" We had tried to induce leading Louisvillians to form a press council, but the effort failed, perhaps because we felt our direct sponsorship might taint a council's independence.[2] So the background was clear about our interest in raising standards.

More, we felt we had the ideal candidate for the ombudsman role in John Herchenroeder, who had been the *Courier-Journal*'s city editor for twenty-five years, and was one of the two best "telephone editors" I every worked with—the other was Aaron Benesch of the *St. Louis Star-Times*. Both could adjust instantly to the countless situational nuances that arise constantly; both were native to their cities, with encyclopedic knowledge of the areas. I gave John a copy of the Raskin article and he told Mr. Bales in 1977, "When I got to the part about an ombudsman for the readers, I knew without asking what Norm had in mind." As to the title, Mr. Bales recorded a conversation in which I had said, "We gassed about the name for maybe an hour. Anything else came up flat. Ombudsman carries with it a sort of shock value. In other words, it had a kind of instant promotional value so we didn't worry about other names." The word is Swedish. *Ombud* is the word for an agency setup to protect the rights of citizens who become victims of the endless spinning of red tape by bureaucrats. The ombudsman practice traces to 1809. In Swedish use, the chief of each office has become an "ombudsman." Now there are several of them (parliamentary, which also includes the military; antitrust; consumer; and press, which was added only in 1969).

Mr. Herchenroeder's work was publicized nationally over the ensuing few years. When he retired in 1979 after twelve years on the job, Robert Schulman, the *Louisville Times* media critic, called him "close to ideal. . . . A gentleman of the old school of manners and of the old school of accuracy, community knowledge and compassion in journalism."[3] The flow of calls from the public grew so much that two other ombudsmen were appointed later, one for advertising and another for circulation. Before the start of the ombudsman function in 1967 both papers carried corrections columns, one named "We Were Wrong" and the other "Beg Your Pardon." After the ombudsman began work, and acting upon the suggestion of a reader, the columns were given fixed positions appearing in exactly the same positions each day.

In 1967 and '68 about a dozen news executives came to see for themselves. Most of them were strongly approving, with some saying glumly that their publishers were unlikely to approve any such expenditure. The *Washington Post* adopted the idea in adjusted form and later added an improvement—a regular column, which we had not felt necessary. Over the years, it was to prove an effective educational tool for both staff and readers. Richard Harwood was the *Post's* first ombudsman; then came Ben Bagdikian, Robert Maynard, Charles Seib, Bill Green, Robert McCloskey, and Sam Zagoria.

It takes time for every news organization to learn how to live with its ombudsman, and the *Post* has been no exception. It went through one unfortunate fall-out in 1972 when Mr. Bagdikian (who now has become dean of journalism at the University of California-Berkeley) held the post. The first strains surfaced in March when a number of black staffers joined in contending that the *Post* was discriminating in not selecting any of their number for desk training and promotion. Mr. Bagdikian wrote a column, supporting their viewpoint. A month later in a symposium he defended the newspaper against charges of racist coverage. During the discussion he expressed the opinion that economic boycotts had been the most effective way of influencing news organizations. Terming it disloyal, Executive Editor Ben Bradlee called on Mr. Bagdikian to resign. He did, but a more composed Mr. Bradlee tore it up. But the episode also tore the relationship. Some of Mr. Bagdikian's critical articles did not appear and in August he abruptly resigned. *Time* (August 28, 1972) called "the divorce both sad and ironic. The *Post* is more willing than most to confess its sins and Bradlee is seeking another ombudsman. Bagdikian concedes the *Post's* relative virtue, but told *Time*: 'There's a feeling here that I should be loyal to the management. When they first put me in this job, they assured me my first loyalty would be to the readers.'" Apparently his point was accepted since all his successors appear to have had full freedom. It was with Mr. Seib that the *Post* started employing able outsiders under specific-term contracts.

Mr. Seib had been managing editor of the rival *Washington Star*. He wrote a syndicated column. His last one in November 1979 is worth quoting: "Newspaper readers," he wrote, "are more perceptive than most editors realize. [They] are quick to notice the flaws that crop up in every newspaper—the headline that goes beyond what follows, the distortions caused by what we in the business call the 'hype' and the 'needle' or the biases of the reporter. While quick to detect these flaws, readers tend to ascribe them to wrong reasons. Too often they see errors of judgment and mistakes caused by deadline pressure and outright stupidities as evidence of a deliberate slanting of the news. We of the press are the blame for this conspiracy theory of journalism. We have a tradition of aloofness from our customers and a totally unjustified posture of infallibility that encourages such suspicions." He went on to say "elitism is an occupational disease in newsrooms and editorial offices, and humility is in very short supply. . . . Compassion is synonymous with softness."[4]

From my point of view, there were a series of key words and phrases in Mr. Seib's column that point directly to my own thrust. He was talking *to* gatekeepers, not reporters, when he dealt with overdisplay and underdisplay. As said earlier, this is an editor's responsibility. The reporter can be victim, as we will see a bit later. An ombudsman's greatest influence is that coming to bear on the tiers of gatekeepers. A good ombudsman can materially raise his newspaper's standards. A weak or timid one offers little more than cosmetic promotional touches. I now am convinced that a regular ombudsman's column is a valuable tool for challenging defensive subeditors and for alerting executive managers to weaknesses in the gatekeeping machinery that, if left untended, can erupt later into highly unfortunate situations.

At any rate, almost two decades after John Herchenroeder's pioneering steps, there now are something like forty ombudsmen at work. To put it in percentage terms of the nation's 1,688 daily newspapers would be unfair. Some 1,200 of them are too small to afford a senior staff member for only this, and it is true that some smaller-city editors serve in the role as best they can. Nevertheless, the slow growth tells a lot about the reluctance of owners to invest in accountability and also, in many cases, resistance of both subeditors and staff members to the idea of oversight regarding their work. In a 1970 report in *Time*, Mr. Herchenroeder said of newspaper people, "Sometimes they're harder to deal with than the public."[5] The two of us ran into that strain of resistance during the first few months of his serving as ombudsman. It seemed to us to be centered among a few of the older, more habit-prone, deskmen and reporters. If the ombudsman function was going to work, they had to know that the news department management had no intention of accepting anarchy. Leaning on the Bovard—Van Anda tradition, I often had expressed an overdrawn doctrine: "Democracy in the newsroom is the refuge of the weak." It was put to use without any trace of subtlety. While there were many instances of misplaced anguish, no one ever again tried to challenge John Herchenroeder's authority.

Although David Shaw is not an ombudsman but a media reporter, he has had a similar reaction to his columns in the *Los Angeles Times*. He said that while some editors and reporters were "supportive . . . some have taken loud (or silent) exception to much of what I've written. One editor complained to the publisher about one of my stories and then didn't talk to me for a year, even when we passed in the hallway. . . . Two reporters have refused to be interviewed by me for stories. A few have put nasty notes on the bulletin board. Others have refused to speak to me after certain of my stories. In fact, when one of these sulky reporters subsequently said hello in the hall, she retracted her greeting a few minutes later and said, "I didn't mean to say hello to you. I didn't realize it was you. I'm not talking to you."[6] All of it adds a bit more flavor to Robert McCloskey's crisp comment in one of his columns in the *Post:* "In the newspaper game, rectification still takes a back seat to righteousness."[7]

Clearly, the ombudsman role calls for both commitment and strength of character. Mr. Zagoria, the *Post*'s newest monitor, found himself obliged to disagree with Editor Ben Bradlee in June 1984, when the newspaper splashed atop page one of its Sunday edition the first article of a series excerpted from reporter Robert Woodward's book, *Wired: The Short Life and Fast Times of John Belushi.* Mr. Zagoria quoted Mr. Bradlee as referring to John Belushi as "one of the major cultural figures of the '70s and '80s" and his asserting that the "social use and abuse of drugs is one of the most significant and untold stories of today. This is a way of doing it." Mr. Zagoria contended that the series "devoted too much attention to a story of an individual who could not cope with meteoric success, and it capitalized on the sensationalism of other entertainment names hooked on drugs. It was a story that belonged in the paper, but the length and prominence accorded it reflected a search for a 'gee whiz' response rather than a desire to educate readers or affirm morality. It was a heavy dose. Were *Post* editors so impressed with the achievement of breaking into the private lives of entertainers that they suspended usual standards of news judgment? Where are the stories of the hard-working, talented Washington area individuals who obey the laws and contribute positively to society? Are they at the top of page one on Sunday?"[8]

Among the News Council's most successful achievements was its publication of *Excerpts,* a monthly newsletter on behalf of the Organization of News Ombudsmen, aptly initialized ONO. It was the brainchild of Richard Cunningham, one of the Council's associate directors, himself former ombudsman for the *Minneapolis Tribune.* From *Excerpts* came a stream of fascinating examples of challenges to gatekeepers who seem unable to break away from the habit patterns that do not take compassion into account in the handling of news. If proof was needed to convince me the ombudsman's columns were an essential, *Excerpts* provided it. Ombudsmen's columns provide early warning signals to directing editors and publishers about weaknesses at the subeditor levels, flawed judgmental capacities that can lead to dangerous mistakes in handling major stories. Mr. Cunningham learned in 1983 that *Excerpts* was being used in 240 college-level journalism programs.

In Sacramento in 1982, a mother shot another mother after their children fought over a seat on a school bus. The *Bee* ran a photograph of the accused mother on the ground being handcuffed and another picture of her three children emerging later from their house with their hands in the air. Complaints poured in. The desk editors said they used the picture because it described the tension existing. Ombudsman Art Nauman pilloried the editors. He called the incident overplayed and wrote, "I suspect that the mere existence of the dramatic hands-up photo was a subtle, but powerful influence on news judgment. Without it, or if it had been adults marching out of the house, the incident would have gotten much less attention." He went on to check *Bee* files and noted that the paper had followed a fairly consistent policy of not naming local juveniles arrested for crimes, no matter how serious "to protect them from the ravages of publicity. Yet now we have these three kids, apparently well known in their community circles, hands aloft, faces reflecting what must be their inner anguish and confusion, arrested for no crime, and dragged into a situation created by foolish adults. . . . I find it very difficult to justify or explain how the *Bee* can protect one set of youngsters, but not the other."[9] Two years later, in July 1984, my mind went back to that episode when I read in the *Washington Journalism Review* a letter from a subeditor on Mr. Nauman's paper, saying that dealing with an ombudsman "is a lot like self-flagellation. To a few it is a religious experience but to the sane and rational many it is just a pain."[10] Intriguing how deep the strain of infallibility runs among some journalists.

Another California newspaper (the *Register* in Santa Ana) found ombudsman Pat Riley confronting gatekeeper overhandling. Readers protested a story about Huntington Beach that said, "Today the buildings are shabby and the streets too narrow." The reporter said he was astounded because he hadn't written it. He also was upset because something he had written, about a $325,000 semi-mall beautification project, had been deleted from his copy. The editor in charge said he had done "considerable cutting and pasting" of the story to get what he considered the main issue up high, and had cut out the improvements portion. "I fully intended to return the information to the body of the story, but failed." He handed the copy to a colleague to check. She added the words "shabby" and the "narrow streets," saying she had seen the streets and thought the story lacked some touches such as these "to make the reader SEE the area." The managing editor sided with the ombudsman, saying, "It's the reporter's reporting, not the editor's reporting." Mr. Riley wrote: "Omitting information that would have better balanced the story was unfortunate enough, but inserting an editor's subjective view was, in my opinion, extraordinarily bad judgment. I hope we don't do it again. Such 'touches' readers can live without."[11]

The *Rocky Mountain News* went through a more embarrassing bit of subeditor misjudgment in the fall of 1983. Police with floodlights were searching woods in a park, and two officers who requested anonymity told reporter Charles Seigel—who was close to deadline—that a man had confessed to the murder of a three-year-old girl two days earlier. Mr. Seigel could not reach higher level police officials to obtain confirmation. He informed his desk of his inability to confirm, but an assistant city editor decided to run the story. The headline read, "Police get confession, seek body of girl, 3." The story was wrong. The *News* acknowledged the mistake in two editions later in the week, citing the unnamed officers as the sources of the misinformation. Ombudsman Mal Deans wrote that the misreport should never have been published. "Reporter Seigal did his job," he said. "He tried to verify. . . . He reported to the newsroom what information he had been given. . . . Without corroboration from higher authorities, the story should have been scrapped. . . . Getting a story first is fine. But getting it right is an absolute necessity."[12]

Some newspapers find the ombudsman title a bit arcane and prefer "reader's representative." Alfred JaCoby built such an outstanding record at the *San Diego Union* that he has become assistant managing editor for metro coverage. He was pungent and perceptive about such matters as unwarranted publicity for those arrested but not charged. That particular issue surfaced late in 1983 when two rape stories came from the police beat. San Diego turns out to be one of those cities where, by the assertion of the mayor, more than 40 percent of arrests never result in the filing of charges. One of the two cases had to do with a marine arrested for the alleged rape of a juvenile. Normally, the *Union* publishes names of those arrested. This time, the editor "had a gut feeling" that this case might merit an exception. All the other news organizations in the city reported the marine's name. But that evening he was released.

However, the paper was not that lucky with the second case. A girl telephoned police, claiming to have been raped and named the man. The *Union* published his name. Next day the girl confessed to having lied and the man was released. Mr. JaCoby contended that the "unwarranted publicity . . . is irreversibly damaging" and he reminded editors and reporters about "two previous cases here in San Diego involving people who were arrested and about whom stories were used in The *Union*. The suspects—innocent men, remember—lost their jobs and couldn't get them back. These were cases in which small stories were used and follow-up stories were also used explaining that no charges were filed. . . . It doesn't seem fair that a person who is unfairly arrested should be penalized by having his or her name publicized. It also seems uncomfortable that a newspaper or the electronic media should have a part in this. . . . What difference would it make not to use a suspect's name until charges are filed? . . . Weren't the stories and not the names the key?"[13]

Given the casual oversight by gatekeepers, the field for the tough-minded ombudsman with broad experience is almost unlimited. There are no better current courses in on-line journalistic ethics than what these monitors are teaching. Dip back to early 1983 in the *Washington Post* for one such example. The quote in that paper was attributed to Dan Alexander, president of the Mobile County (Ala.) School board, and read, "If some-one doesn't give them [the United States Supreme Court] the finger every now and then, nothing ever changes." Mr. Alex-ander protested that he had been "blind-sided." Then-ombuds-man Robert McCloskey checked into it. He found that near the end of a long interview the reporter said, "Dan, some of your critics might say you are giving a finger to the Supreme Court." Mr. Alexander used the words as quoted, but immediately added, "Now, don't print those words. They were yours not mine." The reporter said he had followed the "rule" that a jour-nalist need not honor a request to retract an on-the-record quote and that he thought Mr. Alexander was an astute politician who understood the "rule." Further, the reporter did not tell the *Post*'s editors of Mr. Alexander's disclaimer about the wording. In his talk with Mr. McCloskey, the Mobile official said that he could have provided a strong quote if asked, but resented being maneuvered into using "a gutter phrase." Mr. McCloskey sided with the official, saying: "This kind of journalistic fix—a re-porter graphically summing up a controversy and an official borrowing the expression in response—is not uncommon. Fair play and professional ethics clearly entitle the respondent to be disassociated from it if that is his request. Clearly, that should have been honored in this case."[14]

There are scores of other instances of ombudsmen taking on both reporters and gatekeepers and doing it publicly. For example:

● Lou Gelfand of the *Minneapolis Star & Tribune* chiding the copy desk for passing and then defending a headline that used a word not employed by a public official. "It's one thing for a candidate to be outspoken on a sensitive issue," he wrote. "It's another for a headline writer to put words in his mouth."[15]

● Charles Ware of the *Honolulu Advertiser* finding that an editorial in the newspaper had been "a distortion of fact that has no more place in an editorial than in a news story." (It is worth noting that the complainant, a city councilman, had taken his protest to the Community Media Council, which referred it to Mr. Ware).[16]

• Robert Kierstead of the *Boston Globe* weighing a budding controversy about a talented writer's sports column. An editor conceded that "it was a mistake to have approved it." Mr. Kierstead wrote that the writer was not a racist. "Yet he created a column that could have made a valid point, but which degenerated quickly through his technique of Don Rickles-type one-liners and insensitive use of black language. His mistake was in using a technique which submerged the theme and left him and The *Globe* open to charges of running an article that could be interpreted as racist."[17]

• And to the *Post* again early in 1984, where Mr. Zagoria questioned the fairness of a column attacking the Maryland bottle-return bill and got fast action. The column had devoted only one sentence to arguments favoring the measure. *Post* editors acted defensively, saying columns were by nature opinion. Mr. Zagoria held that the newspaper does not label columns as opinion and pointed out that the writer was a reporter identified as a "staff writer." Promptly there came a second column, giving much more attention to supporting statements for the legislation and, of some importance, it was labeled "Commentary." There may have been no connection, but the paper's entire letters space was given to bottle-bill letters, most of them favoring the bill.[18]

All of it makes Abraham Henry Raskin something of a prophet. What he stressed in 1967 was the need for someone "armed with authority to get something done about complaints and to propose methods for more effective performance of all the newspaper's services . . . particularly the patrol it keeps on the frontiers of thought and action." And that is what has been developing in the ombudsman role.

After a year as ombudsman for the *Kansas City Star* and the *Kansas City Times,* Donald Jones compiled a list based on the most complaints he had received. It ran: inaccuracy, arrogance, unfairness, intrusions into privacy, insensitivity, contempt for the community, sensationalism, and bad writing and editing. All save one speak for themselves. That has to do with gatekeeping. "Our editors," he said, "need to be strong enough to come back

to reporters, to challenge their biases, to force them to get however many sides the story may have to it; they have to instill in
the minds of reporters and subeditors that it is better to be late
and accurate than first and wrong. Surprisingly, many readers
seem to undertand the problems and pressures of getting news.
What they can't understand is the extreme to which many reporters and subeditors will go to keep from saying 'we were
wrong.' "[19]

The question is certain to arise in readers' minds as to why
Mr. Raskin's charm and persuasiveness failed to register at his
own newspaper, the *New York Times*. The large, powerful, and
tradition-minded newspapers of the world ("the elite press," as
educator-author John Merrill termed them) always have been
highly resistant to change. The *Times* even went through some
type of trauma in deciding to drop the period after its name in
the title line a decade ago. The *Times* has since changed in many
ways. In 1983 came what the paper calls "Editor's Note," bearing remarkable resemblance to the ombudsman idea. A number
of "Notes" have been tart, but one in August 1985 was as caustic
as anything I have seen anywhere. It censured a *Times* article
published two days earlier about Mortimer Zuckerman, the real
estate developer, who also owns *Atlantic* magazine and *U.S.
News & World Report*. "Notes" scalded all concerned for the
use of "opinionated wording . . . perjorative phrases . . . and
permitting anonymous criticism."[20]

My regard for Thomas Griffith, who writes on the press for
*Time*, runs very high, but it seemed to me his 1983 column on the
*Times*'s new development, titled "Water-Torture Journalism,"[21]
appeared in the wrong publication. He quoted A. M. Rosenthal
as saying that he wanted to get at the "more serious defects" of
stories that are loaded, overplayed, or underplayed. Mr. Rosenthal had added that the aim of "Editor's Note" was to rectify
"what the editors consider significant lapses of fairness, balance
or perspective." It was he who used the "water-torture journalism" phrase about stories that add one small, new fact and te-
diously repeat old and familiar assertions. Mr. Griffith thought

the ambition admirable, but that too often the notes left "the impression of being things the editors should have thought about earlier." Fair enough, but the impression has lingered that *Time* may have been the wrong one to carry that message. It is among the magazines that believe in media criticism—except about themselves. As editors of the magazine have made clear, the old "Time-erred" phrase disappeared long ago. Corrections no longer are carried because readers of *Time,* as the News Council was duly notified, "understand" that letters published which take issue with *Time* reporting constitute corrections. Clearly, I am an innocent among true sophisticates.

In the last analysis, it matters not what route newspapers, magazines, or broadcast organizations choose to take in order to clarify the public record. If the *Times* has decided that the best way to deliver its executive messages to its hundreds of gate-keepers is through candid criticism in the newspaper's columns, it may develop into one of the best of the "ombud" variants.

In public speeches, I have said frequently there would be no need for press councils or ombudsmen if journalists felt the ethical imperative to instantly request correction space on learning that whatever had been published or broadcast had been in error. In my view, it was put best by Mr. Nauman in a 1982 column, when he reported a challenge to journalists from California Assemblyman Louis Papan, who had written:

If I, as a legislator make a mistake on my financial disclosure report, the press doesn't report the mistake as one made by the California Legislature. I am cited by name, as it should be. But when a reporter makes a mistake, he or she is not cited by name. Instead, the paper says, "the *Sacramento Bee* inaccurately reported . . ." Perhaps if reporters were held more accountable, if they were willing to review their own profession as they do legislators, then perhaps reporters would use more care in checking facts, in writing opinions, in giving both sides of a story, and in writing their pieces in a fair and unbiased manner.

Mr. Nauman wrote:

Mr. Papan makes an important point. Reporters and editors are special and privileged people, I submit. They possess something few other people have: access at no charge to space in a powerful communication medium. They and their employers enjoy a degree of constitutional protection accorded no other sector of private enterprise. In truth, they are powerful and, potentially at least, enormously influential people in the community, a position not achieved at the polling booth.

Moreover, most journalists I've known want to be seen by their readers, their sources, their peers and their employers as professionals, people whose fidelity and truth and ethical behavior is beyond question, and not merely as wage slaves doing the bidding of a corporation.

If all that is true then papers and journalists ought to be willing to provide their readers with a high degree of voluntary accountability that Mr. Papan wants. One way to do it is to admit mistakes freely, prominently and honestly, naming names where it is possible and appropriate—and getting the entire news staff, the 'system,' to carry out this policy. . . . Far from hurting The *Bee*'s credibility or that of any of its journalists, candor will only enhance it.

Furthermore, candor will help fend off an even greater danger: that government, overreacting to concerns like Mr. Papan's, will attempt to impose accountability, thus destroying the system.[22]

## CHAPTER 9

# Conflicts, Conflicts...

"WE ARE GOING to have to kill ethics before ethics kills us," began the long lead editorial in the *Wall Street Journal* in mid-July 1983. Editor Robert Bartley, 46, uses the language with the skill of a heart surgeon with a scalpel, and he was doing his kind of carving on some of Washington's reporters. The operation would have been tidier if he had concluded with more precise stitching. Mr. Bartley was piqued by the press corps' dissecting of columnist George Will (with whom he has not always agreed, by the way). All of it had started with the disclosure that Mr. Will (a) had taken a small role in a coaching run-through for Ronald Reagan just before his debate with President Carter and (b) then had gone on a post-debate TV program and applauded Mr. Reagan's performance. Mr. Will, who had no background in journalism before becoming a columnist, not only had crossed the line that separates writer and participant but also, during the barrage of coverage, said that he had seen on the table of his friend, Budget Director David Stockman (who had taken the Jimmy Carter role in the mock debate), some briefing papers prepared for President Carter and given to Mr. Stockman by one of the Reagan campaign officials. Mr. Will said he glanced at them, and judged "their importance nil."

Mr. Bartley went on to stress that among those offended were journalists who often had flouted the principles they were applying. "The point is," he wrote, "that there's a kind of ethical absolutism that no human institution can sustain. It's not necessary to abandon ethics to recognize that the real world will always be full of cut corners and uneasy compromises." He came to his central point: "Once the ethical issue is raised, everything else stops until the last entrail of morality has been examined. . . . It is as deluding and self-destructive as any other obsession, and we risk going down in history as the first civilization to strangle itself in a frenzy of ethics."[1] In *Time* magazine, William A. Henry III took pretty much the same position. "When a story is legitimately grave," he wrote, frenetic coverage "is worth enduring. If a scandal is overblown, however, the nation is subjected to a deplorable, unnecessary burden. . . . Those who place ethical absolutism above all other interests should bear that in mind."[2]

The *New York Times*'s Sydney H. Schanberg was closer to the mark when he twitted Mr. Will about his post-event comment that "If there's a line and you see a line, you don't step over it." "Pity he didn't follow his own advice," remarked Mr. Schanberg. "Or maybe he's suffering from blurred vision and didn't see the line. . . . The debate within the press should center on two issues: lines that shouldn't be crossed and the press's reluctance to talk about itself in public (and thus its slowness to blow whistles on erring colleagues.)"[3] That Mr. Will hadn't realized there were some tricky lines seemed evident when he said later, "wild horses could not drag me" to accept another such invitation, adding that he thought some of the questions raised about his involvement had merit.[4]

One curious aspect was that no one mentioned that Mr. Will might have blunted much of the press corps' all-out chase if only he had said openly when he was on TV that he had been present during the debate practice run. Ted Koppel of ABC invited just that when he said, "George, it's my understanding that you met for some time yesterday with Governor Reagan and I'm just wondering what you know of his game plan and how you think his game plan worked out tonight?" All Mr. Will had to say was that he had been at the preparatory session and that. . . . But as cerebral as he is, George Will joined the countless others who regularly violate—deliberately or thoughtlessly—one of the most essential of all journalistic ethics: accountability. Mr. Will still would not have escaped criticism for the conflict of interest, but he would have been the one to have made it public. This was the neat "stitching" that struck me as missing in Mr. Bartley's editorial. He was quite right that life is not as tidy as we would like it to be. Author Henry James probably put it best more than a century ago: "There are conflicting obligations in every transaction in life." Journalism repeatedly has trapped itself by insisting on the right to expose every transgression it can uncover, but then holding to a totally different standard for itself.

The fact is that journalism always has been confused about its conflicts of interest, and still is, even though there is a small mountain of evidence that considerable progress has been made in facing and rooting out some of the more obvious embarrassments, corporate as well as individual. If there is any member of the press, in high position or low, who has not strayed over one or another line at some time, he or she ought to be canonized before it is too late. As the result of unhappy or awkward experiences, many of us work hard to build defenses, but most of them are imperfect. My son, Stephen Isaacs, who was metropolitan editor of the *Washington Post* and later editor of the *Minneapolis Star,* and who now is a producer with CBS News, is an ethical purist to the extent that he does not believe it possible for one in news to have any true friendships outside the craft, and that "even some inside it are suspect." At first, I had trouble with that stance, but after wrestling with it for a long time, came to accept it. I exempt only one individual in my life from that blanket—my "brother" Rowland Allen, who, while he talked about journalism, never raised anything that gave me pause. One has friends, surely, but as Steve pointed out, it is inevitable that at some point something arises that instantly reminds you that your access to printing press, microphone, or TV camera automatically brings vulnerability. Richard Leonard, the *Milwaukee Journal* editor, has said candidly that he has declined to maintain social contacts with former college classmates who have become prominent in civic and professional life.[5]

Meg Greenfield put it beautifully in discussing one facet of the equation in a 1983 *Newsweek* column, when she wrote, "We are frequently called on to say, do or support things that run counter to what a friend is trying to do—or to deny that friend some help we could provide. . . . You just do it, that's all. Friendship, if it is real and if there is anything to it, survives. The most poignant and instructive example of this for me came some years ago when a much admired high public figure turned out to have done something truly foolish and unacceptable—and his dearest old friend at the paper, having satisfied himself that the facts were so, wrote the editorial for his resignation."[6] Good news organizations and good professionals follow that principle, but as pointed out earlier, that level of performance is far from standard.

Where conflicts of interest get stickiest is in the realm of civic affairs, extending even into family connections. The Pulitzer-owned *Arizona Daily Star* felt itself obliged to take a position on such an issue late in 1983. "The *appearance* of a conflict is as harmful as an actual one," said the editorial. "The nomination last week by Governor Bruce Babbitt of Edith Sayre Auslander to an 8-year-term on the Arizona Board of Regents undoubtedly will raise questions concerning the *Star's* editorials on the University of Arizona and the regents. Mrs. Auslander is married to the *Star's* editorial page editor, Steve Auslander. . . . It is for this reason that Steve Auslander will not be concerned with any editorial, article or letter to the editor concerning the regents or universities. Instead, the positions taken and the writing and editing of editorials on the subject will be left to the other six members of the board. . . . Editorials concerning the regents and the universities will carry a reminder of the ethical conflict."[7] There are some who will see this as a form of executive intimidation. While holding reservations about the emphasis on the *"appearance* of conflict" being as harmful as many journalists hold, it is difficult to disagree with the basic position taken.

Looking back, there is the wish similar policies had been in effect during my years as an editor who also doubled as a "civic leader," a mistake frankly conceded in speeches. It was an honest miscalculation, following the historical tradition of many American newspapers being leaders in the building of their cities. It is a complex matter. Max Frankel, editor of the *New York Times* editorial page, addressed one aspect of it when he said,

"We are boosters of the economy of this city, and sure, our own welfare is tied to that. Whether that's a conflict or not, I don't know."[8] In many cases, if publishers had not invested their money and time in civic causes, their cities might have gone downhill. The Bingham family in Louisville is a good example of that tradition, investing continually in city and state. They inaugurated the bookmobile movement, heavily funded the arts, endowed university chairs, paid for new college buildings, strongly supported mental health, rebuilt Shakertown, and engaged in scores of other philanthropic undertakings. One unanticipated, enlightened self-interest payback came when General Electric began surveying a number of metropolitan zones for its new "Appliance Park," which would produce large appliances, employing from 15,000 to 20,000 people. GE chose Louisville because it had modern educational and medical facilities and a full range of artistic and intellectual outlets for the many who would come from larger cities—orchestra, opera, ballet, art.

In such an atmosphere as a corporate officer, as well as directing editor, it was a painless (but thoughtless) step into wide-ranging civic duty. Most of those on the news staffs treated those associations with the desired independence of judgment. The orchestra (of which I was president) frequently was panned without mercy. But overall, this was illusory. The motives were pure, but, like other journalists, I had confused myself with ownership. It was right and proper for the Binghams. It was improper for the executive editor. I had blurred the lines. The highest civic duty for editors and reporters is to work to put out the best news products that they can.

That said, owners and publishers have a right, if not a duty, to be deeply involved in their cities' problem and growth. The assertions of some editors and reporters—that *their* credibility and integrity have been compromised by their publishers' interest—strikes me as presumptuous arrogance when no hindrances have been placed on their ability to report and publish all the facts and extent of the corporate activity. The Louisville news staffs were able to expose their own circulation department's inefficiencies, as well as the fact that the company's magazine-printing plant was one of the city's major polluters. Certainly, the circulation and the printing plant executives protested vehemently. The owner and publisher ordered them to clean up the operations. That was public accountability at the highest gatekeeping level.

The fight against a proposal for casino gambling in Florida was a case where publishers crossed a wrong line and news staff members raised a mistaken issue. A statewide vote was pending. Governor Reuben Askew called on the state's news organizations to help fund his campaign against the proposal. A total of $180,000 came from newspapers, newspaper executives, and broadcasters. There was not the slightest attempt to influence the news staffs, but funding a drive on an issue going to a public vote plainly was crossing a dangerous line. Yet, in fairness to all concerned, it was in the open. The *Miami Herald's* executive editor criticized the step—in print. So did columnists. Many reporters contended that their credibility had been impaired. But a careful examination by the News Council found that the coverage had been full, fair, and professional, so much so it was a case of "overkill" in coverage.[9]

Eugene Patterson, the able president and editor of the *St. Petersburg Times,* made a strong case for the involvement, holding that casino gambling would materially alter the Florida ambiance. "I would hate to think newspapers are neutered as citizens by a pacifist mentality when rape is threatened," he said. "The magnitude of the gamblers' financing convinced me this was no time to be spooked by the hobgoblins of little minds. Advertisement of our own virginity scarcely responded to the threat." Not all the Florida publishers agreed. Allen Neuharth, chairman of the Gannett chain, applauded the decision of his group's papers in the state to refrain from contributing. "The whole question of credibility is such a sticky one," he said, "that those of us who own media and identify with one side of a controversial issue, no matter how objective our reporting is, will be suspect." The *New York Times'* newspapers in Florida took an almost identical position. The outcome of the election was 72 percent against casinos, 28 percent in favor. Sigma Delta

Chi put the issue in rational perspective when it adopted a resolution calling contributions to a nonjournalistic political action committee "inappropriate." It was equally clear that the news staffs' claims that their "credibility" had been impaired was proven to be self-serving bombast by the public vote.

Charles C. Reynolds, editor and publisher of the *Atlantic City Press,* had been on both sides of the argument. In 1974, when he was editor, the publisher at the time was chairman of a pro-casino drive and had the *Press* contribute $11,000. "I was appalled," said editor Reynolds. But in 1976, as publisher Reynolds, he was on a three-man executive committee working for a new casino election. This time, his newspaper gave $45,000 to the campaign. Voters approved it, 10 to 1. Mr. Reynolds said the paper's coverage was fair, and that it since has been strongly critical of casino abuses. His revised view is that a news organization's best course is to editorialize, but not invest, in issues where public votes are involved.[10]

Minneapolis was another case where the lines were crossed on both sides. John Cowles, Jr., then principal owner and head of the *Star & Tribune,* was a major force behind a $55 million-bond issue drive for a sports stadium downtown. The newspapers contributed $900,000 in land and pledged $4 million to support a development corporation. Again, staff reaction was hostile. Forty-five staff members joined to buy an ad to make their protests public, also maintaining that their credibility was compromised. One editor wrote a column, saying that Mr. Cowles "should not even contribute to such projects. . . . Editors and staff members too often feel they have to prove to each other and to readers that they are not being controlled."[11]

Stop and ponder the words, "*to prove to each other.* They disclose not an interest in the issue of whether the newspaper should be involved as a pivotal financial element in a bond issue vote, but, to repeat, the oldest of preoccupations—of newspaper people putting out newspapers not for readers, but to impress each other. How was it possible for journalists not to acknowledge to themselves that, without John Cowles' interest and money, the city of Minneapolis might have had to wait a long

time for its Guthrie Theater, Walker Art Center, and Orchestra
Hall? The argument that the newspaper could have contributed
to civic agencies and had them carry out the projects played,
again, to the journalists' idea of their being enshrined above and
beyond community life. Nevertheless, in the instance of the
domed stadium, Mr. Cowles had crossed the line into a public
bond issue vote, with many citizens opposed. Again, a careful
outside study found that the coverage had been full and fair.
Unhappily, the wounds had cut deep. The entire management
has since changed hands, but some executives contend that the
old management had reacted with hostility to the advertisement
purchased by staff members, and had raised objections to recommended salary increases for any who had signed the ad. All of it
was unpretty and discomfiting.

What these various episodes illustrate is how divided and
confused journalism has become in trying to sort out the ethical
verities of its existence. Corporations are not required to contribute to good causes, but those that see a social responsibility
in doing so are living up to a decent ethical standard. Publishers
who want their cities and states to improve educational, artistic,
and other standards are on perfectly sound ethical ground in
contributing to such causes, and deserve praise for their fore-
sightedness. The only relevant issue in journalism is whether the
editorial product is as honest as fair-minded people can make it,
as balanced as possible, and untainted by either corporate or
personal bias.

The same rules that apply to the coverage of public affairs
ought to be practiced about news organizations' affairs. The
double standard—the press's claimed rights to examine everything and everyone in the public eye, and its own resistance to
having its own work and conduct placed under equal scrutiny—
is one of the root causes of the huge loss of journalism's credibility with its audiences. In Minneapolis and Miami the publishers had a right to use their money to support what they
considered to be the best public interest so long as they were
willing—as they were—to let their investments and their roles be
treated precisely the same as every other individual and institution involved in the undertaking. Their open participation in the

two instances was highly questionable because of the public vote element. So long as the journalistic coverage was honest, thorough, and free of taint there was no conceivable ethical issue at stake—judgmental, yes, but not ethical.

For news staffs to go into breast-beating indignation claiming that *their* credibility has been compromised raises serious questions. In what way is reportorial credibility damaged when there is not the slightest hindrance to full coverage, with the public given all sides and all arguments? In the truest sense, is this not how credibility is built? Reporters and editors deal with imperfection at every step in the processes of handling news. Sources can be wrong, sometimes deliberately. Pictures can distort. Judgments often have to be made too swiftly. These and a hundred other things bedevil journalists constantly. They simply do not always know truth. It is asking a great deal of fallible people to reach for perfection every minute of their time. Yet it has to be asked for, even knowing it may not be achievable. It is precisely why the news control system is the most vital part of the whole ethical thrust in journalism. It clearly was operating well in Miami and Minneapolis. One would have thought reporters would have been encouraged by the liberty to report so freely. In chapter 8, dealing with ombudsmen, the record is clear that many newspeople resent and resist criticism of their own performance, which sometimes involves their own conflicts of interest. How do they parse this challenge to their credibility with their feather-preening, when their news organizations' judgment may be wrong but is open to public view and accountability? Journalism's double standard clearly has infiltrated into news staffs. They seem to have forgotten that journalism's role is to tell what is known as truthfully as possible, even when it hurts. Ethics, after all, begins by recognizing right from wrong. In some situations, journalists' own unions demean their credibility by blindly defending sloths and incompetents on the basis that any concession of such truths would imperil the jobs of all others. Where is their credibility here?

Far, far different was the case of the *San Francisco Chronicle* and the *Examiner,* which for years fought closed courtrooms and the sealing of records and yet, when their own interests were involved, appeared to have no hesitancy about destroying the records of a years' long legal battle concerning antitrust litigation against them. The plaintiffs faced court costs they could no longer afford. The newspapers offered to assume the costs in exchange for all of the plaintiffs' files. They agreed. An *Oakland Tribune* reporter dug into the case. What was uncovered led *Tribune* editor-publisher Robert Maynard to write, "The image of a news organization taking 17 boxes of public records in a major antitrust law suit and dumping them into a vat of acid and then incinerating the slurry is lurid to contemplate. It stands the First Amendment on its head." He went on to comment, "When the managing editor of the *Examiner,* David Halvorsen, was asked his opinion, he said it was a 'corporate' matter. No further comment from the former head of the state's Freedom of Information Committee."[12] It was not crossing a line for the *Chronicle* and the *Examiner*. It was obliterating it with a form of Agent Orange.

Columnist Jack Anderson learned to his chagrin that he had hurdled over a line when he became a founding director of the Diplomat National Bank, which had its eyes on Washington's big Asian-American community. In mid-1976 the bank was under attack after reports that much of the stock was owned by followers of Dr. Sun Myung Moon, the controversial religious leader. In November, two Koreans, Tongsun Park and Pak Bo Hi, were being investigated on charges of having spread handsome contributions among members of Congress. They also were reported to have large holdings in the bank. Mr. Anderson had moved up to be chairman of the executive committee of the bank, and was accused by then-representative Donald Fraser of Minnesota (later mayor of Minneapolis) of threatening to use his column to block an investigation. Mr. Anderson would admit only that he wrote two "intemperate" letters. John McMullan, then the executive editor of the *Miami Herald,* now retired, killed a portion of an Anderson column that dealt with some of the Rev. Moon's activities. In a column of his own, Mr. McMullan said Mr. Anderson "is now disqualified because of his bank connection. . . . Jack needs to decide whether he is a banker or a newspaperman. Either is an honorable profession, but he can't be both without inevitable conflicts."[13] Mr. Anderson got the message. He promptly withdrew from the bank and other business activities. He called it removing the appearance of a conflict of interest. It was more a new record time in a reverse high-hurdle event.

In 1965, Bailey K. Howard, then head of Field Enterprises in Chicago, didn't vault over a line. He went into space, arranging with astronauts Virgil Grissom and John Young to put many pounds of gold and silver medallions on board their Gemini 3 capsule. The splashdown on March 23, 1965, was 58 miles short of target. Talking to the *Chicago Journalism Review*, Mr. Howard said, "I don't know how they [NASA] found out about it. But they figured the additional weight that they didn't know about would cause the overshoot."[14]

It was a far different line, but the *Washington Post*'s Ben Bradlee recalls the time "one photographer who covered an anti-war protest for us, then joined the protest herself." Richard Harwood, the *Post's* deputy managing editor, still remembers a woman's march for peace during the Vietnam war. "One of my reporters covering it came back and said, "How am I supposed to write about it? The first woman I saw marching was my wife and the second I saw was yours."[15]

There are dozens of illustrations of crossing the lines. In oversight many seem to come down to where we began with George Will, and his belated recognition of such even existing. "Disclosure is the answer," was the position of historian Arthur Schlesinger, Jr. He said that journalists ought to be free to take part in the normal activities of their communities, taking care not to become entangled in any direct conflicts of interest. When that happens, he said, the news organization should make public disclosure promptly. Back to Miami and Minneapolis, but hardly San Francisco.

A small city paper, the 25,000-circulation *Lewiston Morning Tribune* in northern Idaho, decided to do it in one bite in one of its Sunday editions in April 1978. A full page was devoted to the disclosure of the financial, personal, and political involve-

ments of the newspaper's staff, from publisher down through
editors and reporters. One reporter did all the checking. Only
managing editor Ladd Hamilton saw the story before it went to
the composing room. The account included an offer by publisher
A. L. Alford to show his latest income-tax returns to anyone
calling at the newspaper. The report was that no one took him
up. Mr. Alford's many civic ties were listed, including his being
president of the Idaho Board of Education. There was an analysis of how some stories were written or overwritten because of
his associations. There were reviews of various reporters' involvements, including the business writer who covered the forest
products firm, Potlatch Corp., where her husband worked; a
reporter who was a member of a planning and zoning commission; and another reporter who was on the historic preservation
board and wrote about the issues regularly. There also was an
anlysis of whether the editorial page editor could write independently and adequately about Senator Frank Church since he had
served as the Senator's press secretary. Both the publisher and
managing editor said in print that they thought his posture about
Senator Church was suspect because of his having served with
him.[16]

There appeared no question but that townspeople were impressed. James Boylan, then the editor of the *Columbia Journalism Review,* said he had never before seen "this kind of full
scale undressing. Usually these things are discussed very reluc-
tantly."[17] There were laudatory comments from other newspaper editors, but to this point, there has been no replay of this
kind of "full scale undressing" by any other news organization
that anyone in the industry knows about.

One unusual and unseemly matter surfaced in the summer
of 1984 when a *Wilmington* (Del.) *News Journal* reporter hired a
lawyer to restrain publication of the ombudsman's column. Del-
aware's attorney general had protested that a story the reporter
had written wrongly implied that a union official had received
special treatment in bargaining down drunk-driving charges to
reckless driving. The state official told ombudsman Harry
Themal that the reporter bore a grudge because she had quar-

reled with his chief deputy, and that she herself had once been arrested for driving under the influence. After a check, Mr. Themal wrote a column and gave the reporter a copy. She asked that the reference to her driving case be removed. Mr. Themal said he would not remove it. The record was that she had entered a first-offender program at a time when completing the program did not constitute a conviction. The column was published with these data included.

Many on the staff had supported the reporter's demand for deletion of her driving record. Executive editor J. D. Brandt issued a memo to the staff after the publication, upholding Mr. Themal's position. He cited the attorney general's suggestion that a "conflict of interest" existed and said, "the public credibility of these newspapers would be compromised if we failed to reveal that at the outset." He added, "I want all of you to know that I find an effort to impose prior restraint on the content of these newspapers as reprehensible when it is made on behalf of a member of the staff as I do when it is attempted by any public official."[18] All of this tawdry episode traced to the gatekeeper— the reporter's supervising editor. The editor had known of the reporter's arrest and decided it did not disqualify her from writing about the union official's case. The vulnerability was evident at that point. To have shrugged it off illustrates again how news organizations fumble their way into so many difficulties.

One conflict of interest is rarely mentioned in newspapers, on radio, or on television. Does the public know that some of their tax dollars go to pay for news organizations, rich and poor, using space and equipment in press quarters set aside in government buildings—federal, state, and city? Reporter Patricia Fanning in the *Wall Street Journal,* in August 1978, gave a word picture of what the state of Illinois was doing for the press. It provided a $1-million press suite, with orange desks and matching chairs; three pressroom attendants; the payment of most telephone bills; and sixteen private and semiprivate offices, all at no rent. She wrote that other states were providing similar facilities, including free parking spaces.[19] Howard Covington, Jr., of the *Charlotte Observer,* in a personal letter in 1972, commented tartly on this issue. "I wish more papers had the guts to put their feet down on the obvious and not-so-obvious payoffs that come into newsrooms and eventually make their way into the news pages. Some of the examples of misuse of the media I saw during the recent primary elections would short-circuit your electric typewriter. One TV station in this state, for example, had a capitol correspondent who wrote campaign speeches and did TV commercials for candidates on the side. And somebody said they just couldn't understand why the public doesn't trust us!"[20]

One report in the *New York Times* in 1977 remarked on a TV report by Roger Mudd, then with CBS, of "the perquisities allowed Congressmen—office space, travel allowances, franked mail and medical services, their private dining room, barber and beauty shops and five free parking places each. What he did not say was that he and 3,000 other accredited members of the Hill press corps also have free office space, access to the same dining rooms, the option of having their hair cut in the same shops, and hunting privileges, at least, for Hill parking spots."[21] Some disagreements exist between the major networks about free space and other perks in Washington. NBC's Washington news director said his network was willing to pay its fair share but that there were some freedom-of-press issues to be resolved. "The press in the Senate and House is there because the Constitution says we should be allowed to have access to our government," he said. George Watson, ABC's vice-president, said he believed it was the government's responsibility to provide "ordinary facilities for the news media," including pressrooms and typewriters. CBS didn't seem to agree. It already was paying annual rental for its 80-square-foot broadcast booth in the west wing. Both of the major wire services accept it as a matter of principle that they should pay their own way if it can be worked out.

Sometimes it can't, as the two Louisville newspapers discovered in the early 1970s. They tried to pay for the pressroom space at the state capitol, but the governor refused. So did his successor. So in March 1974, the papers moved out of the statehouse, bought a house, and renovated it, but still sought to pay the money they felt was owed the state. The state wouldn't take it, so the money finally was given to the University of Kentucky, which set up a lecture series. There are stepped-up efforts by editors' groups to get states to agree to prorata rental charges for space and equipment, but the movement is glacial on other matters involving money. But let a reporter find some state or federal legislator taking advantage of regular political perks and his or her newspaper will promptly find page-one space for it. Other papers may have recorded what the *New York Times* did in its article—but it is doubtful more than a handful did—which was to list some of the costs to taxpayers, such as:

• Salaries for 24 press gallery employees, plus doorkeepers and messengers—$592,517.

• 181 free parking spaces on the Capitol grounds—$130,000.

• 180 free telephones—with annual bills totaling $23,000.

• Desks, chairs, typewriters, and other equipment—$40,000.

In a speech on the issue to a Wisconsin press group, Rep. David R. Obey, who was chairman of the House committee on House Practices, said his concern was not perquisites, but hypocrisy, and whether the public was being fully and fairly appraised of the information.[22] What journalists deal with here—or rather, what their home offices deal with—is the double standard, which, to repeat, also plays a role in journalistic credibility.

Much of it is reminiscent of the 1976 article in *The Center* magazine, published by the Center for the Study of Democratic Institutions in Santa Barbara, Calif. It was written by Donald McDonald, the editor:

Ten years ago, Fred Friendly quit CBS News when the network executives refused to air the Senate Foreign Relations Committee's hearings on American foreign policy in Vietnam and insisted on broadcasting a fifth rerun of *I Love Lucy* and an eighth rerun of *The Real McCoys*. Mr. Friendly said the network would not have suffered a net loss that year if they had dropped the reruns for a few days; it would only have made a little less profit. When CBS

officials were confronted by that argument in a discussion
here at the Center, they replied that, for CBS stockholders,
no decrease in net profits is acceptable.[23]

In this instance, Fred Friendly had not just crossed a line. He
had broken through the holy wall.

When the whole huge basket is sifted out, the conflict-of-
interest issue is going to remain one of journalism's greatest
continuing headaches. Former Supreme Court Justice Potter
Stewart summed it up in his comment that "the difference is
between what we have a right to do and what is the right thing to
do." That has been journalism's dilemma from the outset. The
struggle continues.

In recent years, journalists have made much of "the appearance of impropriety," as did the *Arizona Star*. On a pure ethical
basis, it is a troubling thesis. Ethics consists of knowing right
from wrong and following a right course as an honorable duty.
In inserting the word "appearance" as carrying equal force, then
a "right" act—something that *ought* to be done—could be
blocked on the basis that simply the "appearance" makes it
"wrong." Such a hypothetical situation was generated out of the
immensely successful "Media and the Law" seminars, pioneered
by Fred Friendly when he was with the Ford Foundation, and
expanded in the seminars now run under his Media and Society
program at Columbia University.

The fictional situation created was of a leak, presumably
coming from a high-level source, demanding a pledge of absolute
anonymity. A team of five of the country's top psychiatrists has
issued a written report adjudging the President of the United
States to have become mentally unstable, and seriously so. The
report is locked in a safe. It is under 24-hour surveillance. The
source says where it is located, warning that the only way it
could be obtained would be forced entry and overpowering the
guard. David Shaw of the *Los Angeles Times* put the question to
his editor, William B. Thomas. Given such information, would
he order his staff to do whatever was necessary to get it? "Christ,

yes," said Mr. Thomas, "we have to go get it. This is the official with his finger on the button."[24] Posed with the same hypothetical situation, a number of other editors agreed, one of them saying, "Any act necessary has to be taken—even if it came down to the risk of having to commit murder." It makes for a dramatic test of editors' views of their responsibility. All one can say in this instance is that the answers do meet the ethical test of coherence and fall under the "duty for duty's sake" approach of philosopher Immanuel-Kant.

The "conflicting obligations in every transaction in life" come into play constantly with every piece of public relations copy submitted to news desks, with every political "handout," with every sports, entertainment, travel, and other business-oriented subject matter covered or considered for coverage. In practical terms, the list is almost endless, and it is why the gate-keeping functions literally constitute every news organization's last line of defense. As Mr. McDonald wrote in *The Center* magazine, "Today, in some respects the most interesting and formidable threat to consistently responsible journalism comes not so much from government as from the mass media themselves." In his article, he cited a case of Sears, Roebuck and Company, the world's largest retailer, going on trial in Chicago before an administrative law judge of the Federal Trade Commission on charges Sears had engaged in bait-and-switch selling tactics. "The hearings," he wrote, "lasted 11 days. Eighteen former Sears employees from 13 states, and 25 consumer witnesses from 11 states testified." He quoted from a *Columbia Journalism Review* article that reported that the *Chicago Tribune*, which then was receiving $5 million annually in Sears advertising, "carried not one line about the case from the date the trial began . . . until it ended." Mr. McDonald went on to report that the *Tribune* carried a four-paragraph story a week after the trial, a "condensed replay of a report filed by . . . the *Wall Street Journal*'s Chicago bureau. Coverage by the other two Chicago dailies was only a little bit better."[25] As the San Francisco episode of far more recent vintage would demonstrate, when corporate dollars are involved, the editing function in many places tends to become one of making certain the gates are either tightly locked or are opened only the slightest crack for sake of the "record."

To judge from the APME's *Editors and Stress* report in 1983, many editors still have to suffer through such anguish as was revealed in the just-before-Christmas letter in 1973 from DeWitt Scott, then executive editor of the *Express* in Easton, Pa., who now is on the West Coast editing, teaching, and writing. His letter began:

> It happened again yesterday. Only God knows how many times it has happened to me and hundreds—perhaps thousands—of others down through the years. Probably not in Louisville or St. Pete. . . . I raise that because you may not know how bad it is on the small and medium dailies. What happened? The publisher and the ad director braced the editor in the editor's office. Tight-lipped. Angry over a roundup story on page one surveying effects of a major storm on business during the merchants' annual get-well season. No quarrel with the story, which was factually correct, or even with the tone of it. It was an honest enough, though turgidly written, little survey. The quarrel: WHO we surveyed. The upshot: We are never, never again to survey any merchant who doesn't advertise with the *Express*. In taking the economic pulse of our area, to coin a phrase, we do not take the pulse of the non-advertiser because he is dead. He has no pulse. . . . Today, I won a small concession. The publisher agreed there would be times when I'd have to use my judgment. . . . It might even be necessary to elicit such a cretin's quotes. But the underlying fact remains: the advertiser is still No. 1. So even when one of us little editors wins a battle now and then, "they" are still winning the war. The reader is still the ultimate loser.[26]

This is an instance of the worst kind of conflict of interest coming at the top gatekeeper level. But then, on reflection, my mind goes back to reporters grown so close to prosecutors that they were publicly bad-mouthing their newspaper's decision that it no longer would publish any police or prosecutor's office announcement about obtaining a "confession." Once it came up in trial, by all means. But not for public relations purposes.[27] Trivial comparison, to be sure, but it was, and is, the buddy-type of conflict of interest that blights much of journalism at the lowest levels of gatekeeping. But one must concede that getting a wayward publisher straightened out sometimes is next to impossible. It's easier to educate a wayward reporter. Provided, that is, the top newsroom gatekeepers put up with no nonsense and transfer the reporter off the beat, tell him or her why, and add that the next time it happens will be the last. As Meg Greenfield wrote about journalists and outside friendships, and when facts have to be faced: "You just do it. That's all."

## CHAPTER 10

# Chips Off the Block

FOR ANYONE IN JOURNALISM, it was eye-catching. Emblazoned on the magazine cover page were five words: "Do we need Journalism Schools?" It was the November/December 1984 issue of the *Bulletin* of the American Society of Newspaper editors. The subject took 30 of the magazine's 44 pages, covering a broad range of editors' thought. A few months earlier the Associated Press Managing Editors' *News* had focused on the same issue. For me, the most telling ASNE article was pure bellringer (a journalistic term drawn from the old days when the wire service teletypes signaled "bulletins" and "flashes" with a series of bells). It was written by Lauren Kessler, a University of Oregon professor, and too delicious to even think of tampering with. Here it is in full:

Thirty of them sit in straight-back chairs behind long wooden desks. Some shuffle papers; others doodle. A few gaze at the floor. The rest direct their attention to the blackboard at the front of the room.

The teacher points to a sentence scrawled on the blackboard. "The woman (a) who (b) whom detectives believed committed the robbery has been cleared," it reads. "Well," says the teacher, "what do you think: who or whom?" The flourescent lights hiss. The room is so quiet you can hear an infinitive split. The teacher waits.

"It's whom," says one of the doodlers after a long pause.

"Why?" asks the teacher.

The doodler hesitates. "It just sounds right," he says.

"No," says one of the attentive ones in the front row. "'Whom' is stodgy and too formal. We just don't use it in journalism anymore."

The teacher points to the next sentence on the board. It reads: "The man (a) who (b) whom police arrested confessed to the robbery." "Now what do you think?" asks the teacher, eyeing one of the paper shufflers. The shuffler squints at the board. "I don't know," she says. "I guess I'd just rewrite the sentence and avoid the problem."

"Uh, isn't 'whom' an object?" asks someone in the back of the room. "I seem to remember it's an object." "Right," says the teacher. "But what does that mean? Can it help us make the correct choice?" The fluorescent lights buzz. No one speaks.

Who are these people? Indolent journalism students destined to butcher their native tongues once they set foot in the newsroom? Poorly taught, ill-read 20-year-olds ready to confound and exasperate their hardworking editors?

No. These are the hardworking editors themselves. They are attending a seminar on literacy in the newsroom, and they are discovering that grammar is not just something other people have problems with.

These editors hem and haw their way through a half-hour grammar quiz, performing no better than the first-year journalism students for whom the quiz is designed. Then, breathing a sigh of relief, they pour themselves fresh coffee and settle down to discuss the subject closest to their hearts: how poorly their journalism school-trained reporters use the English language.

P.S. The correct usage is who in both instances.

Wait. Stop looking back and puzzling about that "who." There was a postscript. Four of them, in fact: three letters from editors in the February 1985 *Bulletin*, each saying "whom" was right; a following note from the managing editor, agreeing with them and adding that "the solution was garbled in a telephone transmission." How, I wanted to know. Everybody flunked Telephone Journalism 1. Obviously, "who" and "whom" can easily be confused in a telephone checkback, and they were. The *Bulletin* managing editor learned that in the future the best way to do it is to check in writing or, in a hurry, to use the old "w" for whiskey, "h" for hell, and so on. I confided my experience of relying often on the profane, the vulgar, and even obscene to make certain of clarity. "Whom" with an "m" for "masturbation."

Back to Professor Kessler's "class." It would be slandering perhaps a thousand well-schooled American editors who are skilled in correct use of the language to consider them in the same terms as the ones Professor Kessler described. Unhappily, though, the fumblers reflect many more thousands who hold gatekeeping positions on the newspapers they serve. As common scold, I am driven to repeat that this type of editor holds the post because he or she is able with the mechanics of getting the newspaper to press on time and this is what the publisher wants. Publishers who care usually are those willing to invest in ombudsmen. Some of the ombudsmen have become so disturbed by the endless flow of butchered language in their papers, they have moved to issue regular reports to editors and staff members. They are citing specifics, following the pioneering of Theodore Bernstein, who as assistant managing editor of the *New York Times*, began his "Winners & Sinners" reports in 1951. It was to lead him to produce a total of six books and in his last years a syndicated column.[1] The erudite "Teddy" Bernstein raised my sights, as well as those of countless others, and many of us cherish his contributions to sanity in communicating with readers.

There isn't anything new about the country's leading editors agonizing over the weaknesses in the academic system that provides so much of their staffing. It has been going on for more than half a century. Most editors seem incapable of admitting it, but the basic problem is that education for journalism is a mirror image of the industry. The range in quality is the same—from the elite to the dreadful. Top-rank educators are just as contemptuous about the shoddy schools as A. M. Rosenthal of the *Times* is about the papers he thinks print "too much garbage." The late Richard G. Gray, the journalism dean at Indiana University, was equally blistering. "I am ashamed of what is offered as journalism and mass communications at a number of campuses, and of the faculty who want to perpetuate that mediocrity."[2]

In the truest sense, those editors who floundered so during the grammar test can be counted as victims of "the system."

They represent the unconscious contempt so many publishers, and their broadcast counterparts, feel about the need for quality or for professional standards in their newsrooms. The same goes for many university and college administrators. Despite protestations about their dedication to high-quality education, too many also give the identical impression of looking on their undertaking as a business. Whatever high calling it started out to be, it now may be just that in their institutions. Fact is, the historically superior schools always have had a superior clientele for their student product. The inferior schools today are counterparts of cheap, cost-cutting retail stores.

The record is that journalism fouled its educational nesting grounds in the early years and getting it straightened out now is a huge problem. Few have put it more compactly than Dr. Everette E. Dennis, now director of the new independent Gannett Center for Media Studies at Columbia University (former University of Oregon dean and past president of the Association for Education in Journalism and Mass Education). "Mass communications is central to the functioning of society," he said, "but I can't think of a university that acts as if it was."[3]

However, what is new is that after years of caterwauling, there has come a hopeful development. The strong focus in the editors' magazines flows out of a partnership building between the thinking editors and the thinking educators. They are agreed that those who aspire to careers in journalism need to be exposed to courses in history, political science, literature, economics, and languages, and together they look askance at the proliferation of programs that stress technology, public relations, advertising, and other such courses that mark so much of the offerings in many institutions. Given the tenacity of faculty politicians in protecting their turf, the struggle to come may be fierce, but there still may be a way to break what Robert M. Hutchins back in 1938 referred to as "the shadiest educational ventures under respectable auspices."

Forty-five years later, Irving Kristol, editor-educator and social scientist, was on the same theme, although he should have spread the net of blame a lot wider. "Most publications these days," he wrote, "not all, thank God, recruit from schools of journalism. This means they are recruiting from the bottom 40 percent of the college population since, on the whole, bright students do not go to schools of journalism." He said the very bright go into the sciences. Those at the second level go into professional schools or graduate work in humanities and social sciences, at the third level into schools of business, at the fourth level into journalism, and at the fifth level into schools of education. "To the degree that the media recruit from schools of journalism," he argued, "they are recruiting young men and women who don't think very well and who don't have the habit of thinking. When you go out and talk to young people outside New York (there the major publications can recruit the cream of this journalistic community), you find yourself facing a kind of invincible mindlessness."[4] On the basis of my experience, Mr. Kristol's academic-choice listing was astute. Nor can there be much serious challenge about the "invincible mindlessness" factor being a general journalistic problem. It is in New York and Washington as elsewhere. Surely, he recognizes that some good newspapers exist elsewhere in the country and that editors in those cities also manage to enlist some of the cream of the crop. While subscribing to the core of his argument, I hold that it failed to challenge the cause and effect factors that trace directly to the industry.

Journalism education began with general academic approval more than seventy-five years ago at the University of Missouri. It still has that acceptance there, and it is true also of a number of other well-run schools. Where academic journalism went astray was with a surrender to "the trade." Seeking professional acceptance, several schools drifted into "assembly-line" production, preparing students to walk into any small-city newsroom and be capable of covering standard events and writing stories in compact form. Some also had "back shop" skills, as I discovered in my one assignment with an accrediting team years ago at a Midwestern school. We found students receiving credit hours for working at linotype machines, handling type in page makeup, helping the hired pressman run off the campus paper, and soliciting advertising. Small papers in that state were delighted with what they got in the way of ready-to-go-to-work people. After all, they weren't looking for intellectuals. They wanted cheap help, trained for their markets.

Joseph Pulitzer had a sound idea when he put up the endowment for a graduate school of journalism at Columbia University in 1912. But that intelligent step forward was to be contaminated by many schools which proceeded to add graduate-year study on top of their undergraduate work. However, even that might have been useful if it had not been for the proliferation of journalism schools and departments. There now are about 250 universities and colleges offering degrees in various aspects of communications, and in 1984 only 85 of the total number were accredited. Many of the 165 others lacking accreditation undoubtedly did not seek it because of an unwillingness to accept the requirement that 75 percent of every student's college credits must come from courses in the liberal arts. Concentrations offered in some schools of communications included sequences in graphic arts, printing management and the technology of printing, teacher certification, telecommunication, interpersonal communication, film and drama, public relations, advertising, and news-editorial.

Speaking of the 1983 job placements, Thomas Engleman, the executive director of the Dow Jones Newspaper Fund (a foundation established to encourage young people to consider careers in journalism), estimated that as many as 15 percent of the graduates had gone into advertising and public relations. He also said a number of journalism deans told him "we are losing the best" because of the perception of many students that newspaper salaries were too low. They were right, Mr. Engleman found, in checking 1983 entry-level salaries. The median starting salary for journalism school graduates at daily newspapers was $11,180 and the same in local broadcasting. It was $12,740 for those going into advertising and $13,260 for these in public relations. Anyone surprised by the salary figure for broadcasting should know that, other than for anchor people and on-camera weathermen, local television stations tend to pay lower salaries than do local newspapers. None of this applies to the top 25 to 30 newspapers in the country, but there is little innovative thought given to economic administration among the vast majority of news organizations. Most insist on following the formulas given them by the publishers' organizations that collect data. It has gone on all through my career. Still in memory is the bittersweet humor of a witty Missouri editor, Merrill Chilcote, who liked to tell of his being one of the country's first "ten-cent executives." It came after the National Labor Relations Board in the 1930s ruled that an individual could not be considered as an executive unless receiving a salary of more than $36 a week. "I got an instant raise," Merrill loved to recount, "to $36.10 a week."

Another facet of the disdain many professionals hold for some journalism schools is the absurdity of faculties insisting upon doctoral degrees as a requirement for any teaching post. It is a requirement that would have blocked out of journalism education a number of the most distinguished professors and deans. Even an extremely short list will serve to make the point. It includes Elie Abel, Columbia's dean for a decade and now the chairman at Stanford; James Atwater, former senior editor at *Time*, and now dean at Missouri; Fred W. Friendly of Columbia, former president of CBS News; and Vermont Royster, emeritus professor at North Carolina, who was the Pulitzer Prize-winning editor of the *Wall Street Journal*. There are twenty others who could be listed among the group. Each of us would have been rejected out of hand at North Hogwash State, just as would Arthur Schlesinger, Jr., the historian who also has no Ph.D. card but who was good enough for Harvard and New York universities. Professor Abel offers a sound explanation for the insistence on the doctorate. "The state schools have to sell their budget requests to the legislature each year," he said, "and they've figured out the best way to snow them is by claiming to have faculties consisting of 100 percent Ph.D.'s, no matter if the doctoral studies had only the barest connection with journalism."[5] Ah, well, Lyndon Johnson as President used to play the same game. Annoyed by columnists who had compared the quality of his appointees with those of John F. Kennedy, he was given to turning to people like Vice-President Hubert Humphrey and saying, "Tell 'em how many Ph.D.'s we've appointed to key positions." Then he would fold his arms and stare belligerently, as if his point was proved. Heaven knows how many journalists had to go through that bit of playacting.

Beyond that, however, the great majority of journalism school educators—other than a few with outstanding professional backgrounds—have failed one of the prime academic tests, that of challenging the qualitative and ethical aspects of the profession at large. It merits noting that many of the most important breakthroughs in medicine have come through research work in university hospitals. A substantial number of the most eminent jurists have emerged from the law schools, and the leading constitutional scholars customarily are found in residence in the great universities. So, too, in the fields such as philosophy and history. There have been only scattered evidences of this kind of venturesome and probing thought being advanced by those in academic journalism. What was reported in chapter 6 on the long-lived effect of the diagnosis-and-prescription report of the group of men assembled by Robert Hutchins is a case in point. None of the famed scholars had any background in journalism. The challenges they presented were to be hooted down by nay-sayers among the editors and publishers, but the ideas were to take root in many minds.

The autocratic Hutchins had a clear-eyed view of what education ought to be. He said it plainly: "Education is not to teach men facts, theories or laws, not to reform or amuse them or make them expert technicians. It is to unsettle their minds, widen their horizons, inflame their intellect, teach them to think straight, if possible, but to think nevertheless." In essence, this is what the editors and educators working to remodel the academic patterns are saying ever more strongly. Everette Dennis and University of Illinois Dean James Carey, for instance, agree with Frank McCulloch, the new managing editor of the *San Francisco Examiner*, that journalism schools need "to be a lot tougher when it comes to admitting and keeping undergraduates. If the prospect can't, or won't, read, write and spell properly . . . and can't accept with equanimity the frustrations journalism eventually will bring, then send him or her somewhere else for a college education."[6] Dr. Dennis is a believer in competency testing. He believes in "good entrance requirements" and checking regularly to make sure the student is "cutting it." Dr. Michael Burgoon of Michigan State expresses it in stronger terms: "Journalism schools are going to have to abandon all remedial education that leads to the B.A. degree in journalism. They cannot continue to be the refuse dump of students who cannot make it in other, more rigorous, disciplines."

Dr. Burgoon makes another charge, that most of the opposition to reform of journalism education comes from faculty members with "a vested interest in defending what it is they are *now* doing." The temptation has been strong to join in the so-often reiterated denunciation of faculty politics, but exposure to life in general has brought restraint. Some of what goes on in faculty meetings is narcissistic posturing, frustrating for anyone trying to deal with issues in "real world" terms. Implanted in memory is the day Fred Friendly held his hands to his head during a faculty meeting, and exclaimed, "Isn't there a better way for grown people to spend their time?" In so-called real world political maneuvering, the goals are evident: positioning for power and the rewards that go with it. In academe, the objectives often seem tied to egotistical one-upmanship. Columbia's late Wallace Sayre may have described it best when he said, "The reason faculty politics are so vicious is that the stakes are so low."

There are times when the stakes do get high and educators do react to any challenge for change with open hostility. One such episode came in 1957, when the late Norval Neil Luxon, the able and visionary dean of journalism at the University of North Carolina, was president of the Association for Education in Journalism. The mushrooming expansion in journalism schools worried him and he told the association's annual convention that there needed to be a drastic reduction. "Forty or fifty truly professional schools of journalism," he said, "located at institutions with outstanding libraries, and nationally recognized departments in the humanities and the social sciences, with rigid requirements for the first two years of work in the liberal arts . . . will serve the nation's [newspapers and other media] far better than 150 to 175 schools, many of which are inadequately staffed and supported."[7] Members of the organization promptly responded by rejecting him as the association's representative on the American Council for Education in Journalism, the first immediate past president to be so rebuked. It said volumes about the educators' devotion to free speech, as well as about their ethics.

Changing ground for the moment, it is clear that a part of the current problem for journalism educators lies in what can only be seen as the disintegration of "quality" in the primary and secondary public school systems. The international comparisons of achievement were enough to convince any doubter. On nineteen academic tests, American students never scored either first or second and, in comparison with other industrialized nations, were last seven times.[8] While I was aware of the slide downward in the quality of public school education, it nevertheless came as a shock, when I first began teaching at Columbia, to confront the fact that the same equation applied to so many students who had come into graduate work after winning B.A. degrees elsewhere. This is not to say that there was a paucity of brilliant students in the class. Since Columbia put its emphasis on backgrounds in the humanities, there were many who would have been outstanding in any setting. The school's reach was for as great a diversity as possible. But too frequently, I was to realize that an astonishing number of students were sitting in the embarrassed silence of ignorance when topics arose that called for some knowledge of the past, including even recent journalistic history.

Some of us were tempted to place the blame on the unrest of the mid-1960s on college campuses, but we were wrong. Rechecks on college transcripts showed excellent grades in many of the courses taken, along with supporting letters from professors which amounted to "rave" reports. The standards in those schools had collapsed, too.

It has to be conceded that a major mitigating factor was the Congressional intercession that gave students the right of access to professors' reports on their work. As with libel law, the constant threat of litigation clearly has driven many in the teaching ranks to protect themselves from student and family suits to see all recorded information and to seek damages. In the light of more than a few sad-sack experiences, it is little wonder some of us came to look on professorial "rave" reports as defensive evasions. In short, Ralph Waldo Emerson's essay on "Compensation" remains as valid today as when he wrote it some 140 years ago.

Subsequently, I came around to describing the normal Columbia class as consisting of 15 percent of students who needed very little guidance from any of us—who, while not at the same level as a Jim Detjen, were reasonably close. All they needed was exposure to the wealth of journalistic material available in a city like New York, and some tough-minded editing to sharpen their natural skills. At the other end, we had 15 percent of students who—had the admissions committee received a totally accurate rundown—probably would never have been accepted. The other 70 percent ranged from "very good" to "maybe, with the grace of God."

The denouement, if it can be called that, came in the spring with the arrival of recruiters. We had worked with these students for a full eight months. One would think that recruiting editors or personnel officers would seek out professors (and particularly any they knew personally) to do some probing. How astonishing to find that, with a few precious exceptions, the professionals tended to make no such inquiries whatever. It would come as no surprise a year or so later to be told by some editor that he was having reservations about Columbia's students, that they were short on many skills. Some of us solved the problem by dealing in advance by telephone with good news organizations, naming those students who struck us as top quality and well worth taking a long look at. The accomplishment record of many of those students has proved the wisdom of those acts of intercession. The overall results, however, are added proof of the casual approach accepted by the managements of so many news organizations.

There was a chance that the slide in public school quality could have been detected much earlier if more news organizations had the urge—and able staffing—to have done some examining of the educational process long ago. Richard Harwood, now a deputy managing editor of the *Washington Post,* did exactly that for the *Louisville Times* in the 1950s. What he did may not have produced a model system, but it did acquaint the citizens with the central problems and led to a fair amount of restructuring. What Mr. Harwood had begun to show in the 1950s was, in effect, validated in 1983 with the report of the National Commission on Excellence in Education, which bore the title, "A Nation at Risk." Commenting on that report in his book *Megatrends.* John Naisbitt focused on the commission's description of today's school systems producing a "rising tide of mediocrity." Mr. Naisbitt charged, "It is more and more apparent that young high school—even college—graduates cannot write acceptable English or even do simple arithmetic. For the first time in American history the generation moving into adulthood is less skilled than its parents."

Vermont Royster, one of the most thoughtful journalists of my generation, continued to write a regular column for the *Wall Street Journal* after he had become professor at North Carolina. In one such column, he reported on what he experienced when he accepted an invitation at another university to lead an undergraduate class discussion. "The writer today," he wrote, "who trusts to some echo phrase from Shakespeare or Dickens—or even the Bible—to make clear his point leans upon a slender reed. He'd best take care to make his point without assuming such common ground between writer and audience." Prior to the discussion, he had decided to begin an outline of different views by recalling those of Socrates. "I began by asking how many knew the story of Socrates," he wrote. "Not a single hand went up. Not one among these advanced university undergraduates." He went on to say, "After some years now in a belated career on a university faculty I should have been past surprise. What seems to have happened in the educational process of late years is that the unbilical cord to our cultural past has come unraveled if not severed. It's not so much that Johnny can't read as that he isn't asked to read very much."

Mr. Royster's experience addressed the central problem of all education, and of the society as a whole. Major weakness in any of the essential institutions—from government, justice, education, commerce, and particularly communications—endangers the democratic fabric. In the hands of gatekeepers with no purpose other than personal gain, we run the constant risk of even worse disintegration.

What follows may shed some light on one of journalism's, and its educational-support line's, long-range problems. During my last years at Columbia, Edward W. Barrett and I collaborated in working up and conducting in partnership a joint-degree program in "Media Management." It brought together equal numbers of students from the graduate schools of journalism and business and from the school of law. It required joint admission and full course work, meaning a year of graduate journalism study had to be added for both those already in the M.B.A. and LL.D. programs—and a complete M.B.A. course for the journalism M.S.J.'s—before any degree could be granted. Why would these students go through all this? Well, the law school members had a deep interest in communications law. The business school students had their eyes on careers in communications management. Light came when we received a listing showing entry-level salaries (as of 1979) for all three fields. Law was on top, in the $25,000 to $32,000 range. M.B.A.'s were second, in the $20,000 to $27,000 range. The journalism openings were recorded as being in the $12,000 to $15,000 range. Here is where Mr. Kristol's "invincible mindlessness" actually has its central meaning. It is why journalism schools attract so many "fourth level" students.

How cheap-shot journalism intrudes on the business of proper learning was illustrated by George Harmon in an article in *Quill* magazine. Mr. Harmon, former business editor of the *Chicago Sun-Times*, now teaches at Northwestern. He wrote:

"Business journalism is hot, the strongest area of news growth in dailies over the past decade. The kid who twenty years ago might have dreamed of becoming a political columnist now wants to be a business reporter. Undergraduates who have never taken an economics course announce to me they'll be covering business during a summer internship at the *Viperville Vindicator*. They don't know the difference between puts and calls and bases on balls, they say. Isn't there a quickie method of learning about business? You know, man, in a week or two? Nope. . . . When it comes to business, journalism sends out a lot of players who don't know the rules. Newspapers and television constantly assign reporters and editors to business stories without a lick of training." Which applies as well, he might have added, to the coverage of law and the courts, education, public utilities, welfare, and the score of other sensitive areas demanding sound backgrounding and the training of how to research. Mr. Harmon's point was corroborated by Irving Shapiro, former chairman of the Du Pont Company. "In important subject areas such as technology and economic affairs," he said, "many journalists do not understand their subject well enough to report on its responsibly. . . . There, the media's reach has exceeded their grasp and the resulting coverage has been so lacking in perspective as to constitute a disservice to the public."[9]

Similar criticism about science reporting came in the wake of intense coverage of artificial heart transplants, Alzheimer's disease, and other health subjects, as well as of such technology as nuclear power. The *Wall Street Journal* quoted a number of researchers who expressed concerns, perhaps expressed most pointedly by Professor Dorothy Nelkin of Cornell University, who said science reporting had become "just entertainment—cute science—and doesn't give the readers the idea that there are important public choices to be made." Jay Winsten, a researcher at the Harvard School of Public Health, had completed three years of study of science coverage and said writers sometimes "hype" news to get prominent display for their stories. He added that editors striving "for the strongest possible statements" in stories also cause distortions. Mr. Winsten may not have been sure how close he was to the central target, or he had chosen care in his choice of language. The fact is that only those science writers who have the cachet of impressive work records can exert any control over what is published or broadcast. Following the J. Edward Murray formula by which news editors operate, science reporters lacking such muscle have to adjust to what their desk editors decide is to be published or broadcast—including what if any "hype" is to be applied.

The same control factor is constantly at work in the area of coverage of international news. That was demonstrated by Professor Marion Lewenstein of Stanford's communications faculty, who directed a study of foreign news used in 32 newspapers across the nation. It encompassed 6,500 stories carried on 25 wire services and syndicates. She found that in selecting foreign news, editors strongly favored stories that mentioned the United States. "The United States was mentioned 45 percent of the time," she said. "It shows you the kind of bias in stories we call foreign news." She added, "Except on the very largest papers there isn't anybody with any sort of training in foreign news who's in charge of the copy."[10]

This, of course, traces to two primary shortcomings. One lies in the skewed educational patterns of the last several decades, and the other in the creativity gap that exists at the management levels of so much of communications. Alfred Balk, editorial director of *World Press Review,* believes that the majority of those assigned to edit world news copy "don't know what to look for." He makes the point that their directing editors should have recognized long ago that "there no longer is such a thing as foreign news. Everything affects us these days." What needs to be done is to be as selective about such desk personnel as is the case with reporting specialists in the sciences, health, law, the arts, and other fields. Those considered for foreign desk editing need to understand from the start that the work requires extensive outside reading and that the news organization stands ready to provide whatever subscriptions and books are required to broaden and deepen knowledge and understanding.

As encouraging development has come in higher education with the moves by a number of universities and colleges moving to what a *New York Times* report called "a new wave of curriculum reform that is radically changing what college students will be learning in coming years." Reporter Edward W. Fiske linked the change to Harvard's 1975 move "to restore some structure to curriculums that had been denuded of requirements in the student rebellions of the previous decade." A new curriculum required of all students for graduation at Harvard calls for taking courses from a list reflecting six of what the university calls "modes of inquiry—literature and arts, historical study, social analysis, moral reasoning, science and foreign cultures."

If this spreads generally through the best of the country's institutions of higher education, added pressure is certain to be placed on schools of journalism to adapt. What all the agencies of communications need urgently are increased numbers of individuals with a working knowledge of the nation and the world, of governments and major issues confronting them, of literature and the arts, of science, philosophy and ethics and, strikingly, of history, particularly American history. Many in journalism declaim glibly of their First Amendment rights but precious few have ever studied the debates and papers about its formulation, and they understand next to nothing of the checks and balances of the national charter.

Were Neil Luxon alive today, surveying the educational scene, my guess is that he might be urging not two, but four, years of intensive study in history, government, public affairs, science, and ethics—and only then would graduates be eligible to apply to any of the 40 to 50 "truly professional *graduate* schools," where the concentration would be on marrying the depth and breadth of liberal arts knowledge to reporting and writing. All of this adds up to one of the crisp descriptions voiced years ago: "We can teach them journalism. We can't give them an education."

One answer to the basic relationship of journalism schools and the field of professional communications also appeared in that "focus issue" of the editors' *Bulletin*. The answer came from Claude Sitton, a Pulitzer Prize winner who is editorial director of the *News & Observer* and the *Raleigh Times* of North Carolina. He told his colleagues that the one way to cure the problem of judging graduates was to hire only those coming out of schools that have won accreditation. He did not say it explicitly. I will. When and if those who run newspapers and broadcast stations make it a rule to employ only from universities and colleges on the accredited list, then will come a genuine revolution in journalism education. Fiery words may emerge from a lot of faculties, but without a clientele, they will be out of business.

However, before professional communications arrives at that kind of tough-minded resistance to nonaccredited schools, it seems clear that the Association for Education in Journalism and Mass Communications needs to do some careful reassessment of its present blanket rules covering accreditation. Pam Johnson, president and publisher of the *Ithaca* (N.Y.) *Journal,* who holds a doctorate from Wisconsin and formerly was a professor at Norfolk (Va.) State University, and who also has served on accrediting teams, makes the point that there are many different shadings between the elite independent schools at the top levels and schools that operate on an "open admission" basis. "What is needed," she holds, "are probably as many as four different models for accrediting teams." The end-product, of course, has to be a commitment to a sound humanistic education, as distinct from any crass trade-school approach, a commitment open to careful appraisals that lead to an accredition that becomes meaningful to professionals.

One other portion of Mr. Sitton's advice was directed to what he called "the publisher's Midas touch. Who knows better than he or she that there's no free lunch? Until newspapers improve salaries, there'll be little improvement in the quality of those who aspire to work for them. Today's market for glamour has fled to television where, as a reporter making the switch once told me, 'You don't have to know how to spell.'"

## CHAPTER 11

# Keepers of the Dollars

H E WAS 5 feet, 2 inches tall. Born to an immigrant family living at the edge of poverty, he went through grade school, took a summer course in bookkeeping, typing, and stenography, and went to work for a lawyer, who owned the *Bayonne Times,* in New Jersey, just across from Manhattan. At 16, he was told to take care of the newspaper. He did it so single-mindedly that 68 years later in 1979, when he died at 84, he was billionaire king of one of the dozen or so largest communications empires in the world. He was S. I. Newhouse, named Solomon at birth, called Sammy from childhood, and known in the news industry as Sam, most often simply by his initials. He took a law degree in his young years so he knew the basics of law, but his forte was in bookkeeping. He may have had the skills of one born to be an auditor, but he was far wiser than that. He knew how to bail out of difficult situations, almost invariably coming forth with a profit. In large part, this chapter focuses on him because, while not the first major chain builder in journalism, he appears to have been three decades ahead of the brokers and bankers in recognizing the financial potentials in what now has developed into a form of mania in Wall Street for communications mergers. As is the case with most of today's money market deal makers, Sam Newhouse was not interested enough to do more than glance at the more than score of newspapers he owned, cared nothing about their editorial positions or how the papers looked.

One of the most interesting journalistic books of 1983 bore the tongue-in-cheek title, *Newspaperman.* Author Richard Meeker, by hard investigative work, had done a biography of S. I. Newhouse. Summing up, Mr. Meeker stressed this facet of the billionaire's career, saying, "For [him] a newspaper was not a newspaper at all. It was a package whose purpose was to carry advertising."[1] When it couldn't get the advertising, S. I. Newhouse had other strategies and he used them all. They worked to build an empire that in 1984 brought in almost $2 billion in revenues. *Advertising Age*'s 1985 report put the Newhouses' Advance Publications (a name taken from his first newspaper success, the *Staten Island Advance*) seventh in the list of companies in the billion-dollar plus group, as follows:[2]

| Rank | Company | Media Revenues |
|------|---------|----------------|
| 1 | ABC Companies | $3,650,000 |
| 2 | CBS, Inc. | 3,340,000 |
| 3 | Time, Inc. | 2,576,000 |
| 4 | RCA Corp. (NBC) | 2,370,900 |
| 5 | Times Mirror Co. | 1,988,300 |
| 6 | Gannett Co. | 1,960,200 |
| 7 | Advance Publications | 1,900,000 |
| 8 | Knight-Ridder Newspapers | 1,664,700 |
| 9 | (Chicago) Tribune Co. | 1,596,700 |
| 10 | Dun & Bradstreet | 1,400,000 |
| 11 | Hearst Corp. | 1,400,000 |
| 12 | New York Times Co. | 1,229,000 |

There are other, differing, rankings which never mention Advance. There is no question that CBS is larger than ABC by at least $1 billion in revenues. I lean to *Advertising Age*'s reports because print and broadcast revenues are separated from "non-media activities" and also because they deal with privately held companies, like Advance. Sam Newhouse must have gloated privately about leading the *New York Times,* since its flagship newspaper may have been the only one he ever really read. This disinterest in editorial content was what led several newspaper families to sell to him. His union-busting record was no black mark where newspaper executives were concerned. His breakthrough into major newspapers came in 1950 when he bought the *Portland Oregonian,* which had a great reputation, but had overextended itself.

Checks with Newhouse editors brought verification that there was never any interference with editorial policies. Later, Sam Newhouse brought the *Oregonian* under ruthless expense control, but the early years encouraged a model that led to other acquisitions. A 1956 expose of racketeers and gambling by Bill Lambert and Wallace Turner won a Pulitzer Prize for local reporting. Editorial autonomy was there, but the cost-control thumbscrews were being applied.

The explosion was to come in 1959, and by coincidence it bore a relationship to what occurred in St. Louis, where the theme of local control had brought him the *St. Louis Globe-Democrat* in 1955.[3] It was the same appeal that year for the *Birmingham News,* along with its satellite, the *Huntsville Times.* S. I. Newhouse didn't seek out either one of them. They sought him. "The decisive reason for selling to Mr. Newhouse," said Clarence B. Hanson, Jr., the publisher in Birmingham, "was his established reputation for insisting that his newspapers be operated locally and independently."[4] So it was in St. Louis, where things were to develop in different patterns and show Sam Newhouse as a master gatekeeper where dollars were concerned.

The Newhouse experience in St. Louis is worth taking a look at. He and his son, S. I., Jr., were able to parlay a $6.5 million investment in a barely profitable newspaper in a city with obvious problems into what now—and for the next fifty years— is a share of profits in a major paper, without the Newhouse family having to do more than deposit dividend checks.

It began when the trust company responsible for the estates of the owning family persuaded 70-year-old Lansing Ray, publisher of the morning and Sunday *Globe-Democrat,* that earnings, running about $300,000 a year, had reached a danger point and that it was only prudent to sell.[5] One part of Mr. Ray's trouble was a relatively new building far too big for the paper's needs. Part, also, was that the *Post Dispatch* always had been the No. 1 advertising choice of the merchants and remained so even though St. Louis was starting to show signs of the central city decay that followed the first wave of the flight to the suburbs. At the time, Mr. Newhouse's mind was set on buying as many newspapers as he could. That the *Globe-Democrat* was the morning paper undoubtedly had an influence on his calculation of its potential. At least two local men well able to meet the asking price were interested, but Mr. Ray vetoed both.[6] He was determined to have the paper continue in the family tradition.

It was the bank that drew Mr. Ray's attention to the Newhouse record of "local autonomy." Mr. Ray needed little selling after Mr. Newhouse said he wanted Mr. Ray to stay as publisher and his nephew, James Burkham, to continue as the president. All Mr. Newhouse proposed to take over were the paper's general business operations—budgeting, purchasing, advertising, and circulation. Mr. Ray's delight was evident in his statement at the time of the sale. "To me," said Mr. Ray, "the vital feature of his operations is that each of his newspapers is complete master of its own destiny."[7] Five months later, Lansing Ray died on his seventy-first birthday and Mr. Newhouse received his first, unanticipated bonus: $1 million from a life insurance policy payable to the company. James Burkham was released and Newhouse executives moved into full control.

Conservative though he was, Lansing Ray might have found the new editorial stridency hard to swallow. In the 1970s, *More,* a magazine of press criticism, published a list of the "ten worst" newspapers in the country and placed three Newhouse papers among the ten: the *Cleveland Plain-Dealer, the New Orleans Times-Picayune,* and the *Globe-Democrat.*[8] *Time* described the *Globe*'s editorial policies as including "cartoons depicting Communist leaders with hands dripping blood and editorials terming Federal Judge William Hungate, who ordered citywide school desegregation, as 'Attila the Hungate.'"[9] Aside from this, however, during the first years under Newhouse management, the paper demonstrated more local coverage enterprise and its circulation had grown.[10]

Things broke apart in 1959. The Newspaper Guild, representing news, clerical, and circulation staff employees, demanded a pension plan comparable to that of the *Post Dispatch.* The union claimed that when Mr. Newhouse took over, there had been 400 people in the union jurisdiction, and that this had dropped to 292.[11] Mr. Newhouse had a long record of hard dealing with unions and he refused. The union went on strike. It lasted 99 days, with the company finally acceding to a pension plan, to be secured by the assets of the Herald Company, the subsidiary of Advance Publications for the St. Louis operation. One week later Mr. Newhouse calmly dropped a bombshell on the *Globe*'s employees and one that raised eyebrows among newspaper executives all across the country.

Well before the strike, the *Post-Dispatch,* concerned about its old building and its aging presses, had made inquiry as to whether Mr. Newhouse was intent on keeping his oversized building. After the strike took hold, Mr. Newhouse had expressed interest in talking and serious discussions had begun. The bombshell was the announcement that he had sold his building and all its equipment to the *Post-Dispatch,* had rented space for the *Globe*'s staffs in an office building two blocks away, and had signed a contract with the *Post-Dispatch* to print the *Globe-Democrat.* The sales price for the transaction was not made public, but local estimates put it at $8 million. The newspaper had proved to be no profit cow, but in four years Sam Newhouse had more than made up the $6.5 million he had invested. Since both newspapers had Sunday editions, obviously the *Globe* had to make an adjustment. Its Sunday sections were printed on Saturday and a four-page green wrapper, updating news and sports, was run off late Saturday night on the press of the *Sporting News.* Later, the pretense of it being a full-fledged Sunday was dropped and it was promoted as a "a weekend edition." Around the country, the transaction had news executives asking each other questions. What was the point of a morning-and-Sunday newspaper selling its building and equipment to its afternoon-and-Sunday rival, and as a direct consequence, placing itself in a less-than-competitive position on Sunday, the most profitable edition of the week? Sam Newhouse had an answer, but he wasn't talking about it just then.

One reason that he wasn't might have been the developing uproar at the *Oregonian.* Sterotypers there objected to a new piece of labor-saving equipment and called a strike. Anticipating that possibility, the Newhouse executives had prepared to publish, no matter who struck. In his detailed account, Mr. Meeker wrote that the Portland strike lasted "five years, four months, and twenty-five days. It cost hundreds of employees their jobs and wrecked countless other lives. It also cost the city the independence of its afternoon paper. But nowhere was the toll greater than at the *Oregonian*." The loss of many of its outstanding editors and reporters, Mr. Meeker wrote, could have been avoided. But Mr. Newhouse "helped his people prepare for the worst, thus assuring trouble; and when it occurred, he chose to let events run their course, knowing that, ultimately, he would be that beneficiary."[12]

That could be read into Mr. Newhouse's long-range view of the situation in St. Louis. The "answer" referred to earlier traced back to 1933, when the two Albuquerque (N.M.) newspapers devised a way to cut costs dramatically and still have the papers survive as separate entities.[13] They had been publishing in separate buildings, each with its own typesetting machinery and costly presses, and each maintaining individual advertising, bookkeeping, and circulation departments and their own fleets of trucks. They decided on single-plant operation, each newspaper using the printing facilities during the individual cycles of operation, and using the same trucks. One business office would operate for the two papers and one advertising staff. What would remain separate and independent were the news and editorial departments, each with its own quarters. That and determining how the profits were to be shared completed the framework. The split was worked on the basis of the records of each newspaper's advertising and circulation revenues. They came to agreement on a satisfactory formula, and then set up a separate corporation to service both newspapers in all the necessary fields, except news and editorial. The cost savings of single-plant efficiency was obvious and there were delighted followers: El Paso in 1936; Nashville in 1937; Evansville in 1938; Tucson in 1940; Tulsa in 1941; Chattanooga in 1942; Madison in 1948; three in 1950—Birmingham, Lincoln, Neb., Fort Wayne; Salt Lake City in 1952; Shreveport in 1953; Franklin-Oil City in 1956; Knoxville in 1957; Charleston in 1958.

More were to come, but Sam Newhouse knew precisely how it worked from his experience in Birmingham. Sometime in

1960, he suggested quietly and privately to the *Post-Dispatch* that the idea was worth exploring for St. Louis. It was duly studied and the financial records were examined. Based on the two newspapers' incomes and costs, they agreed that 70 percent should go to the Pulitzers as the *Post-Dispatch* share, 30 percent to the Newhouse side. It became effective January 1, 1961. A Newhouse lawyer later said the formula also was based on the heavy expenses the Pulitzers would carry in operating the printing plant functions. The agreement, not made public, was to bring criticism from Department of Justice officials.

But bigger things were to come that not even Sam Newhouse could have anticipated. The Department of Justice was to challenge the agreement that the two Tucson papers had devised in 1940, where one of the papers was strong, the other barely hanging on.[14] In 1969, the Supreme Court held the agreement to be in violation of the Sherman Anti-Trust Act in that it had ended "any business or commercial competition between the two newspapers" and that it had brought price fixing, profit pooling, and allocations of market.[15] The decision aroused immediate counter action, led by the American Newspaper Publishers Association. A bill was introduced in Congress, called the "Failing Newspaper Act," but this later was changed to the more felicitious "Newspaper Preservation Act." As could be expected, the bill had strong support from congressmen from those areas where joint operations were already in effect. It was not, however, universally popular in the newspaper industry. Many middle-of-the-road publishers were concerned about appealing to Congress on economic grounds, and worried openly that it could open a door to other types of legislation affecting the press. Nor was it palatable to some congressmen who argued that the new provisions amounted to legitimizing for the press activities that had been judged to be illegal. The Attorney General agreed with them, but the congressional majority was with the publishers. Mr. Nixon was much too shrewd to get caught in the argument and he signed it into law in 1970.[16]

Whether Mr. Newhouse's original checking on St. Louis was thorough will never be known. He was so eager to buy newspapers that he might not have cared. But he could have been told that the city boundaries were fixed for good, ordained by a state legislature always dominated by Missouri's rural sections. When the movement out of the cities became flight, it was to become a case of vast suburban sprawl. The adjourning city of Clayton became a high-rise community, with big department, furniture, and specialty stores. The downtown section of St. Louis sagged. As is true in most American cities, the advertising pot grew, but so did the number of hands reaching out to share in it. The total metropolitan St. Louis zone was recorded by the 1980 census as having a population of roughly 2.5 million. Once the eighth largest city in the nation, St. Louis was down to about 450,000, half of what it once could claim.[17] Both the newspapers by 1980 had seen an erosion of 30 percent in their circulations since 1959. They were competing with 100 or more local newspapers, most weeklies but some of them dailies; a number of local and regional magazines; 7 television stations, not counting the cable input; and 37 radio stations. Reconstruction of the downtown area had begun, but this, as has always been the case, took until mid-1985 to start to show major results.

The *Globe-Democrat* had built a small circulation advantage, but it was never able to cut into the *Post-Dispatch*'s appeal to major advertisers. It can be likened to the *New York Times'* advertising dominance. Major advertisers keep their focus on those with the highest spendable incomes and in St. Louis, the *Post-Dispatch* held that type of audience. In 1983, as example, the "agency" record in St. Louis—"agency" being the term used in all the cities where agreements had been reached under the Newspaper Preservation Act—was to show how this pattern had held. "Combination advertising," ads that ran in both papers, produced 54 per cent of the advertising revenue. *Post*-only advertising brought 36 per cent, with only 10 per cent attributable to *Globe*-only advertising.[18] The disparity had held at those relative levels all through the agency history, and any change seemed improbable. More, the agency was no cornucopia of riches for the two sharing newspapers.

So it made common sense for S. I. Newhouse, Jr., to meet with Joseph Pulitzer, Jr., in January 1982 to talk over mutual problems. What developed out of that talk and future discussions was an agreement that would need approval of the Department of Justice's antitrust division. The *Globe-Democrat* was willing to go out of business, provided that the Herald Company, the Advance Publications' arm, could continue as minority partner in the agency. The theory was simple enough. The Act was passed by Congress as "Newspaper Preservation" legislation. The *Globe-Democrat* had to be a demonstrable failure. By June, the two papers agreed to commission Lexecon, Inc., a Chicago economics consulting firm with strong ties to the University of Chicago's law school. By May 1983 the survey was completed. It covered the national patterns, as well as the St. Louis zone. The record was that suburban growth had worked against more than one major central city newspaper being able to survive. Where St. Louis was concerned, advertisers would benefit if the *Globe* no longer existed. There would be only one major paper in which to place advertising and because of the strong area competition, the *Post-Dispatch* would be compelled to hold to competitive pricing.[19]

In June, the discussions moved to Washington. The critical question: Would the government permit the *Globe* to close and let the agency arrangement stand? It was a new approach under the Act and the antitrust lawyers needed time to study it. First, the records had to be examined. The eventual conclusion was that it was clear the *Globe-Democrat* was failing and there was no hope of it becoming viable. Justice asked the newspaper to try to find a buyer. On November 7, 1983, the *Globe-Democrat* announced that unless a buyer appeared beforehand, it would cease publication on December 31. What was offered for sale was the name and goodwill along with the liability of the 1959 pension plan—$3.2 million as of January 1, 1983. *Not* included was the Herald Company's share in the joint agency. That the *Post-Dispatch* intended to move into the morning field was clear. Thus any prospective buyer faced enormous problems. If any attempt to go morning was contemplated, adequate press capacity would have to be found.

A brief divergence seems indicated about this latter aspect. Two bells rang for me when I read the terms. One rang for mid-

June 1951, when the *Star-Times* was sold to the *Post-Dispatch*. The first arrivals were outside mechanical crews, come to disassemble the typesetting equipment and the presses. The presses left the plant first, one line going to Madison, Wis., the other line to a Southern newspaper. The second bell sent me back to Mr. Meeker's biography. He had written an account of Sam Newhouse's first try at owning a newspaper of his own in 1920. With borrowed money for his half, and his lawyer-employer's half, he bought the unsteady *Fitchburg* (Mass.) *News* for $15,000.

The experience was unpleasant. The townspeople didn't care for him; he didn't have much of a paper; a fire razed his offices. He went to see the owner of the dominant *Sentinel* and sold him on a deal. If he bought the *News* for $15,000 and folded it, the *Sentinel* could raise street sales prices and get its money back in a year, and make even more by raising ad rates. The *Sentinel* owner speculated about new competition. Sam Newhouse's answer was that he would take the printing press and printing equipment out of town with him, along with the contract for newsprint. The owner agreed and paid the $15,000. The Bayonne newspaper needed the press and equipment, and the advantageous paper contract. Everyone made a handsome profit. Many things changed in the period from the 1920s to 1980s,[20] but Sam Newhouse's sons had learned the fundamental lessons well. One of them plainly was that even in a losing situation there can be ways to win.

St. Louis was such a case. There was community confusion all through November and December 1983, stretching into January 1984. Late in January, Joseph Pulitzer, Jr., held an unusual press conference. He said he wanted to dispel the "fog, smog and hot air" that had come with the *Globe-Democrat*'s announcement it was giving up. But there had come a surprise. A buyer had surfaced—30-year-old Jeffrey M. Gluck of Columbia, Mo., former student at the University of Missouri, who at the end of 1982 had bought the old *Saturday Review* magazine. On December 23, he and the Herald Company made an announcement that they had signed a contract. It wasn't to hold because the agreement included a waiver that would have prevented employees from suing the Herald Company. Many questions were raised about his financial capacity. He refused to divulge his resources, saying, "If you're privately held, it's your own business. There is no public right to know. The money is there and that's all that matters." Repeatedly, he accused the Newhouse interests of trying to avoid selling the *Globe* to anyone. It came together under double pressure—from an injunction suit filed by city officials to prevent the closing of the *Globe* and from Justice Department warnings that it might have to take the matter to court. Finally, the Herald Company agreed to pay severance benefits to as many as 120 employees who left the newspaper before or by February 25. Mr. Gluck agreed to assume responsibility for all others. Apparently, he paid less than $1 million, payable in installments, for the name and goodwill. He was reported to have made a first payment of $50,000.

All through this period the newspapers and the broadcasting stations in the area gave extraordinary coverage to the struggle and the implications.[21] Yet, oddly, St. Louis editors seemed not to have remembered during the excitement that, earlier in 1983, two family-owned St. Louis suburban newspaper chains had been sold to Ingersoll Publications of Lakeville, Conn., for $80 million. Ralph Ingersoll who died two years later called the deal "well worth it." So may have been the feeling of the Newhouse brothers. Their Herald Company emerged from the turmoil with a fifty-year minority partnership in the Pulitzer-operated *Post Dispatch*, with no voice over either the business or editorial affairs and obligated only to pay half of capital investment exceeding $500,000, with the proviso that neither party could sell its interest without the other's formal, written agreement—a "silent partner," in Mr. Pulitzer's words. But, then, old Sam Newhouse always took a silent role, other than making sure about the cash flow.

For his part, Mr. Gluck began newspaper life struggling to find a way to succeed. At the outset, with three different arrangements for press runs, he went head-to-head against the *Post-Dispatch*'s new big morning. In March, the *St. Louis Journalism Review* surveyed the two morning papers and reported that the

*Post* was clearly superior in every measure. . . . Right now the *Globe* has an incredibly steep uphill climb on its hands." At the end of March, Mr. Gluck halted Sunday competition, calling it "a mistake," and moved back to a Saturday weekend paper. He announced and started a new afternoon paper, the *St. Louis Evening News,* but it lasted only four weeks. During that period, Mr. Gluck confirmed that his *Saturday Review* was for sale and there was a transfer of ownership shortly thereafter. It was a difficult year for him. Late payments for printing bills, medical insurance premiums and a break with a delivery firm made it clear he was fighting cash flow problems.[22] Meanwhile, *Post-Dispatch* circulation was rising and the *Globe-Democrat*'s was falling. In early 1985, Mr. Gluck said "We are making it. But we take whatever painful measures it takes to make sure that we're making a profit." As the *Christian Science Monitor* put it, "Still, his reasoning flies in the face of the common wisdom that there is simply not enough advertising to support two daily papers."[23]

According to *Advertising Age*'s 1985 rankings, the Pulitzer Publishing Co. looked quite able to wear down the competition. It was No. 46 on the list with revenues of $256 million from its St. Louis and Tucson papers, and seven TV and two radio stations; and in June 1985 bought the 300,000-circulation Lerner chain in Chicago—45 weeklies, 4 Sundays, and 3 free "shoppers."

Even so, the Pulitzers well knew they were not in the same league with the Newhouse family's Advance Publications. Advance is deep into cable and video operations all across the country; into magazines under its Conde Nast umbrella, which produced in 1985 almost $500 million in revenue (*Vogue, Glamour, Gourmet, House & Garden, Mademoiselle,* and *Vanity Fair*), and owns such book publishing firms as Random House, Knopf, Ballantine, Modern Library and Vintage. It grew more late in 1984 when S. I. Newhouse, Jr., paid $25.5 million for 17 percent of New Yorker Magazine, Inc., and still more in March 1985 when he paid $142 million for the remaining 83 percent. There were strong words of protest from members of the *New Yorker*'s staff,[24] but given the family record, it seemed unlikely there would be any interference with editorial policy.

This isn't to say that the Newhouse family is without problems. The biggest is a long-continuing dispute with the Internal Revenue Service over the size of Sam Newhouse's estate. The IRS put it at more than $1 billion and the family has been fighting the appraisal.[25] It is trivial by comparison, but there also is a legal problem in Cleveland, an important Newhouse holding since 1967 and more so now because its *Plain Dealer* there not only is Ohio's largest paper, but the only daily in the city since July 1982, when the *Cleveland Press* went out of business—paid by the Newhouses to fold, according to suits filed.[26] Federal Judge Ann Aldrich in Cleveland wrote an opinion in March 1985 saying that "a jury could find, as a matter of fact, that Plain Dealer and Newhouse wanted to assure that the *Press* went out of business and that Plain Dealer acquired a newspaper monopoly."[27] The opinion held that the Newhouses paid $22.5 million to a company that had paid only $8 million for the struggling *Press* only 20 months earlier.

This aside, the Newhouses have not had to fret about any hint of the family discord (or lack of interest by heirs) that has brought on the sale of so many independent newspapers to the chains. Richard Wald, an ABC-TV vice-president, is author of the quip, "The single greatest force for the distribution of wealth is the children of the wealthy." John Morton, the perceptive analyst of the newspaper industry, agrees. "By the third or fourth generation," he said, "company shares usually are dispersed widely among cousins, in-laws and shirttail relatives, many of whom have little sense of allegiance to the family business."[28]

Whatever any of the reasons for selling, by mid-1985 there were fewer than thirty American cities that still had competing newspapers. And in twenty-two of them, those operating were doing so under the "agency" provisions of the Newspaper Preservation Act. The sellout syndrome also seemed at work in the book publishing field, but it was less significant because for every merger a number of new book firms spring up. Benjamin Compaine, executive director of Harvard's Program on Information Resources Policy and editor of the book, *Who Owns the Media,* said, "Book publishing is a very diverse industry. It's a less concentrated industry than it was forty years ago."[29]

One other arm of communications—magazines—not only

is diversified, but is in constant turnover. Certainly, there are giants, but the 1985 N. W. Ayer Directory figure of 11,090 magazines being published in the United States speaks volumes about entrepreneurial activity in the field. Here is a table on top-tencirculations, as recorded by the Magazine Publishers Association:

| Rank | Magazine | Circulation |
|------|----------|-------------|
| 1 | Reader's Digest | 17,866,798 |
| 2 | TV Guide | 17,115,233 |
| 3 | Modern Maturity | 10,770,668[a] |
| 4 | National Geographic | 10,392,548 |
| 5 | Better Homes & Gardens | 8,058,839 |
| 6 | Family Circle | 6,920,333 |
| 7 | Women's Day | 6,517,684 |
| 8 | McCall's | 6,311,011 |
| 9 | Good Housekeeping | 5,184,559 |
| 10 | Ladies Home Journal | 5,058,538 |

[a]Listed just under Modern Maturity by the MPA is NRTA/AARP News, a monthly newsletter with a circulation of 10,421,921, going to approximately the same audience.

Two things strike me instantly about these numbers. One has to do with the senior citizen bloc. The other is that six of the top ten are directed to "women's interests." Both are areas which too many newspaper gatekeepers, particularly, have shrugged away as unimportant.

Going back to the 100 companies on Advertising Age's 1985 list, only seven of the news organizations in the daily newspaper field did not yet have a stake in broadcasting, and one of them, Rupert Murdoch's News America Publishing, had moved in mid-1985 for a stake in 20th Century-Fox Film Corporation and to buy Metromedia's seven major-market TV stations.

It was hard keeping up with the moving and shaking. It is pertinent to mention the chase for the Des Moines Register & Tribune, Gannett outbidding all others with a $200 million offer. Discussing the the stepped-up pace of communications industry turnovers, Robert B. Ladd, a publishing analyst in Chicago, offered an intriguing insight into what fuels the acquisition fervor. Mr. Ladd estimated that the $200 million for

*The Register* would dilute Gannett profits for 1985 by five cents a share.[30] For all his nerve, young Mr. Gluck in St. Louis had plunged into a game of high-stakes poker with what looked like a very thin bankroll, playing against professionals comfortable with million-dollar gambles. *Newsweek* added a fillip about Allen H. Neuharth, Gannett's energetic chairman. Asked once whether the company name was pronounced "Gan*nett*" or "Gan*nett*," Mr. Neuharth's reply was quoted as, "The accent is on the net."[31]

Take what is contained thus far in this chapter as an overview of one part of print journalism as it moves into the last fifteen years of the twentieth century. The steep rise in values put on newspaper properties came primarily because of monopoly—owning the only game in a city. When I became president of the Wilmington (Del.) *News-Journal,* the morning and evening combination had a valuation put on it by a leading broker of $24.4 million. My one economic contribution was adding a Sunday paper. Two years later, Gannett won ownership with a $60 million bid. Gannett needs no broker or bank counseling, but in recent times some of the major transactions have been promoted and orchestrated by the big investment firms.

When we turn to television, we find companies more driven than any other branch of communications to produce ever-growing profits. That it impacts on the journalistic approach surfaced as 1984 was coming to an end. "I am heartbroken," exclaimed Richard Salant, former president of CBS News, in commenting on the network's announcement that it had hired Phyllis George, a former Miss America, to be a co-anchor on the "CBS Morning News." Calling it demeaning, Mr. Salant said, "If they want to do that, put the show in the entertainment division or the record division or the toy division. But get it out of news. Once we start playing those games, we lose all our credibility."[32] The reports put Miss George's salary at around $700,000 a year.

That wasn't surprising. Led by ABC's million-dollar deal with Barbara Walters in 1976, all three big networks escalated salaries for anchors to figures matching those of movie box office stars. Bill Leonard, Mr. Salant's immediate successor as CBS News president, also was candid about it. "It's very difficult to make a case for an anchor being a simple journalist when he earns five times as much as the President of the United States," he said. "This is nothing against Dan Rather or Barbara Walters or Bill Kurtis, but it does not further the sincere effort of those who believe that broadcast journalism is as legitimate and serious an arm of journalism as the print media—that it is not show business."[33]

What we hear in this is the TV editors' version of the APME study, *Editors and Stress.* The Messrs. Chancellor, Cronkite, Kuralt, Leonard, Moyers, Salant and hundreds of others are, in their own varying ways, expressing personal anguish over the chasm that divides their strong individual public service aspirations from their corporations' drives to produce the profits that keep stockholders happy and the takeover raiders at bay. This means grubbing for audience—and that translates to escapist entertainment. It is in sharp contrast with Edward Murrow's view that without strong public service as the basic principle, it was all "merely lights and wires in a box." As is clear, there are a number of *good* newspapers, TV stations and magazines, even though they are a minority of the total. One major depressing aspect of the incessant banker-broker-lawyer acquisition pressure can be observed in the lessened number of top-quality documentary programs. Over the years, TV has produced many brilliant and informative documentaries but there are fewer as times goes on. It is in no way a dearth of talent for TV has producers, reporters, photographers, writers, and film editors who have enormous skills. What they lack is access to time on air—and, as Mr. Moyers made plain, in prime time to provide the greatest informational value for the nation's citizens.

When people in TV journalism evoke a hero image, it is that of Mr. Murrow (1908–1965). In a speech to radio and TV news directors in Chicago in 1958, Murrow told of President Eisenhower delivering a television address to the nation. "He was discoursing on the possibility or probability of war between this nation and the Soviet Union and Communist China—a reasonably compelling subject. Two networks, CBS and NBC, delayed that broadcast for an hour and fifteen minutes. If this decision was dictated by anything other than financial reasons, the networks didn't deign to explain those reasons. That hour-and-fifteen-minute delay, by the way, is about twice the time required for an ICBM to travel from the Soviet Union to the United States. It is difficult to believe that this decision was made by men who love, respect and understand news." He went on to say, "I am frightened by the imbalance, the constant striving to reach the largest possible audience for everything. . . . Unless we get up off our fat surpluses and recognize that television in the main is being used to distract, delude, amuse and insulate us, then television and those who finance it, those who look at it and those who work at it, may see a totally different picture too late."[34]

In his provocative book, *Due To Circumstances Beyond Our Control,* Fred Friendly's story of his leaving CBS, he wrote of a debate with William S. Paley, builder and chairman of the network, over the effect news costs had on earnings. Mr. Paley had argued that if management failed to maintain growth and profits, it risked losing control of the company. "Then," wrote Mr. Friendly, "the chairman of the board, who owns over a million and a half shares of CBS stock, was silent for a moment; looking at [Frank] Stanton, he said, "I suppose the mistake we made was in ever going public."[35]

Mr. Friendly's date on that exchange was October 3, 1965. Twenty years later, with the corporate raiders in high gear, it was no surprise to read of one big communications company after another—each of which once saw great advantage in "going public"—plunging into aggressive campaigns to buy back public shares, just as CBS did in fighting Ted Turner.

Nothing in communications has been under more continuous scrutiny over the years than the ratings of what viewers watch. There has been instant equation of those ratings on earnings projections by stock market analysts and their thoughts and opinions appear regularly. After all, each rating point translates to approximately $50 million in advertising revenues over the year. The money market analysts are doing what they are paid to do for those who invest in public companies. In the case of television, the end result is persistent pressure on the quality of programming.

The agreement of ABC to be sold to Capital Cities Communications in March 1985 for more than $3.5 billion came as a stunning surprise. The surprise was legitimate. It was the first change in ownership for a major network; other than in the oil industry, it was the biggest acquisition in corporate history; the company taking over was a fourth the size of ABC; there had been no leak whatever about the months-long discussions and negotiations. And yet—

There was a spate of stories all through the last four months of 1984 about ABC being the target of a takeover. One article in the *Wall Street Journal* said, "If ABC's ratings don't improve, it may face additional hostility from Wall Street."[36] ABC's whole programming strategy was examined in a Sunday *New York Times* story in December, and one sentence referred to the network constituting "a continually tempting takeover target." This *Times* story reported market analysts as saying that ABC's "worst mistake by far was the shift away from comic programs appealing to young families."[37] It must be hell to be an editing executive in television working under such economic pressures.

The new CCC-ABC operation may be an improvement because of the skills of chief executive Thomas S. Murphy. His record has been one of running "tight ships," but also supporting high-quality operations. One of his key partners in the ABC deal was Warren Buffett, the Omaha financier, who also is committed to good journalism. He owned the *Omaha Sun* when it won a Pulitzer Prize in 1973 for its bold coverage of Boy's Town. Both Messrs. Murphy and Buffett, interestingly, were strong financial supporters of the National News Council.

Merger fever shows no sign of abating, particularly in the field of communications. Assessing the scene in May 1985, *U.S. News & World Report* commented: "Wall Street has discovered that ownership of TV stations is tantamount to running a money machine that churns out profits in good times and bad. Helping to fuel the frenzy is the laissez-faire stance of the Federal Communications Commission, which, under Chairman Mark Fowler, has opened the door to a video revolution on two levels—the rapid turnover of local stations and hostile takeovers of powerful networks, including Ted Turner's recent bid for CBS." *U.S. News* termed TV profits "almost unbelievable" and cited as an example the sale of a Tampa station to Taft Broadcasting of Cincinnati for $197.5 million—a station that the seller, Gulf Broadcast, had purchased for $17.6 million only six years earlier.[38]

As the *Wall Street Journal* noted: "If the fight has been long and expensive for CBS and Turner, their lawyers and investment bankers will come out of it richer."[39] Yes, indeed. Reporting its 1985 second-quarter operating figures to the Securities and Exchange Commission, Turner Broadcasting put its thwarted-bid expenses at $18.2 million. E. F. Hutton & Co. received $8 million in advance. On the CBS side, Morgan Stanley got $10.4 million for the CBS buy-back placement.

Perhaps of more far-reaching importance was the move by Rupert Murdock, already half-owner of 20th Century Fox, to buy the Metromedia TV chain for $2 billion. It involved Mr. Murdoch applying for and receiving U.S. citizenship since FCC rules bar foreigners from owing more than 20 percent of a broadcast license. It also meant divestiture of his newspapers in New York and Chicago since the rules do not allow ownership of both newspapers and broadcast stations in the same city. What the deal appeared to offer was the creation of a fourth network, at least in the area of entertainment to begin with. Metromedia owned seven major TV outlets in New York, Chicago, Los Angeles, Washington, Dallas, Houston, and Boston. John Kluge, owner of Metromedia, agreed to sell WCVB in Boston to Hearst for $450 million before his selling to 20th Century-Fox. This spared Mr. Murdoch the prospect of having to sell his *Boston Herald*. Mr. Murdoch called the other six "the choice group if you are looking for a network by next year. But we would hope to become a fourth force over the next few years."[40] *Time* speculated that he might "have an even grander plan: to build a global TV empire linking Europe, America and Australia." He already was operating a satellite station supplying English-language programs to almost two million homes in Britain and Europe.

He quickly sold *Village Voice* and there appeared no barrier to selling his *New York Post* and *Chicago Sun-Times*. The *Sun-Times* has been marginally profitable. The *Post* has been a steady loser, even though circulation has risen sharply. Estimates have put the annual loss at $10 million. An apocryphal story has depicted Mr. Murdoch going to a major department store president in New York to question why the store was not advertising in the *Post* in light of its large circulation gains. The store chief has been portrayed as replying, "Rupert, you don't understand. Your readers are *our* shoplifters." As of mid-1985, the chief potential purchasers were regarded as being the Tribune Company (owner of the *Daily News*) and the Times-Mirror Company (owner of *Newsday*, which is now pressing to establish a firm foothold in the New York City market).[41] If Mr. Murdoch sold to either, it clearly would mean the end for the *Post*. All either the *News* or *Newsday* would want is an unimpeded run for the circulation and the *Post's* press capacity. It would be the last of New York's blatantly sensationalist tabloids, many of which passed from the scene despite huge circulations. It may work elsewhere (England, and perhaps several other countries), but the record in the United States is not one in which noisy flamboyance in daily publishing has ever turned a lasting profit. If there is a better argument to be made for quality control in journalism I'd like to hear it.

There are network executives who believe healthy changes are to come. They think that within the span of the next few years, one of the networks is going to go to a full hour of evening news and that the others will promptly follow, no matter how loud the affiliates protest. Let us all hope they are talking out of inside knowledge, and not wishful thinking.

Old Sam Newhouse was of a somewhat different cut than most of today's entrepreneurs in print and broadcasting. He shared with no one. He built one of the major communications empires as a purely private preserve. He surely would have been pleased by S. I. Jr.'s handling of the *Globe-Democrat* problem and particularly of the *New Yorker* deal. It probably could be assumed he would have been displeased by the IRS's position on valuing his estate. Chances are he would have viewed that as an invasion of his personal privacy.

Certainly, he would have understood the new business environment in which the money market people have come to play such major roles. As he did, they are not concerned about how the newspapers, magazines and broadcasting stations they hustle to buy and sell handle news and editorial opinion. For them, the business of communications is no different than dealing with automobiles, computers, food, toothpaste, soap, shoes, or anything else. It wasn't their doing, by any stretch, but they certainly have helped in making obsolete so many of the basic values that built journalism into one of the major institutions in the American society. Time, as always, brought hundreds of changes, many for the better. Some, unhappily, as with the soul of journalism, not always for the better.

If there is hope, I am afraid little of it will come out of the brokers, bankers, and lawyers. Quality in journalism is nothing that concerns them. The one freedom that registers with them automatically is the freedom to make money in handling communications properties. There seems little point in raising the subject of journalistic obligations with them. They probably would react with genuine surprise. "What's journalism got to do with it?" they might ask. It reminds me of one excellent communications lawyer's quip about some colleagues in the law. "They'll defend you right down to your last dollar," he said, and laughed uproariously.[42]

## CHAPTER 12
# The Gathering Storm

ONE OF THE OLDEST of questions must be, "Knowing what you know now, would you . . . ?" The instant answer is yes. For all of the arrogance, hypocrisy, and anti-intellectualism that have tarnished the great dream of Jefferson and Madison, for many of us journalism remains the most challenging and inspiring of all callings. Several signs point to the next ten to twenty years as possibly being the most crucial for journalism to survive as a freestanding entity. My generation has lived through an astonishing series of history-making developments. Now we find ourselves with what may be one of the biggest stories of our lifetime—difficult to deal with because its beginnings remain hazy, all the ramifications have not yet unfolded, and because it is subject to constant reinterpretation.

The story centers on the massive change in the attitudes of the American people toward their government, their leaders, and the major institutions in the society. Alvin Toffler, the talented futurist, defined it in 1971 as "a special moment in history . . . a system break. . . . Sweeping changes are roaring through the society and to a considerable degree are out of control. The reality is that the order is breaking up."[1]

We see it in scores of polarizations over issues: crime and the criminal justice system, drugs, poverty, welfare, abortion, nuclear power, education, pollution, public and private corruption, child abuse, terrorism, equal opportunity, invasion of privacy, on and on. Once national problems like these were not so clear and the extent of public feeling was debatable. But no longer is this the case with skilled public polling reflecting attitudes with remarkable accuracy.

Polling in the scientific sense began in 1935. The pioneers were George Gallup, Elmo Roper, and Archibald Crosley. All three came out of marketing research. The Roper polls began appearing in *Fortune,* and Gallup and Crosley polls were syndicated to a number of newspapers. The *Literary Digest* dug its grave in the 1936 presidential campaign between Franklin D. Roosevelt and Alfred M. Landon. At the same time, by almost a 90 percent majority, the country's publishers and editors were helping to undercut the self-created myth of newspaper credibility by ridiculing Mr. Roosevelt's chances for reelection.

Two and a half years before his death in 1971, Elmo Roper in a long interview described both the public attitudes and the naivete of editors.[2] "People had had four years of Roosevelt," he said, "and had made up their minds that he was a sort of near-God or sort of a near-devil and they all knew what they were going to do anyhow and the sentiment changed very little from the week after the conventions. The *Literary Digest* continued to predict a Landon victory. They were using telephone interviews. There was nothing like the saturation of telephones then as there is now and in addition it was still the depression and a lot of people who once had telephones were having them disconnected. So they [the *Digest*] were missing almost entirely the bottom segment, the very people who comprised the great wealth of Roosevelt's strength. But you couldn't tell the *Digest* people that. They were absolutely certain they were right. They were derisive about these young upstarts. Newspaper editors by and large across the country looked upon us as interlopers. They had been the people who told the readers what the people think."

Mr. Landon carried only Maine and Vermont.

As Mr. Roper said in 1968, the result made professional polling instantly respectable. "The three of us became instant heroes. We were telling the same story and this was important. And we weren't claiming perfection. We were admitting we were learning. There was an awful lot that we had to learn in the area of question asking. You can ask a question in such a way as to get any answer you want. Unconsciously, we all did that occasionally."

This brief background is useful if only to underline the degrees of expertise that have come into use in the half century of polling since 1935, and why professional testing—carefully weighted by size of sample and census tracts, along with economic status, age, political bent, religion, and other balancing—can be relied upon to be reasonably accurate in gauging public moods. Not all polls, by any means. As in everything, there always will be quacks, some because of the gullibility of so many untrained gatekeepers in journalism. These seem unaware of the importance of insisting on knowing who did the polling and how (personal, mail, telephone?), wording of questions, the size of the sample.[3] This kind of care was being taken by the top two score newspapers in 1984, but probably 95 percent of the nation's newspapers and broadcast stations still have no idea that standards exist to protect the public. Thus, some news organizations report as fact what often is propaganda. The professionals in the field miss by some degree on occasion, but not over the long pull, or they would no longer be in business. To note how close good well-trained surveying becomes, the Gallup Poll in its final 1984 report said Ronald Reagan would draw 59 percent of the vote. That is precisely what it was. Some others were only a few points off.

There is general agreement among social scientists that the late 1950s marked a high point of citizen trust in the society. The turn in public attitudes apparently began around 1963 and 1964 and misgivings have deepened with each major episode. The Vietnam war. President John F. Kennedy's assassination in 1963. The Watts riots in 1965, leaving 35 dead and the Los Angeles suburb a shambles. The campus uprisings. Riots in other cities: Newark, 26 dead and 1,500 injured; Detroit, 40 dead, 2,000 injured, 5,000 left homeless; torches put to downtown Washington minutes after the bulletin April 4, 1968, that Martin Luther King had been assassinated. Stores looted, trashed, burned. Before 1968 was over Robert F. Kennedy was assassinated.

It was not only an American trauma. Between 1963 and 1984, a total of thirteen chiefs of state were slain, including Hendrik Verwoerd of South Africa, King Faisal of Saudi Arabia, Park Chun Hee of South Korea, Anwar Sadat of Egypt, Bashir Gemayel of Lebanon, and Indira Gandhi of India. During that period, Americans, in increasing numbers, were enlisting in causes: to curb nuclear proliferation; for women's rights; for quotas to provide jobs for minority citizens; and the many others so well known.

In 1977, Daniel Yankelovich, social scientist turned pollster, reported, "Trust in government declined dramatically from almost 80 percent in the late 1950s to about 33 percent in 1976. . . . More than 61 percent of the electorate believe there is something morally wrong in the country. . . . The change is simply massive."[4] Mr. Yankelovich's findings were supported by the reports of the Center for Political Studies at the University of Michigan, which had been posing "trust in government" questions since 1958. One Center query has been whether citizens believe government officials are honest. After the Watergate scandals the figure for believing public officials *dishonest* rose to 45 percent. Strikingly, 1980 returns showed a rise to 47 percent.[5]

One more point about all this is that journalism meanwhile was acting oblivious to the fact its own performance was under attack. As a result, it now runs the risk of having its First Amendment freedom challenged if a full constitutional convention was to come into being. By no means is this to suggest that such a convention would be called with an openly declared intention of reviewing sections of the Bill of Rights. What is a fact is that the possibility of a constitutional convention exists so strongly as to have brought teams of scholars into coordinated study, under the sponsorship of the American Historical Association and the American Political Science Association. Should the legislatures of two-thirds of the states (34) petition Congress to call such a convention, Congress would have no recourse but to authorize the procedure. By September 1985, thirty-two state legislatures had passed such petitions. California would have become the thirty-third in November 1984 had not that state's supreme court struck from the ballot a proposition that, if passed, would have required the legislature, under threat of pay and benefits suspension, to join in petitioning Congress for a constitutional convention. As was the case in other states, the central thrust was for an amendment to bind the federal government to a balanced budget.

The reason for the concern of the two scholarly organizations is that there is nothing in the Constitution that restricts what subject matter could be considered by a convention. An introductory report, *The Constitutional Convention as an Amending Device,* was published in 1981. The preface said, "Critics of the never-used convention method worry that it is fraught with hazards. . . . They believe that . . . its delegates could add other special-interest questions. . . . The many divisive issues include abortion, busing, civil rights, pornography, drugs, treaty and war powers, welfare, and women's rights. Potentially limitless agendas and a convention of endless length can be imagined. There is also the derivative fear that no check will exist on the conduct or product of such a convention. . . . Only popular voting in states will determine ratification. . . . The balloters must accept or reject whatever terms the convention prescribes. In short, the expressed fear is that democracy will generate a runaway national constitutional convention unlike anything known in American governing processes."[6]

In the light of what is presently known about public attitudes, is it not likely that any representative group of delegates would be certain to include some individuals determined to vent anger against the press and to propose some restrictive language? The fact that no legislature had petitioned Congress with that in mind would be of no consequence. If any such proposal ever survived a convention debate, the press would find itself blind-sided—and facing a national referendum on the freedoms so casually taken for granted by so many journalists for so long.

How justified are the fears expressed? The late Senator Sam J. Ervin, who earlier had been on North Carolina's supreme court and was a Constitutional scholar in his own right, twice persuaded the Senate to vote unanimously for a proposal stipulating that once a convention was mandated, the petitioning states would be required to agree upon an agenda of the subject matter to be considered by the convention.[7] The Ervin bills in 1971 and 1973 never emerged from House committees.

However, with the possibility growing of a mandated call for a convention, Senate action resumed in the late spring of 1985. The Senate subcommittee on the Constitution voted unanimously for a balanced budget amendment to be submitted to the states. If the move would muster Congress' approval, there would be seven years for the legislatures of three-fourth of the states to ratify and the nation would have a new amendment. With only two states needed to bring a full convention into being automatically, it seemed clear that the senators were seeking to avoid the prospect the scholars warned about: a convention "unlike anything known in American governing processes."

That this was on their minds was evident by the subcommittee simultaneously voting out a bill establishing procedures for calling and convening conventions. The proposal stipulated a 585-member convention (the same size as the House and Senate combined). The bill stipulated a six months' life for any such convention unless Congress voted an extension. Reflecting Senator Ervin's thoughts, a convention could not consider amendments differing from the states' calls for the issue or issues to be considered. Legal scholars promptly said Congress lacked the constitutional authority to control the agenda and it seemed probable that, if passed, the proposal would meet a challenge that could be settled only by Supreme Court review.

Apart from this skirmishing, some polling organizations have tried periodically to keep abreast of the public mood. The Roper firm, headed by Burns Roper, Elmo's son, has posed four questions regularly. In 1979, 43 percent felt no need for fundamental changes, 5 percent did not know, or did not answer. But 37 percent said the Constitution should be thoroughly revised and 15 percent said the country needed a new form of government. Add them up. As of 1979, 52 percent either were for a new form of governance or for thorough revision.[8] Late in 1984, the Gallup Poll reported that while memories of Watergate might be fading, public attitudes toward the nation's major institutions were no higher than they were in 1974, and in some cases, had fallen. In 1979, 51 percent of the public approved of newspaper performance. By 1984, this figure had dropped to 38 percent.[9]

Earlier, the Gallup Poll had been commissioned to measure the public mood by the First Amendment Congress, an organization founded in 1979 by the nine principal print and broadcast associations and the two major wire services. Reporting in 1980, George Gallup, Jr., said, "The press in America is operating in an environment that is increasingly indifferent—and to some extent, hostile—to the cause of a free press. . . . The survey shows Americans leaning heavily, 2 to 1, to the view that present curbs on the press are not strict enough." He urged "greater efforts to give journalists . . . a renewed sense of the need for professional standards."[10] Later that same year, the Public Agenda Foundation issued its survey report, *The Speaker and The Listener,* and Mr. Yankelovich, as president of the foundation, wrote a preface saying he believed that "freedom of expression will face a serious challenge in the decade ahead. General social forces will produce new problems . . . and the First Amendment itself may well be subjected to reexamination."[11]

The documentation is so strong one would expect even confirmed optimists to agree that we might be approaching a "clear and present danger" period. Yet in many discussions, few leaders in journalism seemed willing to accept the possibility. One of the few who did, A. M. Rosenthal of the *New York Times,* nodded glumly. "If we had to be voted on today," he said, "we'd lose—and lose big. I've thought about it a lot and decided there isn't anything I can do about it in direct terms. It seems to me it's a problem for the lawyers and the legal scholars. My job, I think, is to try to put out the best paper I can. If we do it right, my hope is that it will stand as one of the main arguments and examples of why we need the First Amendment left intact."[12] It is a valid posture—for the *Times,* and for papers like the *Los Angeles Times,* the *Wall Street Journal,* and the *Washington Post,* the country's four outstanding newspapers.

Caught in the constant ratings competition, those directing the television networks' news divisions seemed ambivalent about the issue. During 1984 they were warned by Burns Roper that their insistence on continuing the increasingly criticized practice of exit polling was "a foolish decision."

> The networks are running a risk to themselves and, possibly more important, to the nation as a whole in persisting in making early projections. I do not seriously think that

the First Amendment is going to get revised and that freedom of the press will be knocked out of it. However, if there is a rising tide of public indignation over what people view as excesses of the press, it is quite possible that we will see court interpretations that define freedom of the press in more restricted and limited terms. This can constitute a kind of tightening censorship—even if the First Amendment is never touched.

Mr. Roper pointed out that the state of Washington had passed a law making exit polling so difficult and potentially so inaccurate that it could not be done, and that Florida, Massachusetts, and Hawaii were moving in the same direction. "It is not exit polling per se that these states are objecting to," said Mr. Roper. "It is the reporting of exit poll results prior to the close of the polling places. . . . It is the presumed interference with the election process they object to."[13]

Congressional resolutions urged the broadcasters not to announce a winner until all the polls closed. The networks issued statements couched in high ethical terms, but on election night did what journalists have traditionally done. They went chasing the scoops. CBS's Dan Rather declared Mr. Reagan the winner at 8:01 P.M. Eastern time (5 P.M., West Coast), and the others followed in quick order. *Broadcasting* magazine pointed out that the push to proclaim the winner had stripped suspense out of the evening, resulting in the networks having had "a tough time holding their own against the offerings of independent and cable TV systems."[14]

Roone Arledge, head of ABC News, had commented that the networks knew the exit polling results "by noon or 1 o'clock or so on election day. Editorially, the *New York Times* asked some key questions: "Yet, the networks don't rush to trumpet their findings till evening. So the question for them remains: If you are willing to delay reporting the results to exit polls for hours, why not wait another hour or two or three to protect the democratic process? You practice restraint now; why not real restraint?"[15] Post-election, Mr. Arledge retreated to embracing the Frank Stanton formula, saying the real answer rested with the Congress. It should, he said, "pass a law—whatever it takes, so that there is a common closing of the polls across the country." It wasn't the networks' most brilliant journalistic period.

If any significant documentation of the trends in public stance was needed, it was coming from jury actions in libel suits against newspapers and broadcasters. What had happened in the libel field in the past two decades had been stunning. When the Supreme Court issued its 1964 decision in *New York Times v. Sullivan*, lawyers hailed it as a landmark victory for the press. The case arose out of the civil rights movement. An advertisement in the *Times* described alleged police violence against demonstrators in Montgomery, Ala., who had protested discrimination. One of two suits brought against the *Times* was by L. B. Sullivan, a Montgomery commissioner. The jury found for Mr. Sullivan and awarded him $500,000. Alabama's supreme court upheld the judgment.

For well more than a century, the United States Supreme Court had held that the First Amendment did not cover libel; that the press was subject to common law suits and had to prove either that statements were true or were privileged (that is, open to public dissemination). *Times v. Sullivan* was a total reversal of that concept. The new formulation held that "debate on public issues should be uninhibited, robust, and wide open." The new position was that an official could recover damages only if he could prove actual malice, defined as "knowledge that it was false or with reckless disregard of whether it was false or not."[16] Subsequently, the Court expanded the doctrine beyond public officials to cover "public figures."[17]

On the face of it, the lawyers who proclaimed the press virtually freed of major libel burdens seemed to be on firm ground. It turned out to be more the consistency of quicksand. Libel suits by public figures increased sharply in number. Arguments about "why?" have ranged from bitter criticism of the surge in expensive litigation of all kinds to the press having overrun the bounds of prudence through arrogance.

There was no argument, however, about the striking differences in cases involving the press decided by juries and those where judges made the decisions. In non-jury cases, the press won 75 percent of the cases. But when juries were involved, the press lost almost 90 percent of the time.[18] However, on post-trial motions and appeals, many jury verdicts were reversed by judges and most large damage awards were substantially reduced. All of it has been staggeringly costly. More, the press now worries about what may lie ahead as openings come on the Supreme Court. The Center for Business and Economic Communication at American University said in mid-1984 that "press critics are mounting a new assault in the hope and belief that the Supreme Court in the not-too-distant future will be receptive to their arguments that *Times v. Sullivan* and its progeny afford the press too much libel protection."[19]

None of us have yet heard the last of the two court battles that never should have taken place—involving two generals on the attack against two giants in journalism: *Ariel Sharon v. Time* magazine and *William C. Westmoreland v. CBS*. From the start, veteran journalists could see only headaches ahead for the press as a whole. Fred Friendly expressed it well long before the trials started. "Even if both win on the absence-of-malice argument," he said to me, "there will be enough fallout casting doubts about journalism's fairness to haunt everyone." Van Gordon Sauter, executive vice-president of the CBS Broadcast Group, said much the same thing. "There'll be no walking wounded," he said.[20]

It was particularly so in the Sharon case. *Time* was flogged by writers generally. Richard Cohen, a *Washington Post* columnist, was perhaps the bluntest. "The fight between the repugnant Ariel Sharon and the arrogant *Time* magazine ended in the most wonderful of ways," he wrote. "They both lost. Sharon lost his suit and *Time* its credibility. . . . The statements of *Time*'s editors indicate that they still don't understand where they went wrong. From the very first, what was on trial was not whether the law would shield *Time* from the wrath of Sharon, but whether the magazine would be willing to admit that it had made a mistake. From the top of the Time-Life Building to the sub-basement, the answer came back: *Time* admits nothing. But in so doing it admitted plenty—arrogance."[21]

The crux of the suit was a statement in the magazine reporting on the finding of an Israeli commission on the massacre of Palestinian refugees in Lebanon refugee camps in 1982. The commission criticized General Sharon for disregarding the risk of a massacre when he allowed Phalangists to enter the camps. *Time*'s story added that a secret appendix described a meeting of General Sharon with the family of the assassinated Phalangist leader, Bashir Gemayel. General Sharon, *Time* went on to say, "discussed . . . the need for the Phalangists to take revenge." General Sharon called it "a blood libel." After some delay, the Israeli government permitted lawyers from both sides to see the appendix. It contained no such passage.

In three separate stages, an obviously conscientious jury found that *Time* 1) had defamed General Sharon; 2) had been guilty of falsehood; but 3) had not acted with "actual malice." It added a statement rebuking "certain *Time* employees" for "acting negligently and carelessly in reporting and verifying" their information. In a column in the *New York Times,* Richard M. Clurman, who for some years had been chief of correspondents for *Time* and *Life,* wrote, "Mr. Sharon was defeated in law. But *Time*—and journalism—suffered a worse defeat by having to invoke the privilege of laws that allow but hardly applaud inaccuracy or unfairness."[22]

What was uncomfortably open for the news magazines was disclosure of what *Newsweek* even-handedly reported as "*Time*'s multilayered editorial process [similar to *Newsweek*'s] in which New York-based writers assemble stories from 'files' sent by correspondents in the field. The news-magazine fact-checking apparatus usually means fewer mistakes than a daily newspaper makes, but is nonetheless vulnerable when it requires the checker simply to accept a correspondent's word on files involving highly confidential sources, or allows a writer's 'interpretation' of a file to prevail."[23] *Newsweek* later quoted Michael Kinsley of the *New Republic* who, even before the trial ended, had accused both *Time* and *Newsweek* of using an "elephantine procedure that is supposed to provide depth and accuracy [but] seems to function more like that party game of 'rumors.'"[24] *Time,* meanwhile, followed its long-standing position of standing by its system.

General Westmoreland's suit against CBS, captioned early by the newsmagazines as "the libel trial of the century," went eighteen weeks, cost the two sides something like $8 million, and fizzled out like a dud firecracker only a week before it was to have gone to the jury. A tired and discouraged General Westmoreland agreed with his lawyer's urgings to accept a hedged testimonial to his patriotism and withdrew his suit. The last weeks had been difficult for him, hearing former aides take the witness chair in CBS's behalf. A majority of the jurors told news people later that they were siding with CBS, but a number of them apparently were not convinced he had been engaged in a conspiracy to deceive President Lyndon Johnson and his other superiors. One juror said, "I have a hunch he might have come away with more than he settled for."[25]

The journalistic reaction generally was that while CBS had been a clear winner in the trial, the documentary that began it all, "The Uncounted Enemy: A Vietnam Deception" and introduced as the exposure of a "conspiracy," had been flawed. Broadcast in January 1982, it had portrayed General Westmoreland as having systematically underreported the size and strength of Vietnam forces. General Westmoreland called the program "a vicious, scurrilous and premeditated attack on my character and integrity." He demanded an apology. CBS refused. Six months later, *TV Guide* emblazoned on its cover, "Anatomy of a Smear" and a subtitle, "How CBS News Broke the Rules and 'Got' General Westmoreland."[26]

Mr. Sauter, then president of CBS News, quickly asked Burton Benjamin, the division's highly respected senior producer, to study *TV Guide*'s charges. Mr. Sauter issued a statement in July 1983, saying that some of the network's regulations had been violated, but that none of them had changed the substance of the broadcast. The text of Mr. Benjamin's report was not released until April 26, 1983, after Federal Judge Pierre N. Leval ordered that it be given to General Westmoreland under the legal discovery procedures. CBS had held it to be an internal document, but

Judge Leval said CBS had forfeited its right by the July 1983 disclosure of portions of the findings.[27]

Judge Leval undoubtedly was correct in interpreting the legal niceties, but his ruling may have damaged good journalistic oversight. As already argued, both responsible oversight and public accountability are urgently needed in journalism. If news organizations have to fear the consequences of legal discovery in the event of court action, they can become hesitant to do any formal reviewing, and lacking it cannot adequately make any considered public comment. It is an area legal scholars might well apply themselves to in the interest of encouraging intelligent journalistic review. True, Judge Leval did not permit Mr. Benjamin's report to become part of the trial proceedings, but other, less wise, judges might well go all the way.

Mr. Benjamin's report disclosed eleven "principal flaws" in the preparation of the documentary by producer George Crile, a number of them violations of CBS regulations. Mike Wallace, the narrator on the documentary, admittedly spent little time working on the reporting and editing. After the case ended so suddenly, Fred Friendly wrote one of the best summations in a column in the *Washington Post*.[28]

> What is clear is that this suit had little to do with libel, and its resolution was never appropriate for a court of law. It was a controversy over sloppy journalism, and serious journalism may suffer the greatest penalty. . . . "The Uncounted Enemy" may have been even unfair, but that does not answer the rigorous test of libel. Crile admitted several serious journalistic sins—for example, hiring a consultant for $25,000 and then using him as a central interviewee in the documentary. The payment was not mentioned in the program. Another ethical problem: After interviewing a former CIA agent, Crile decided to take him into the editing room to show him the original rushes of his interview and several others before interviewing him again. Such practices are *unacceptable* in any newsroom, broadcast or print.

It is no secret that others much closer to Westmoreland advised the general against a protracted, exorbitantly expensive lawsuit, but the hurt and angry soldier permitted himself to be manipulated, mostly by ultra-conservative media bashers. . . . What emerges from the Westmoreland litigation is a crying, almost desperate, plea for access, particularly air time. The stark reality is that unless there is some imaginative, creative way of answering back, documentaries such as "Harvest of Shame" and "The Selling of the Pentagon" will disappear from the air. . . . Neither television nor print publications are immune from the public perception that editors and producers—the gatekeepers—are insensitive, often arrogant, and unwilling to listen to serious viewers and readers who sometimes believe "they got it wrong."

Early in this chapter I quoted Alvin Toffler. In discussing the changes in our society, Mr. Toffler referred to our losing "the very glue that holds the society together—shared values, shared experiences, ways of looking at reality." One major ingredient in that glue, I believe, was journalism. My claim that dysfunctional patterns hamper journalistic performance was supported in 1973 by Douglass Cater who, in 1958 as a widely admired Washington reporter, wrote *The Fourth Branch of Government*. Later, he became an aide to President Lyndon Johnson, then was associated with the Aspen Institute, and now is president of Washington College in Chestertown, Md. In a paper written at Aspen, Mr. Cater said "I marvel at the maldistribution of reportorial resources. Scores of reporters are dispatched to ride a candidate's campaign plane. Less than a handful give any systematic coverage to the education crisis in America which affects the lives of millions of children."

Communications, he said, "have a vast power to shape government—its policies and its leaders. This is not a strictly editorial power. It is the power to select—out of the tens of thousands of words spoken in Washington each day and the tens of dozens of events—which words and events are projected for

mankind to see. Equally powerful is the media's capacity to ignore. Those words and events which fail to get projected might
as well not have occurred. My criticism of the media is that they
don't take themselves and their role seriously enough. A number
of my colleagues in the press were offended by the title of my
book. . . . They refuse to admit that those who are involved in
the communications of a democracy play a major role in its
governance."[29]

There can be no questioning of television's dramatic force
in public affairs. Don Oberdorfer of the *Washington Post*
explained it succinctly in 1981. "A real life Big Event," he wrote,
"must meet three requirements: it must be accessible to television cameras and transmission facilities; journalistic gatekeepers
must see it as of extraordinary interest and importance; and it
must be symbolic of an idea or trend that has been gathering
force, 'proving' something which people are ready to believe."[30]

A reference again to the global shock over the Ethiopian
famine is in order. Pictures taken by *Denver Post* photographer
Anthony Suau in Ethiopia in 1983 won a Pulitzer Prize six
months later. As Tom Rosenstiel wrote in the *Los Angeles
Times*, it was only then that more than two American newspapers would "even print his pictures." Late in 1984, his pictures
were in demand, "in large part," wrote Mr. Rosenstiel, "because
NBC rebroadcast the BBC footage of dying children in Ethiopian
refugee camps and the famine became a dominant international
concern."[31]

Much of the coverage out of Washington ties directly into
the failures at the gatekeeping levels of journalism. It was made
clear in a 1981 book, *The Washington Reporters,* by Stephen
Hess, senior fellow at the Brooking Institution.[32] His study disclosed a broad lack of involvement by the key gatekeepers on
newspapers in the work of their correspondents. The relationship, Mr. Hess found, was one of "benign neglect. . . . For most
journalists in Washington, the home office is far away and out of
sight. . . . The low level of disagreements between Washington
reporters and their home offices need not be because the report-

ers have been housebroken . . . but because they so often get their way. It is not necessary to push against an open door."

To questions of how much editing was done at home offices, 51 percent of Mr. Hess's respondents said none at all, and nearly all the rest said only minor editing. Only 3 percent of the stories Mr. Hess checked had been substantially edited. His study also made it clear that the problem of source anonymity had been generated out of Washington practice. All of this adds up to a worrisome portrayal of a large part of journalism wallowing in bureaucratic anarchy.

It is far from what was intended by those who took part in our only Constitutional Convention 200 years ago. Arthur Schlesinger, Jr., recapitulated it in 1973, writing, "Few themes were more insistently repeated by the statesmen of the early republic than the idea that government would work only if it were based on an enlightened and informed public opinion." He quoted James Madison's famous statement: "A popular government without popular information, or the means of acquiring it, is but a Prologue to a Farce or a Tragedy; or perhaps both. Knowledge will forever govern ignorance: And a people who mean to be their own Governors must arm themselves with the power which knowledge gives."[33]

From where does the concerned American get this necessary information? Obviously, from the few great and the striving-to-be-great newspapers, magazines, and books of substance, and from the several well-managed television properties. The great new arm among the news media has changed little since 1976 when Walter Cronkite leveled with his broadcast associates, saying: "We fall short of presenting all or a good part of the news each day that a citizen would need to intelligently exercise his franchise in this democracy. So as he depends more and more on us, presumably the depth of knowledge of the average man diminishes. This clearly can lead to disaster in a democracy."[34]

Alfred Balk, editorial director of *World Press Review*, and a former editor of *The Columbia Journalism Review*, is a compulsive student of journalism's output. He divides American com-

munications into two sections—"those news organizations with
their eyes on stories of consequence and which cover them in
depth, and those which are willing to settle for mediocrity."[35]
Were it not for lax editing, he thinks it would be hard to conceive
the *Wall Street Journal* as having the largest daily circulation in
the country. "For readers in so many cities and towns," he says,
"it is the only source for citizens who feel it urgent to get serious
information and mature perspective." In addition to his own, his
monthly magazine preferences are the *Atlantic,* and *New Republic,* and among the weeklies, *U. S. News & World Report*
and *Business Week.* He has regard for quarterlies like *Foreign
Affairs* and *Public Interest.* He considers *Newsweek* and *Time* as
popular weeklies, serving a useful purpose in summarizing and
putting in focus the week's news, a good deal of which many
newspapers fail to publish. No American weekly, Mr. Balk
holds, matches Britain's *Economist,* in writing skill, discipline,
and dispassionate approach. Some 100,000 Americans and Ca-
nadians are regular readers. Mr. Balk points out that the
*Economist,* like the *Wall Street Journal,* began as a publication
for businessmen, "whose vital interests depend upon expert
analysis of matters of consequence."

There are fewer regional and local newspapers of good quality than was the case twenty-five years ago. As noted earlier,
some chain-owned papers are much better; many more are under
less-committed ownerships and, coupled with so much uninspired local television, the result has been that the average citizen is often short-changed on information.

Worse, we face a growing crisis in literacy, with 27 million
Americans incapable of reading. All through our history,
thoughtful observers, from de Tocqueville on, have seen public
education as being a linchpin for democracy's success, and this is
where the system has lurched into its greatest danger. Those in
charge of public education—school boards, superintendents,
teachers content with "how-to-teach" methods rather than master course substance, and virtually driven into lock-step union-
ism by short-sighted taxpayer resistance—bear much of the
blame, but so do journalism's gatekeepers, as Mr. Cater noted.

Walter Lippmann was one who always saw the relationships between press power and education. In 1940, in a major speech, he tendered a blistering attack on educators. "During the past 40 or 50 years," he said, "those who are responsible for education have progressively removed from the curriculum of studies the Western culture which produced the modern democratic state. . . . The schools and colleges have been sending out into the world men who no longer understand the creative principle of the society in which they must live. . . . Deprived of their cultural tradition, the newly educated Western men no longer possess . . . the ideas, the premises, the rationale, the logic, the method, the values, or the deposited wisdom which are the genius of Western civilization. The prevailing education is destined, if it continues, to destroy Western civilization, and is in fact destined, if it continues, to destroy Western civilization, and is in fact destroying it."[36]

A few years earlier, deploring sensational journalism, he was advocating a journalism that would open its doors "to the use of trained intelligence in newspaper work. . . . For the ability to present news objectively and to interpret it realistically is not a native instinct. . . . It is a product of culture which comes only with knowledge of the past and acute awareness of how deceptive is our normal observation and how wishful is our thinking."[37] At that stage particularly, he was asking too much of an editing craft more interested in cops and robbers than in being the slightest concerned about how the schools were doing and how, or other subject matter equally essential for the citizens. The unprofessional gatekeeper system clearly has to be judged as being one of the root causes for the steady slide of public confidence in journalism.

I nurture hope that a constitutional convention, with a potential for ruinous mischief, will not come about. If it should, one can only hope that it might be the shock treatment that would impel those who sit at the top echelons of the giant journalistic organizations to order thorough expert appraisals of their enterprises. I am certain that expert, outside examination would disclose the degrees of outworn habit woven into the fabric of the undertakings, as well as the extent of incompetence preordained by a lack of substantive training. Surely, I tell myself, the top executives would understand at what risk these weaknesses are placing the future of the nation's basic freedom.

But it is an uncomfortable assumption. Do the dynamics of the new postindustrialism allow for such flexibility? Would even such a crisis intervention ʾas a constitutional convention jar owners of newspapers and broadcasting stations to invest some of the ample profits toward increasing quality information for readers and viewers? Uneasiness also comes from the recognition that major reform takes a great deal of time, and none of us can even guess how much time may be left.

More uneasiness flows out of trying to assess the extent of ownerships' commitment to quality service. There are a number of individuals in ownership and executive positions in communications who are profoundly tied to freedom of the press. If one judges by the quality of their newspapers and broadcast properties, there are far more who apparently look on communications purely as a money-making industry and who—Heaven forbid— might be subject to the temptation I have speculatively attributed to market analysts and bankers: that of putting such high priority on making money that they might be persuaded to acquiesce in accepting some limitations on press freedoms in exchange for tranquil dealings with government.

It does not seem logical to assume that a majority of political officeholders are willing to dig in and fight for the cause of a free press. The average politician, after all, is in it (a) to be reelected and (b), if possible, to be elected to a higher post. For these officeholders, the press is a tool to be used, provided it is a favorable press. Their primary interest is getting as much exposure on television as is possible. What most politicians desire is a tractable press. "Responsible" is the operative word. I am for a "responsible" press, too, but suspect that if we had to spell it out, our definitions would be as far apart as Jupiter is from the Earth.

However, little of this answers the question of how journalism can rebuild its reputation and standing, lest it fall victim to Alexander Hamilton's warning two centuries ago that the security of a free press, "whatever fine declarations may be inserted in any constitution respecting it, must altogether depend on public opinion, and on the general spirit of the people and of the government."[38]

My prescription is evident. It is that every news organization of any nature or form, reflects its top leadership, whether that be an individual, a group of owners, or a massive corporation operating through tiers of executives. Organizational purposes and intent need to be laid out cogently. The APME's *Editors and Stress* report showed how far most newspaper organizations are from any such kind of partnership in intent. In the vast majority of newspaper and broadcast operations there no longer is any need to pretend to economic hardships. The huge sums changing hands for communications properties would seem to offer ample proof of that assertion.

What it all boils down to is values. I confess that my tolerance thermometer runs low for those in journalism who see it either as a money machine or as some kind of exciting game. Part of this internal philosophy, as said earlier, came out of early exposures, and part of it by fascinated reading of the remarkable group of men who founded this country. Much has changed since then. Yet for all its spiritual questionings and political polarizations, this remains a unique place; unique in the sense that doors do open for those with ability, desire, and capacity. Still, one would be a fool not to recognize that this isn't the same kind of culture Madison and Jefferson lived in. They appreciated creature comforts, too. But that was not what drove them. When that is all there is to life you find ever fewer people with a deep and abiding faith in broad, humane democratic values.

It may sound stilted in this era of careless language, but I remain captivated by the words and spirit of the 56 men who signed the Declaration of Independence: "... *we mutually pledge to each other our lives, our Fortunes, and our Sacred Honor.*" If only our journalism had that kind of passion and spirit.

My satisfactions have come from having had a role, even if it has been a small one, in helping to build ethical conscience among a number of earnest and talented men and women. There is a glow in seeing them working in all the ways open to them to live up to the dream that the only way democracy can work successfully is through a value system that puts honorable public service in the reporting of events as accurately as possible, interpreting them honestly, and analyzing them fairly. That kind of journalism can win back the confidence of the citizenry.

But it cannot come without a lot of painful reappraisal and reorganization. Given budgets allowing for the employment and training of the most qualified and the best educated men and women they can find, and given also reasonable space and/or time, those in charge of news in both print and broadcast who have a sense of mission, will find the operative code words so elemental as to sound like a Scout pledge. Knowing newsrooms, getting the words enforced can exhaust an editor. But enforced they must be or there is no hope of rebuilding. Accuracy. Balance. Fairness. Compassion. Depth of coverage. Ethical performance. Objectivity in reporting, insofar as the honorable journalist can produce it. Add Accountability, both in personal and organizational terms. An end to granting source anonymity without prior approval by the top editor. Within this framework should come a reconstructing of reportorial priorities and stopping wolf-pack assignments. The dollars saved will make possible far more important information through systematic coverage of the decisive issues citizens in every area need to face. Along with all this must be a steady patrol over every one of the gatekeeping functions, accompanied with a demanding insistence on intelligent planning, assigning, and final editing.

As said, all primitive. Carr Van Anda and O. K. Bovard stuff. But primitive though it be, this is pretty much what it will take to recover—slowly and painfully—what has been squandered over so many years in the wild drives to be first and to keep driving for extensions of "press rights" to the point that journalism seems to have succeeded in convincing tens of millions of Americans, perhaps a majority of the population, that it places its freedoms to do as it wishes above every other institution in the society. It hasn't washed. It won't wash. Reporters and photographers and cameramen can act and perform professionally, but only if those who are in the control posts are thoroughly professional to start with. A sense of proportion has to come into the undertaking.

General Westmoreland's post-trial remarks put this in a rational perspective. There was a wistful tone to his comment when he said that resort to the courts fails to serve the public issue. He mentioned the life and death of the National News Council and its "non-binding and non-punishing opinion" function. "No one is perfect or infallible," he said.[39] Even Mr. Crile seemed to agree. At a broadcasters' meeting, he remarked: "In a sense, I think we pushed too hard."[40]

Until the nation's press—print and broadcast—can see the way clear to build a new, more effective press council, much wider use of ombudsmen would be helpful. Mr. Friendly added a suggestion for all of television in his article: "An auspicious beginning would be the announcement that CBS is setting aside one half-hour, once a month, for creative redress. It would be expensive but not compared with the cost of doing nothing."

Take a moment to think back to the page-one coverage and the TV talk-show attention given to the Equal Rights Amendment drive. How much coverage can anyone recall about the legislatures of thirty-two states petitioning Congress to call a constitutional convention? Once in a while, I wake up toying with a scenario in which the thirty-fourth state has just passed the petition call for the full convention—and imagine the scene of God-knows-how-many news editors on newspapers and local TV stations glancing at the wire story, and deciding quickly it is another dull governmental story.

All, the years of experience say, coming about because they were listening so intently to a reporter's excited talk about some new tale of a politics-sex-and-drug scandal they couldn't hear the roar of the great gathering storm.

# NOTES

## 1. "I'VE GOT A CRAZY ON THE LINE"

1. *The Autobiography of William Allen White* (New York: Mac-Millan, 1946), p. 629.

2. A. J. Liebling, *The Press* (New York: Ballantine Books, 1961), p. 30.

3. Letters from James Detjen, November 15, 1983 and March 14, 1984.

4. Confirmed with A. C. Nielsen Co., New York, November 9, 1984.

5. Simply to get the statistical record current, a recheck with the Federal Communications Commission March 11, 1985, disclosed that there are 1,581 TV stations operating—903 commercially licensed; the others spread fairly evenly between educational (public TV) and low-power frequencies. Total radio stations as of that date: 9,693.

6. Quoted in *U.S. News & World Report,* September 20, 1982, p. 68.

7. Judee K. Burgoon, Michael Burgoon, and Charles K. Atkin of Michigan State University, a 1981 study; issued as a research report, "The World of the Working Journalist," 1982, by the Newspaper Readership Project of the Newspaper Advertising Bureau.

8. Clifford Christians, "Instruction in Media Ethics," a study done in April/May 1984 for the Association for Education in Journalism and Mass Communications, *Journalism Educator,* summer issue, 1985.

9. *U.S. News & World Report,* October 1, 1984, pp. 69–70.

10. *U.S. News & World Report,* February 21, 1983, p. 83.

11. *Wall Street Journal,* February 7, 1985, p. 84.

12. From the text of Charles Kuralt's Scripps Lecture, University of Nevada/Reno, March 29, 1984.

13. Walter Lippmann, "Two Revolutions in the American Press," *The Yale Review,* March 1931, p. 437.

14. Sir William Haley, "News and Documentaries on U. S. Television," in Marvin Barrett, ed., *Survey of Broadcast Journalism, 1968–69* (New York: Grosset & Dunlap, 1970), p. 60.

15. Doris A. Graber, of the University of Illinois at Chicago, in *Political Science Quarterly* (Summer 1984), pp. 370–372.

16. Elisabeth Bumiller, "The Battle of Packaging the Presidency," *Washington Post*, November 5, 1984, pp. C1 and C8.

17. Interview with A. M. Rosenthal at the *New York Times*, August 10, 1983.

18. The Gallup organization's studies of public attitudes toward journalism go back over two decades. *Editor & Publisher* on September 28, 1968, p. 11, headlined its story of a New York conference, "Gallup: Public is fed up with journalistic excesses."

19. Ruth Clark, "Relating to Readers in the '80s," *Bulletin* of the American Society of Newspaper Editors, June/July 1984, pp. 4,5.

20. Walter Lippmann, "Two Revolutions," pp. 434–441.

21. *ASNE Bulletin*, June/July 1984, pp. 8–9, excerpts from the final presidential address of Creed C. Black, publisher of the *Lexington* (Ky.) *Herald-Leader*, delivered May 9, 1984. Earlier correspondence with Mr. Black, June 18 and July 7, 1981.

22. Letter from Arnold Rosenfeld, April 25, 1984.

23. The Pulitzer records show that the AP ranks second in awards only to the *New York Times*, which has received 54 over a much wider range. The two run far ahead of all other rivals.

24. John Morton, quoted in the *New York Times*, April 30, 1984, in story on Harte-Hanks Communications (27 daily and 25 weekly newspapers, 4 TV and 9 radio stations, a cable TV operation and a marketing company).

25. *Advertising Age*, "100 Leading Media Companies," 1984 edition, June 28, 1984. pp. 7–83; 1985 edition, June 27, 1985, pp. 1–64.

26. Daniel Yankelovich, *New Rules* (New York: Random House, 1981), preface, p. xiv.

27. *The Speaker and the Listener* (New York: Public Agenda Foundation, 1980), p. 7.

28. The American Historical Association and the American Political Science Association joined in issuing *The Constitutional Convention as an Amending Device* (1981) as part of the two organizations' "Project '87."

## 2. THE INTELLECTUAL DIABETICS

1. Paul H. Douglas, *Ethics in Government* (Cambridge: Harvard University Press, 1952), p. 45. The remark was made earlier by the senator in a lecture at Harvard.

2. The quote is attributed to F. H. Brennan and appears in *Braude's Second Encyclopedia*, compiled by Judge Jacob M. Braude of Chicago (Englewood Cliffs, N.J.: Prentice-Hall, 1957), p. 246.

3. Mr. Kristol first used the "underdeveloped profession" expression in an article in *Public Interest* (Winter 1967), no. 6. It has been quoted often in the years since.

4. Dr. A. C. Ewing, *Ethics* (Kent, England: Hodder & Staughton, 1953) and subsequent reissues. Mine is the eleventh impression, 1976.

5. *The Ethics of Journalism,* by Nelson Antrim Crawford (New York: Knopf, 1924), was the first book issued in the United States on the subject. Dr. Crawford was head of the Department of Industrial Journalism at Kansas State Agricultural College. Though the book dates back more than sixty years, the problems discussed are strikingly similar to many of the criticisms heard today. Dr. Crawford collected codes of ethics then existing in journalism. There were seventeen such sets of codes by both state organizations and individual newspapers.

6. The admirable *The Press and America* by Edwin Emery and Henry Ladd Smith (New York: Prentice-Hall, 1954) had this to say, "The first definitely organized curriculum in journalism was offered at the University of Pennsylvania from 1893 to 1901. . . . The University of Illinois organized the first four-year curriculum in journalism in 1904. . . . The first separate school of journalism, with newspaperman Walter Williams as dean, opened in 1908 at the University of Missouri.

7. The late Branch Rickey, operating head of the Dodgers, filed suit in the St. Louis Federal Court against the Mexican League and named the assistant sports editor as one of the chief defendants. The case later was withdrawn because of the complexity of jurisdiction.

8. The "tidbits" that follow all are contained in files built up over the years. They are represented by actual letters, telegrams, clippings from national publications, and other supporting matter.

9. Part 8, "Hearings before the Committee on Foreign Relations, United States Senate," 88th Cong., 2d sess., May 6, 1963, pp. 883–887. The letters of Wayne C. Sellers, publisher of the *Evening Herald* of Rock Hill, S.C., to Talbot Patrick, president of the newspaper.

10. William Rowland Allen was ten years my senior. As a reporter, I became interested in the criminal justice system. It was an interest that continued after I became an editor, so much so that I took the time to report and write a major series on the dreadful condition of Indiana's institutions, including not only the prisons, but those for the mentally ill and for the aged. Rowland was a member of the state's civil service board and held an open contempt for the state's crude, low-paying staffing. We met as result of this mutual interest. He "adopted" me, so to speak, and after a year or two, there was never a night when, on his way home, he did not stop at my home to review the day. He became "Uncle" to my Steve and Roberta, and when I moved to St. Louis later, he was a frequent visitor, and all the more so when we moved to Louisville. I held that kind of kinship for his two daughters. I still miss his zest for trying

to move society forward, for his immense sense of proportion, and his great, good humor. Steve set his mind on Harvard from boyhood, just because of "Uncle Rowland."

11. Satirical stage play though it was, *The Front Page,* by Ben Hecht and Charles MacArthur (New York: Covici-Friede, 1928), was a perceptively accurate, ripping expose of the rambunctious kind of newspaper exaggeration that marked so much of Chicago's wild newspaper competition in the 1920s. I still break into laughter reading the final words of Walter Burns, Hildy Johnson's managing editor. I *knew* his type.

12. Elie Abel, former Columbia journalism dean, now Stanford's chairman, recounts similar experiences of his young newspaper days in Canada. His refusal to accept cash gifts handed out by political figures to newsmen at functions brought only the indignant scorn of journalistic colleagues who thought it their "due."

13. The Ku Klux Klan took on enormous political influence across the South and spread north to the Midwest in the 1920s. There were frequent parades of klansmen in their sheets and hoods in downtown Indianapolis. They controlled much of city and state government. Under a courageous editor, Boyd Gurley, the *Indianapolis Times* crusaded against the Klan, publishing lists of members obtained by a shrewd and able investigative reporter, Frank J. Prince. Some of the paper's printers and pressmen turned up listed as Klansmen. A circulation boycott was called for, and pressure was put on the advertisers. Memory can sometimes be bitter and my recollections of certain advertisers remain unkind ones. I recall that the only major advertiser to coolly defy the Klan boycott was the big store, L. S. Ayres & Co., where Rowland worked. It was the only major store in the city owned and operated by Protestants.

14. Managing editor, *Indianapolis Times,* 1936–43; editorial director, *Indianapolis News,* 1943–45; managing editor, *St. Louis Star-Times,* 1945–51; managing editor, *Louisville Times,* 1951–62; vice-president/executive editor, *Courier-Journal* and *Times,* 1962–70; president and publisher, the *News-Journal,* Wilmington, Del., 1975–76.

15. *New York Times,* March 6, 1985, p. 14.

16. The best detailed analysis of this issue I know about is Chris Argyris' *Behind The Front Page* (San Francisco: Jossey-Bass, 1974). Dr. Argyris is James Bryant Conant professor of education and organizational behavior at Harvard. In his book the major newspaper he studied was the *Planet.* In *More,* a journalism review in New York in the 1970s, David M. Rubin, now chairman of the journalism department at New York University, identified the newspaper as the *New York Times.* In the 1978 winter/spring issue of *Nieman Reports,* Dr. Argyris dealt with some of the issues he had studied. The tenor of it was accurately described in the headline: "The Media's Capacity for Self-Destruction."

3. WHAT THE SCOOP HATH BEGAT

1. *The Artillery of the Press*, published for the Council on Foreign Relations by Harper & Row, 1966, pp. 49 and 93. Mr. Reston drew the title from a phrase in Thomas Jefferson's second inaugural address.

2. *Press Watch* (New York: MacMillan, 1984), p. 300.

3. Edwin Emery and Henry Ladd Smith, *The Press and America*, (Englewood Cliffs, N.J.: Prentice-Hall, 1954), pp. 414–416. Although it has not been updated, this 794-page volume remains one of the best historical overviews of the American press up to 1954.

4. W. A. Swanberg, *Citizen Hearst* (New York: Scribner, 1961), pp. 107–108.

5. Emery and Smith, *The Press and America*, p. 445.

6. Messrs. Patterson, Roberts, and Thomas, quoted in Mr. Shaw's report, "Scoop: Rush to Judgment in Newsroom," *Los Angeles Times*, March 2, 1977.

7. John Tebbel, *An American Dynasty* (New York: Doubleday, 1947), pp. 108–110; also in John J. McPhaul, *When the Merry-go-Round Broke Down* (Englewood Cliffs, N.J.: Prentice-Hall, 1962), pp. 224–225.

8. Gene Fowler, *Timber Line* (New York: Covici-Friede, 1933), pp. 462–464.

9. Tebbel, *An American Dynasty*, p. 202.

10. James McCartney in *The Bulletin* of the American Society of Newspaper Editors, October 1984, pp. 14–15.

11. Frank Stanton, speech at the California Institute of Technology, Pasadena, June 11, 1965.

12. Tom Wolfe, *The New Journalism* (New York: Harper & Row, 1973).

13. John Hulteng, *The Messenger's Motives* (Englewood Cliffs, N.J.: Prentice-Hall, 1976), p. 200. This is one of the best of examinations of ethical considerations in journalism.

14. Mr. Sevareid in *Nieman Reports*, December 1970, titled "The Quest for Objectivity," p. 13.

15. Personal conversation with Mr. Felker, May 28, 1985.

16. All of the following episodes were drawn from the detailed report made to the National News Council by A. H. Raskin, published in *After "Jimmy's World": Tightening Up in Editing* (National News Council, 1981). The documented material referred to is from a chapter titled "Journalistic Hoaxes," pp. 121–130.

## 4. "I DON'T WANT TO KNOW"

Formal, numbered reference notes for this chapter struck me as probably overly cumbersome in providing the reader with source information. The basic documentation is contained in the 180-page book, published in 1981, by the National News Council, titled *After 'Jimmy's World': Tightening Up in Editing*. All of the documentation, along with the remaining supply of copies of the book, now are in the hands of the School of Journalism at the University of Minnesota. The school also possesses the tapes made of the Council's discussions during its deliberations.

Follow-up conversations in early 1985 with the Messrs. Green, Coleman, and Simons also are reflected in the writing.

One of the things most useful to readers may be a calendar of how the series of events unfolded:

SEPTEMBER 28, 1980.—Janet Cooke's story published in the *Post*.

FEBRUARY 1, 1981.—Deadline date for submission of 1980 work to the Pulitzer Prize office. The Cooke story submitted well before this deadline.

MARCH 2, 3, and 4.—Pulitzer juries meet to read, appraise, and reach votes on their choices, and file reports.

APRIL 3—Pulitzer Prize Board meets and makes its decisions.

APRIL 13—The 1980 prizes are announced.

APRIL 14—The Associated Press notifies the *Post* that Janet Cooke's biography does not match official records. A prompt examination is begun at the *Post*.

APRIL 16—Janet Cooke confesses the hoax; resigns.

APRIL 19—Ombudsman Bill Green's long report is published.

APRIL 22—Editor Ben Bradlee talks to the annual convention of American Society of Newspaper Editors in Washington, providing his newspaper's overview of the hoaxed story.

APRIL 24—Complaint filed with the News Council in Washington against the *Post* by the journalism faculty of Howard University.

JUNE 12—Council meets in New York. By overwhelming vote, the Council rejected all but two of the charges contained in the complaint. The Council agreed that the story had impaired journalistic credibility in general and it agreed that *Post* editors had been negligent in failing to investigate the validity of charges made after publication by members of the public and from within its staff. The Council expressed concerns about other phases not raised in the complaint, which, in the foreword to the book, I described as "flawed because it was overstated and suppositive."

The Council book contained five chapters: one, the first dealing with the complaint, the joint work of Messrs. Cunningham and Raskin; the second by Mr. Raskin on the Pulitzer Prizes; the third on the role of ombudsmen by Mr. Cunningham; the fourth on hoaxes, done by Mr. Raskin; and the fifth, the responses and views of thirty-four leading editors, originated and handled by me.

Where the information on the prizes was involved, it should be mentioned that the late Professor Richard T. Baker, secretary of the Pulitzer Prize board, was one of my closest friends. Much of what Mr. Raskin learned independently was backstopped by prior knowledge confided to me by Professor Baker. I was a member of the prize board until becoming a member of the Columbia faculty. The experience on both juries and board led Professor Baker to request me to write a general outline for jury procedures. At various times, Dick Baker served as both acting dean of the school and associate dean. He was a lovely, dedicated man, but at the time already ill and preparing for retirement. He died in the summer of 1981.

Mr. Maynard, as said, is an old, dear friend. He also served as a member of The News Council. We had our first conversation about Miss Cooke's story and his experience the evening of April 20, 1981, when we had gathered in Washington for the ASNE meeting. I asked him much later, to consider putting his memoir into writing. He did so in a four-page letter May 3, 1984.

Readers, it is to be hoped, will agree that this informal accounting provides more rounded detail than standard notes.


### 5. "HOW DO YOU MAKE AN EDITOR?"

1. Ben Bradlee to A. H. Raskin, early May, 1981.

2. The late Reed Hynds, music and drama critic of the *St. Louis Star-Times*. As many a colleague commented, he could "write like an angel." The remarkable thing, however, was that Mr. Hynds could produce at high speed typewritten copy that invariably was letter-perfect.

3. "The Editor's Trade," *Harper's Magazine,* July 1965, pp. 20–23.

4. To appreciate the scope of Carr Van Anda's abilities and the breadth of his interests, one is urged to read *The Story of the New York Times—1851–1951,* by the greatly, and justly, admired Meyer Berger (New York: Simon & Schuster, 1951).

5. Another version, attributed to Irving Dilliard, who for some years was editor of the newspaper's editorial page, appears on p. 57 of *Bovard of The Post-Dispatch,* by James W. Markham (Baton Rouge: Louisiana State University Press, 1954).

6. Personal conversation with Malcolm Mallette, May 1984.

7. *The Story of The New York Times*, attributed to Alva Johnston, p. 267.

8. In 1921, by executive order, President Warren Harding transferred control of naval oil reserves at Teapot Dome, Wyo., and Elk Hills, Calif., from the Navy to the Interior Department. Without competitive bidding, Interior Secretary Albert B. Fall leased the Teapot Dome fields to oil operator Harry F. Sinclair, and the Elk Hill fields to Edward L. Doheny. Intimations of scandal caught Bovard's attention. He assigned Paul Y. Anderson to cover the Senate investigation and for weeks Anderson was the only newsman present. It developed that Doheny had lent Fall $100,000, interest free; and that after leaving his post at Interior, Sinclair also "loaned" Fall a large sum of money. Subsequently, Fall was convicted of bribery, fined $100,000, and sentenced to a year in prison. Doheny and Sinclair were acquitted in trials, but Sinclair was sentenced to prison for contempt of the Senate. A Supreme Court decision in 1927 restored the oil fields to the government. Bovard felt there was even more to the case and kept Anderson at work. It was to disclose a wide-reaching conspiracy in dividing something like $3 million in bonds among those tied into the oil field plan. Anderson was awarded the Pulitzer Prize in 1929 for his reporting.

9. Edwin Emery and Henry Ladd Smith, *The Press and America* (Englewood Cliffs, N.J.: Prentice-Hall, 1954), p. 491.

10. Gerald W. Johnson, *An Honorable Titan* (New York: Harper, 1946). The journalist who doesn't hunt this up is missing the biography of a remarkable journalist.

11. *Editors and Stress*, a 160-page book published by the Associated Press Managing Editors, 1983.

12. Fischer, *Harper's Magazine*, July 1965.

13. Malcolm Mallette, personal conversation.

14. Robert Townsend, *Up the Organization* (New York: Knopf, 1970), p. 63; also in *Further Up the Organization* (1984), p. 77.

15. Published in *RTNDA Communicator*, May 1984, pp. 28–29. The study was conducted by Dr. Vernon A. Stone, director of Southern Illinois University's School of Journalism.

16. "Washington Ways," *Washington Post*, August 29, 1984, p. B4.

17. *Roper Reports*, 81–1, p. 123.

18. Obviously, national policy on courtesy titles has certain limits. Convicted felons hardly deserve the consideration. Further, the policy does not seem indicated in covering sports events.

## 6.   THE SEED BED OF HERESY

(Author's comment: In addition to being incapable of dissemblance, I see no point in even trying to sidestep the facts of deep personal involvement in many of the undertakings noted).

1. Published in Louis W. Hodges, ed., *Social Responsibility: Journalism, Law, Medicine* (Lexington, Va.: Washington and Lee University, 1982). Much of the summary is drawn from the text.

2. Ronald Steel, *Walter Lippmann and the American Century* (Boston: Atlantic Monthly Press and Little Brown, 1980), pp. 363–364.

3. The formal report, *A Free and Responsible Press*, edited by Robert D. Leigh, was published by the University of Chicago Press in 1947. The other books, also published by Chicago University Press were: *Freedom of the Press: A Framework of Principle*, by William Ernest Hocking; *Government and Mass Communications*, by Zechariah Chaffee, Jr.; *Freedom of the Movies*, by Ruth A. Inglis; *Peoples Speaking to Peoples*, by Llewellyn White and Robert D. Leigh; *The American Radio*, by Robert D. Leigh; *The American Press and the San Francisco Conference*, by Milton D. Stewart, with introduction by Harold D. Lasswell.

4. Herbert W. Brucker, *Communication is Power* (New York: Oxford University Press, 1973), p. 203.

5. H. Phillip Levy, *The Press Council: History, Procedure, Cases* (New York: MacMillan and St. Martin's Press, 1967), pp. 3–18.

6. Following the 1952 presidential campaign, the membership of Sigma Delta Chi, the national professional journalistic fraternity, called for a study of news coverage of that campaign. The national council of SDX ruled against it. The membership at the 1954 meeting called for a study of the 1956 campaign. It was approved and I was called on to serve as chairman of what was titled the Committee on Ethics and News Objectivity. Was such a study feasible? The Council on Communications Research, a branch of the Association for Education in Journalism, agreed to study that aspect, provided $5,000 would be made available for the expenses involved. After an original refusal, the Fund for the Republic, on the urgings of some journalists, provided the money. The researchers, twenty-six of them, under the leadership of Dr. Raymond Nixon of the University of Minnesota, later reported unanimously it was feasible. It would have cost in the $650,000 range, and there was a possibility the Ford Foundation would be interested if a majority of the press was agreed. The draft of the proposal was sent in late December 1955 to 76 publishers and editors representing 238 newspapers, plus 2 magazine publishers. It was voted down, 59 to 17. A reasonably detailed summary of the 38-page proposal was carried in *Editor & Publisher*, January 7, 1956.

7. The society's resolution stipulated that the study "should be conducted exclusively by trained newspapermen," and that their "approach should be frankly professional and even subjective." I was asked to be chairman of the three-man committee. The other two were Carl E.

Lindstrom, former editor of the *Hartford Times* and first editor of *The American Editor*, published by the society; and Arthur Edward Rowse, then a desk editor at the *Washington Post*, who had formerly been a New England newsman, and had written a book, *Slanted News*, a case study of the Nixon-Stevenson 1952 campaign. The report was delivered by me to the society in Northamptom, Mass., December 1, 1961.

8. From these experiences came *Back-Talk: Press Councils in America* (San Francisco: Canfield Press, 1972) by William L. Rivers, Stanford University; William B. Blankenburg, University of Wisconsin; Kenneth Starck, University of South Carolina; and Earl Reeves, University of Tulsa.

9. *A Free and Responsive Press*, report of the task force to the Twentieth Century Fund, background paper by Alfred Balk (New York: Twentieth Century Fund, 1973).

### 7.   THE EAGLE-HEARTED KIWI

1. No more detailed exposition can be found than in *The Kingdom and the Power*, by Gay Talese (New York: World, 1969). Other informative matter appears in *My Life and The Times*, by the late Turner Catledge (New York: Harper & Row, 1971).

2. See note 5 for chapter 6. Turner Catledge arranged for me to meet with then-publisher Orville Dryfoos and other members of the executive staff to outline the proposal of the researchers.

3. In addition to those named, others on the task force were Lucy Wilson Benson, president of the League of Women Voters; Stimson Bullitt, president of King Broadcasting Co., in Seattle; Hodding Carter III, editor of the Greenville (Miss.) *Delta Democrat Times;* Robert Chandler, editor of the Bend (Oreg.) *Bulletin;* Ithiel de Sola Pool, professor of political science at MIT; Hartford N. Gunn, Jr., president of the Public Broadcasting System; Richard Harwood, assistant managing editor of the *Washington Post;* Louis Martin, editor of the *Chicago Defender;* and Jesse Unruh of Los Angeles.

4. "Standards Relating to Fair Trial and Free Press," American Bar Association, 1966.

5. Over a period of a few years I had periodic associations with the Ford Foundation concerning journalistic matters and did the testing of sentiment.

6. Talese, *The Kingdom and the Power*, p. 338.

7. "In The Public Interest," National News Council report, 1973–1974. Chairman's foreword, p. 4.

8. "In The Public Interest," pp. 23–32.

9. Associated Press story from Washington, Dec. 8, 1972.

10. "In The Public Interest," p. 44.

11. The report was carried in full in "The Public Interest—II 1975–1978," pp. 415–419. The committee was chaired by Judge George Edwards of the U.S. Court of Appeals, Cincinnati. Serving with him were William L. Bondurant, Winston-Salem, N.C.; Dean Burch, Washington; Lloyd Morrisett, New York; Pauline Frederick Robbins, Westport, Conn.; and Harrison Salisbury, New York. As a result of a new assignment at Public Broadcasting Service, Miss Frederick resigned from the panel after the first few meetings.

12. The complete record appears in "Public Interest—II," pp. 385–392.

13. Testimony given at Michigan Employment Security Commission hearing in Escanaba, Mich., February 14, 1978.

14. Henry Gelles letter, October 14, 1977.

15. *Washington Post,* November 19, 1984, p. A3.

16. ANPA's *Presstime.* October 1980.

17. "Public Interest—III, 1979–83," pp. 532–552.

18. From an adaptation in *feed/back,* Fall 1984, pp. 35–37.

19. "Public Interest—III," p. 125–141.

20. *feed/back,* ibid., p. 37.

21. Catledge, *My Life and The Times,* p. 226.

### 8. FIGHTING INTELLECTUAL HERPES

1. "The Courier-Journal & Times' Ombudsman: A Retrospective View," by Fred V. Bales, University of Texas, April 12, 1977.

2. Bales. John Herschenroeder quoted on his knowledge of efforts to form press council.

3. Column in *Louisville Times,* August 30, 1979.

4. Column in *Washington Post,* November 9, 1979.

5. *Time,* July 6, 1970.

6. From Mr. Shaw's text, annual Burnett Lecture, University of Hawaii, March 8, 1983.

7. *Excerpts,* July 11, 1983, p. 4.

8. Zagoria, *Washington Post,* March 6, 1985, p. A20.

9. *Excerpts,* June 8, 1982, p. 1.

10. *Washington Journalism Review,* July 1984.

11. *Excerpts,* July 8, 1982, p. 3.

12. *Excerpts,* October 20, 1983, p. 4.

13. *Excerpts,* December 7, 1981; prior cases, November 15, 1983.

14. *Excerpts,* April 8, 1983, p. 3.

15. Gelfand, *Minneapolis Star & Tribune,* October 2, 1982, p. A14.

16. *Excerpts,* February 7, 1982, p. 3.

17. *Excerpts,* April 8, 1983, pp. 3–4.

18. *Excerpts*, February 13, 1984, p. 1.
19. *Excerpts*, March 8, 1983.
20. *New York Times*, August 7, 1985, p. B-1.
21. *Time*, May 23, 1983.
22. *Excerpts*, February 7, 1982, p. 3.

## 9. CONFLICTS, CONFLICTS...

1. Editorial, "Ethicsgate," *Wall Street Journal,* July 15, 1983.
2. Column, *Time,* July 25, 1983, p. 74.
3. Column, *New York Times,* July 26, 1983.
4. Syndicated column, July 14, 1983.
5. Richard Leonard to David Shaw in *Los Angeles Times* article, July 15, 1983.
6. Column in *Newsweek* magazine, July 25, 1983.
7. Editorial, "A Statement of Policy," *Arizona Daily Star,* December 6, 1983.
8. Max Frankel, quoted in David Shaw column, March 3, 1978.
9. "In The Public Interest—II, 1975–1978," The National News Council, pp. 393–414. Gives the entire record on the casino gambling matter.
10. "In The Public Interest—II," ibid., p. 410.
11. *Wall Street Journal,* "Owners of Newspapers Stir Debate by Taking A Role in Public Affairs," August 24, 1979, p. 1.
12. Column, *Oakland Tribune,* July 7, 1983, p. B9.
13. The entire Anderson episode covered in "The News Business," *Washington Post,* November 26, 1976.
14. *Chicago Journalism Review,* February 1970, pp. 3–5.
15. Confirmed by Mr. Harwood, May 28, 1985.
16. Full story on Associated Press wires, April 13, 1978.
17. AP, ibid.
18. "Ombudsman" column, *Quill,* September 1984, pp. 11–12.
19. "Are Perks for Media Vital to a Free Press Or Just Freeloading?" *Wall Street Journal,* August 29, 1978.
20. Howard Covington, personal letter, June 13, 1972.
21. "Capital Press Corps Challenged on Costs," *New York Times,* July 6, 1977.
22. *New York Times,* ibid.
23. "The Media's Conflicts of Interest," *The Center* magazine, November/December 1976, p. 20.
24. David Shaw's *Press Watch,* p. 140.
25. *The Center* magazine, ibid., p. 19.
26. DeWitt Scott, personal letter, December 21, 1973.
27. An episode out of the author's Louisville incarnation.

## 10. CHIPS OFF THE OLD BLOCK

1. Serving as adjunct teachers at Columbia's Graduate School of Journalism, Theodore M. Bernstein and Robert E. Garst collaborated in writing *Headlines and Deadlines* (New York: Columbia University Press, 1933). Several editions of it were to follow. In 1958, Mr. Bernstein wrote *Watch Your Language* and from this followed a number of other volumes on writing with clarity and precision.

2. The 1983 report of the Journalism Education Committee of the Associated Press Managing Editors, p. 7.

3. Quoted in the *New York Times,* June 3, 1984.

4. *Bulletin* of the American Society of Newspaper Editors, November 1983, excerpting from Mr. Kristol's comments in *Our Country and Our Culture* (New York: Orwell Press, 1983), pp. 79–88.

5. Taped interview with Dean Abel, Palo Alto, Calif., April 5, 1984.

6. ASNE *Bulletin,* November/December 1984, p. 30.

7. APME Journalism Education Committee report, pp. 23–24.

8. *New York Times,* April 27, 1983, excerpting from "A Nation at Risk," the report of the National Commission on Excellence in Education.

9. Quoted in the July/August 1984 newsletter of the National Center for Business and Economic Communication, based at The American University, Washington.

10. From highlights presented to the Associated Press Managing Editors convention, Louisville, Ky., November 4, 1983. Published in *APME Red Book 1983,* pp. 66–69.

## 11. KEEPERS OF THE DOLLARS

1. Richard S. Meeker, *Newspaperman: S. I. Newhouse and the Business of News* (New Haven and New York: Ticknor & Fields, 1983), p. 252. Mr. Meeker's book reflected two-and-a-half years of intensive research. It is an important study of one type of chain newspaper management.

2. *Advertising Age,* June 27, 1985. Annual edition of "100 Leading Media Companies." Crain Communications, Inc., Chicago.

3. Meeker, pp. 149–155.

4. Meeker, p. 167.

5. I figured briefly in these moves. A vice-president of the St. Louis Union Trust Co. telephoned to ask the favor of my inquiring if Barry Bingham, Sr., owner of the Louisville newspapers, would be interested in buying the *Globe-Democrat.* The essential details were provided. Predictably, Mr. Bingham instantly declined, saying he never had harbored any thought of chain ownership. When this was relayed to the banker, a

proposal was made that I consider becoming publisher, the financing to be arranged through certain leading Louisville industrialists. It was an unenticing prospect and also declined.

6. *St. Louis Journalism Review,* January 1984, p. 6.

7. Meeker, p. 167.

8. Meeker, p. 252.

9. "St. Louis Blues," *Time* magazine, November 21, 1983, p. 55.

10. *St. Louis Post-Dispatch,* January 23, 1984, reporting *Globe-Democrat* circulation as 255,141 daily, 25,000 more than the *Post-Dispatch.*

11. *St. Louis Journalism Review,* January 1984, p. 6.

12. Meeker, pp. 196–197.

13. Many reports have been issued on the background of joint operating agreements and on passage of the Newspaper Preservation Act in 1971. One of the most compact was published in the *St. Louis Journalism Review* in January 1984, pp. 14–18. It was researched and written by Paul M. Keep in 1982, when he was a master's candidate at the University of Missouri's School of Journalism.

14. Department of Justice press release, November 8, 1983.

15. *Citizen Publishing Co. v. U.S.* (394 US 131), decision delivered by Justice William O. Douglas for the Supreme Court in 1969.

16. During the five years of Congressional debate, magazines and newsletters serving journalism reported competing views about the "Preservation Act." The *Post-Dispatch,* in its January 29, 1984 report, headlined "Newspaper Act Nearly Failed Here," pp. 3F–6F, made the point that the question of a newspaper failing under the act had never arisen until the *Globe-Democrat's* decision to cease publications.

17. The basic depiction of the St. Louis area is drawn from my experience as managing editor of the *Star-Times,* 1945–51. The *New York Times,* December 9, 1983, published a short, colorful report of St. Louis' population loss and the growth of the adjoining areas, p. A20.

18. *St. Louis Post-Dispatch,* January 29, 1984.

19. *Ibid.*

20. Meeker, pp. 28–33.

21. All of the foregoing material was covered in the St. Louis newspapers and the *St. Louis Journalism Review* in its January and February 1984 issues.

22. Again, all of the foregoing information appeared in the publications already named, and in *St. Louis Business Journal.*

23. Mark Clayton in the *Christian Science Monitor,* January 2, 1985, pp. 3–4. In this account, the *Post-Dispatch* daily circulation had risen to 264,000 and to 479,000 on Sunday. The *Globe's* weekday figure was listed at 221,000 and its weekend paper at 194,500.

24. *New York Times,* March 9, 1985, pp. 1–31.

25. Internal Revenue Service documents filed with the U.S. Tax Court in Washington placed a $1.5 billion evaluation on Advance Publications as of February 29, 1980, the appraisal date selected by the estate. The IRS file showed that the estate had placed a $90.9 million figure on the taxable value. The IRS valued Mr. Newhouse's shares at $1.2 billion and contended the taxable value was $961.7 million, or ten times the amount entered by the estate. The IRS filed for $609.5 million in estate taxes and a $304.8 million civil fraud penalty. The estate has appealed those decisions.

26. *New York Times,* January 19, 1984; *Washington Post,* January 22, 1984; and *Washington Journalism Review,* December 1984.

27. "Newhouse Conspired to Form Monopoly, Judge Suggests," *Wall Street Journal,* March 21, 1985, p. 21.

28. Quoted in *U.S. News & World Report,* February 11, 1985, p. 59.

29. Quoted in *Washington Post,* November 6, 1984, p. E2.

30. Quoted in *Newsweek,* February 11, 1985, p. 53.

31. *Ibid.,* p. 54.

32. *New York Times,* December 4, 1984.

33. Quoted in Barbara Matusow, *The Evening Stars* (New York: Houghton Mifflin, 1983), p. 370. This is a detailed and colorful examination of the broadcast side of journalism.

34. Text, in Edward Bliss, Jr., editor, *In Search of Light* (New York: Knopf, 1967), pp. 354–364.

35. Fred W. Friendly, *Due To Circumstances Beyond Our Control* (New York: Random House, 1967), p. 183.

36. Bill Abrams, "Heard on the Street" column, *Wall Street Journal,* October 19, 1984.

37. Sally Bedell Smith, "An ABC Strategy Goes Wrong," *New York Times,* December 9, 1984, pp. F1 and F26.

38. *U.S. News & World Report,* May 13, 1985, p. 60.

39. *Wall Street Journal,* August 15, 1985, p. 20.

40. *Time,* May 20, 1985, p. 56.

41. *Ibid.,* p. 58.

42. Wilson W. Wyatt of Louisville, 1968.

## 12. THE GATHERING STORM

1. Alvin Toffler, to the American Society of Newspaper Editors, Washington, April 15, 1971. Text in *Problems of Journalism: Proceedings of the ASNE 1971,* pp. 76–87. (At the risk of appearing snide, the author finds it difficult to refrain from mentioning that Mr. Toffler, welcome at every great university in the nation, could not meet require-

ments at any of the North Hogwash State colleges since he has no Ph.D., but merely a degree in English and a small raft of honorary Litt.D.'s).

2. *Roper At 50—October 1933–October 1983* (New York: The Roper Organization, 1983), an 80-page book to mark the fiftieth anniversary of the company, and devoted exclusively to the interview conducted August 14, 1968.

3. Modesty thrown overboard: the February 1972 Newsletter of the National Council on Public Polls commented: "As far as we know, the very first newspaper to adopt political polling standards was the *Louisville Courier-Journal,* in 1969. Norman Isaacs, then editor, issued a memorandum to the newspaper staff and to political parties and candidates." The report went on to name the *New York Times, Washington Post,* and *Charlotte Observer* as having similar policies. The list remains "very small," reports NCPP.

4. "Emerging Ethical Norms in Public and Private Life," Columbia University Seminar, April 20, 1977, pp. 2–3.

5. Center report distributed by Michigan's Inter-University Consortium.

6. Kermit L. Hall, Harold M. Hyman, and Leon V. Sigal, eds., *The Constitutional Convention as an Amending Device.* Washington, D.C.: The American Historical Society and the American Political Science Association, 1981.

7. Report of the Committee on National Constitutional Conventions, of the American Bar Association Section on Individual Rights and Responsibilities, September 20, 1972.

8. Roper Reports 73-10 (October 1973), pp. 11–14.

9. *New York Times,* September 12, 1983, p. B13.

10. "Public Opinion and Freedom of the Press," report by George Gallup, Jr., to the First Amendment Congress, Philadelphia, January 17, 1980.

11. *The Speaker and the Listener* (New York: Public Agenda Foundation, 1980), p. 7.

12. Interview, August 10, 1983.

13. "Early Election Calls: The Larger Dangers," Burns W. Roper, to the American Association of Public Opinion Researchers, Delavan, Wis., May 18, 1984.

14. *Broadcasting,* November 12, 1984, p. 35.

15. *New York Times* editorial, November 15, 1984.

16. 376 U.S. Reports 254.

17. *Gertz v. Robert Welch, Inc.,* 418 U.S. 323 (1974).

18. Newsletter of the National Center for Business and Economic Communication, American University, Washington, D.C., May 1, 1983, quoting from studies of the Libel Defense Resource Center.

19. Newsletter, National Center, June 1984 issue.

20. Quoted in the *Wall Street Journal,* October 1, 1984, p. 22.

21. Richard Cohen, "The Arrogance of Time," the *Washington Post,* January 26, 1985, p. A19.

22. Richard Clurman, "Journalism Loses," *New York Times,* January 30, 1985.

23. *Newsweek,* January 28, 1985, p. 48.

24. *Newsweek,* February 4, 1985, p. 56.

25. *New York Times,* February 20, 1985, p. B6.

26. Don Kowet and Sally Bedell, "Anatomy of a Smear," *TV Guide,* May 29, 1982, pp. 6–15.

27. *New York Times,* April 22, 1983, pp. 1 and C12.

28. Fred W. Friendly, "After the Westmoreland Case: How Can the People Talk Back?" *Washington Post,* February 20, 1985.

29. Douglass Cater, "Communications and Society: Toward a Public Philosophy, the Aspen Institute," January 1973.

30. Don Oberdorfer, "The Press Needs to Reflect on Its Role," *Washington Journalism Review,* May 1981, pp. 37–38.

31. Tom Rosenstiel, *Los Angeles Times,* December 16, 1984.

32. Stephen Hess, *The Washington Reporters* (Washington, D.C.: Brookings Institute, 1981).

33. Arthur Schlesinger, Jr., "Freedom of the Press: Who Cares?" *Wall Street Journal,* January 5, 1973.

34. Address to Radio and Television News Directors Association, Miami Beach, Fla., December 13, 1976.

35. Alfred W. Balk, interview, December 2, 1984.

36. "Education vs. Western Civilization, address given under the auspices of Phi Beta Kappa to the American Association for the Advancement of Science, University of Pennsylvania, December 29, 1940. Published in *The American Scholar* (1941), 10:184.

37. Walter Lippmann, "Two Revolutions in the American Press," *The Yale Review,* March 1931, p. 441.

38. Alexander Hamilton in *The Federalist,* No. 94, May 28, 1788.

39. William C. Westmoreland, "A Court's No Forum," *New York Times* February 24, 1985, p. E19.

40. *Washington Post,* May 3, 1985, Associated Press account of regional RTNDA meeting, Albany, N.Y. Headline: CBS PRODUCER CRITICIZES WESTMORELAND PROGRAM.

# INDEX